中国国家对外汉语教学领导小组办公室规划教材
Project of NOTCFL of the People's Republic of China

NEW PRACTICAL CHINESE READER

Textbook

新实用汉语课本

1

主编：刘　珣
编者：张　凯　刘社会
　　　陈　曦　左珊丹
　　　施家炜　刘　珣

英译审定：Jerry Schmidt

北京语言大学出版社
BEIJING LANGUAGE AND CULTURE
UNIVERSITY PRESS

图书在版编目（CIP）数据

新实用汉语课本. 第一册/刘珣主编
—北京：北京语言大学出版社，2012重印
ISBN 978 - 7 - 5619 - 1040 - 5

Ⅰ. 新…
Ⅱ. 刘…
Ⅲ. 对外汉语教学 - 教材
Ⅳ. H195.4

中国版本图书馆 CIP 数据核字（2002）第 006477 号

书　　名：新实用汉语课本. 第一册
责任印制：陈　辉

出版发行：北京语言大学出版社
社　　址：北京市海淀区学院路 15 号　邮政编码：100083
网　　址：www. blcup. com
电　　话：发行部　82303648 ／ 3591 ／ 3650
　　　　　编辑部　82303395
　　　　　读者服务部　82303653 ／ 3908
　　　　　网上订购电话　82303668
　　　　　客户服务信箱　service@ blcup. net
印　　刷：北京画中画印刷有限公司
经　　销：全国新华书店

版　　次：2002 年 3 月第 1 版　2012 年 7 月第 30 次印刷
开　　本：889 毫米 ×1194 毫米　1/16　印张:16.75　插表 1
字　　数：160 千字
书　　号：ISBN 978 - 7 - 5619 - 1040 - 5/H · 02008
　　　　　05800

凡有印装质量问题，本社负责调换。电话：82303590
Printed in China

目 录
CONTENTS

1

三. 练习与运用　　Drills and Practice

　　喜欢不喜欢　　Likes and dislikes

　　解决语言困难　　Solving language problems

　　买东西　　Shopping

四. 阅读和复述　　Reading Comprehension and Paraphrasing

五. 语法　　Grammar

　1. 介词词组　　Prepositional phrase

　2. 双宾语动词谓语句(1)："给"、"送"

　　Sentences with double objects (1)："给" and "送"

　3. 形容词谓语句和副词"很"　　Sentences with an adjectival predicate and "很"

六. 汉字　　Chinese Characters

　　汉字的结构(3)　　Structure of Chinese characters (3)

一. 课文　　Text

　　生词　　New Words

二. 注释　　Notes

　　"一点儿"　　The indefinite measure word "一点儿"

　　"哪里"表示否定　　"哪里" with a negative connotation

　　"还"(2)：表示现象或动作的继续　　"还"(2)：expressing the continuation
　　　　　　　　　　　　　　　　　　　of a state or action

三. 练习与运用　　Drills and Practice

　　问时间　　Asking about time

　　表示能力　　Expressing one's ability

　　表示允许或禁止　　Expressing permission or prohibition

四. 阅读和复述　　Reading Comprehension and Paraphrasing

五. 语法　　Grammar

　1. 钟点　　Telling time

　2. 能愿动词谓语句(1)：会、能、可以、应该

　　Optative verbs (1)："会、能、可以、应该"

　3. 连动句(1)：表示目的

　　Sentences with serial verb phrases(1)：Purpose

　4. 双宾语动词谓语句(2)：教、问

　　Sentences with double objects (2)："教" and "问"

六. 汉字　　Chinese Characters

　　汉字的结构(4)　　Structure of Chinese characters (4)

四．阅读和复述　　Reading Comprehension and Paraphrasing

五．语法　　Grammar

  1．助词"了"（1）　　The particle "了"（1）

  2．兼语句　　Pivotal sentences

  3．能愿动词谓语句（3）：可能、会　　Optative verbs（3）："可能、会"

六．汉字　　Chinese Characters

  部首查字法　　Consulting a Chinese dictionary using radicals

前　　言

　　《新实用汉语课本》是新世纪之初，我们为以英语为母语或媒介语的学习者学习汉语而编写的一套新教材。本教材的目的是通过语言结构、语言功能与相关文化知识的学习和听说读写技能训练，逐步培养学习者运用汉语进行交际的能力。全书共六册 70 课，前四册为初级和中级以前阶段，共 50 课；后两册为中级阶段，共 20 课。海外专修或选修中文的学习者可用作一至三年级听说读写综合教学的汉语教材，基本上每周学一课，每学期用一册书；也可以作为学习者的自学教材。每册书均配有《综合练习册》和《教师手册》及录音带、光盘。

为什么叫《新实用汉语课本》

　　本书之所以起名为《新实用汉语课本》，是因为我们希望能继承原《实用汉语课本》深受使用者欢迎、并经过时间考验的一些主要特点，但它又是一本全新的教材。《实用汉语课本》是 1981 年开始陆续出版的。20 年来这套教材一直得到世界各地的汉语教师和汉语学习者的支持与关爱。书中的主人公古波、帕兰卡和丁云等，伴随了一届又一届的各国汉语学习者度过了他们的汉语启蒙阶段。现在，古波、帕兰卡、丁云已经人到中年，该他们的孩子辈——《新实用汉语课本》的主人公丁力波（丁云与古波所生的孩子，加拿大学生）、马大为（美国学生）和林娜（英国学生）等在学习汉语了。今天，汉语作为第二语言学习的环境、条件和基础比起 20 年前已有了很大的变化；不论在中国还是在海外都积累了更丰富的教学经验，取得了更多的研究成果。新的时代，新的形势，对汉语教材也提出了新的要求。我们希望《新实用汉语课本》在很多方面将有创新和突破。

新教材，新理念

　　正如愈来愈多的汉语教学领域的同行们所主张的那样，语言教学的根本目的在于培养学习者用目的语进行交际的能力。为达到这一目的，语言教材的编写首先要体现"以学习者为中心"的原则：即教学内容要适合学习者的需要，有利于学习者创造性地学习，使学习者不断增强学习动力并获得成就感。在教学方法上，需要汲取从语法翻译法到交际法的各种教学法流派的长处：既重视学习语言的交际功能，又要牢固地掌握语言结构；既要让学习者通过大量操练和练习培养四种基本技能，又要让学习者懂得必要的语法知识和组词造句的规则。语音、词汇、句型、语法和话语等语言结构的学习是语言交际的基础，要特别注意体现由简单到复杂、由易到难、循序渐进、不断重现的原则，才能使学习过程更为容易，更为顺利。语言教材还应该有助于学习者了解目的语的文化和社会，从而更好地运用目的语进行交际。这就是我们编写《新实用汉语课本》所主张的主要理念。

《新实用汉语课本》的新特色

　　1. 改变以往汉语教材线式编排的做法，本教材不论是语言结构、语言功能或是文化因素的教学均采取圆周式的编排，多次循环重现，螺旋式上升。以语言结构教学为例，六册中共进行四次大的循环。第一册前六课，在集中学习语音的同时，通过掌握简易的口语会话让学习者先接触多种基本句式，但暂不作语法的系统讲解；第一册的后八课及第二册全册 12 课共 20 课，是语言结构教学的第二次循环，逐个介绍并练习主要句型结构。这样，学习者在学习汉语的第一年内就能初步掌握汉语基本句型。第三、四册共 24 课，为第三次循环，进一步巩固、扩大并深化语法句型教学和词语教学；第五、六册共 20 课，除了词语和语法教学外，更把重点放在以往教材不太强调的复句和语段教学方面。这种四次大循环以及课与课之间又有小循环和单元复习、环环相扣的安排,不仅可以通过多次重现加深学习者对语言结构和功能的掌握,更重要的是让学习者在学习的每一阶段——第一个月、第一学期、第一年都能在一定的水平上运用汉语进行交际,时时有成就感。

2. 改变以往教材重结构、轻功能的做法,本教材加强功能项目的教学。从第一课学习语音开始,就把功能放在突出的地位,结合各课的音素教学,练习学生急需的功能项目(如问候、介绍等)。前四册强调基本功能和话题的教学,着重培养学习者运用语言结构进行交际的能力。第五、六册强调培养理解和表达高一级的功能和话题的能力,特别是成段交际的能力。功能项目的教学贯穿全书,以保证学习者听说读写交际能力不断提高。书中附有一定的实物图片及原文材料,如时刻表、菜单、广告、启事、报刊、经典作品片断等。

3. 改变以往绝大多数汉语教材未突出汉字教学的缺陷。本教材考虑到非汉字文化圈学生的难点,第一、二册特别强调按汉字的规律,由易到难,从基本笔画、部件和独体字学起。为此,第一册前六课采用语、文适当分开的做法:先选学六十个常用、易学、组合能力强的基本汉字和一些部件,让学习者在先掌握汉字部件的情况下,再组合成合体字。

4. 改变基础阶段大多数教材内容局限于学校生活的做法,本教材扩大题材范围,加强教材的趣味性。本书前四册情节主线索围绕上述三个外国学生在中国的生活及与中国学生宋华、王小云、记者陆雨平、导游小燕子和几位中国教师的友情、恋情、师生情而展开一些风趣的故事。第一、二册结合校园及日常生活,介绍与汉语表达和理解有关的习俗文化;第三、四册围绕青年学生感兴趣的话题进行中西文化对比;第五、六册着重介绍中国社会的方方面面,体现中国传统文化和当代文化。

5. 克服以往教材的教学模式过于机械、单一、弹性不够的缺点,加强教材对不同起点和不同需求的学习者的适应性。本教材一方面适当加大输入的内容、词汇量和练习量,同时通过板块式的安排注意处理好核心内容和补充内容的关系。在保证学好核心内容的基础上,增加补充内容,有利于学习者根据自己的需要自由习得;也有利于教师根据本班学生的水平因材施教。

此外,为有助于学习者更好地掌握汉语的规律,培养交际能力,本教材在突出词语结构的教学、加强语素和话语的教学以及书面语教学等方面,也力图作一些新的尝试。

《新实用汉语课本》第一——四册体例

课本

课文 为各课提供一定的话题与情境,第一、二册课文基本上用对话体(每课两段),以利于基础阶段在听说读写全面要求的基础上,加强听说的训练。第一册1－6课语音阶段突出拼音课文,第7－14课转入以汉字课文为主,下注拼音;第二册课文不再注拼音,只留调号;从第三册起,不再有调号。由利用拼音到逐步摆脱对拼音的依赖。

生词 对组成生词的语素(汉字)进行分析,便于学习者理解和记忆,同时强调通过连词组的练习掌握生词的用法。补充生词由学习者量力吸取。

注释 主要内容为:解释词语的用法,补充已学过的语法点,介绍必要的文化背景知识。对课文中已出现但先不讲解语法点的句子,通过翻译让学习者弄懂意思。

练习与运用和会话练习(前六课)"重点句式"体现了本课所介绍的主要语言结构及主要功能,希望学习者熟练掌握。通过操练词组、句型替换、会话练习、交际练习等步骤,完成由机械操练到交际运用的过程。

阅读和复述 重现已学过的句型与词汇,着重培养口头与书面连贯表达的能力。从第二册开始,扩展阅读短文的内容,加强阅读能力的训练。

语音、语音练习(前六课) 针对汉语语音的特点和以英语为母语学习者的难点,有重点地介绍汉语语音规律和发音、拼写的方法,并通过拼音、四声、辨音、辨调、变调、声调组合、双音节或多音节连读以及朗读课堂用语等步骤,逐步练好语音。

语法 针对汉语的特点和以英语为母语的学习者的难点,对本课出现的主要语言结构进行必要的说明。着重介绍句子组装的规律,不求语法知识的全面系统。每册有两课复习课,帮助学习者对已学过的语法点进行小结。

汉字 先介绍部件,后组合成汉字。适当介绍汉字的结构规律和书写规律,帮助学习者认写汉字。

文化知识 开始多用英文介绍,便于学习者了解与汉语有关的必要的文化知识。随着汉语水平的提高,文化知识将逐渐融合到课文中去。

综合练习册

主要供学习者课下练习用。除了汉字练习外,还有语音、句型、词汇的练习,以及听说读写全面的技能训练。

教师手册

《教师手册》就每课的教学目的、教学步骤和方法等提出建议,并对教材内容进行说明。对语音、语法、词汇的有关知识作较详细的介绍,供教师参考。每册书有两套单元测试题,供教师选用,此外还附有测试题与练习的答案。

鸣谢

本教材为中国国家对外汉语教学领导小组办公室(简称"国家汉办")所主持的一项重点科研项目的一部分,委托北京语言文化大学承担。国家汉办严美华主任、姜明宝教授、李桂苓女士进行了整个项目的策划与组织工作。北京语言文化大学校长曲德林教授、校务委员会主任王路江研究员对北语所承担的此项教材编写工作一直给予关注和大力支持,保证了我们编写工作的顺利进行。为了解海外汉语教学的现状,我们于开始编写教材前对加拿大六所大学的中文教学情况进行了考察。特别感谢我国驻温哥华总领馆许琳教育领事,她为我们与加拿大不列颠·哥伦比亚大学亚洲学系建立有关本教材的协作关系及实施协作计划提供了极其宝贵的帮助。国家汉办教学业务处宋永波先生在我们完成此项目的整个过程中给我们很多具体的帮助,特此一并致谢。

感谢加拿大麦吉尔大学、蒙特利尔大学、多伦多大学、不列颠·哥伦比亚大学、西蒙菲莎大学及维多利亚大学在我们的考察访问中对我们的热情接待和各校中文教学同行们所提供的宝贵建议。感谢皇后大学、西安大略大学休伦学院、约克大学、兰格拉学院、道格拉斯学院、卡莫森学院等校的同行热心参加有关汉语教材的座谈讨论。要特别感谢不列颠·哥伦比亚大学陈山木博士、郑志宁先生,多伦多大学吴小燕博士和麦吉尔大学王仁忠先生同意担任我们教材的加方咨询委员。

作为我们这次编教工作的加拿大协作方的负责人、不列颠·哥伦比亚大学亚洲学系中国语文主任陈山木博士和郑志宁先生全程参与了协作活动的组织和协调工作,并进行了全书的中英文总校读,提出了很多宝贵的建议。陈山木博士、程茂荣博士、何冬晖博士、李天明博士、郑志宁先生和夏蔚女士承担了本书的英文翻译工作。郑志宁先生、吕鸣珠女士和夏蔚女士参加了第一、二册中文稿的校读,牟怀川博士、何冬晖博士、李天明博士参加了第三、四册中文稿的校读,程茂荣博士、林惠敏女士、杨丽琼女士参加了第五、六册中文稿的校读。该校 Mr. Allen Haaheim 和 Mr. Paul Crowe 编校了英文译文的初稿,施吉瑞教授进行了全书英文译文的总校读。郑志宁先生和夏蔚女士进行了本教材第一、二册的样课试教;何冬晖博士、杨丽琼女士进行了本教材第三、四册的样课试教;程茂荣博士、林惠敏女士进行了本教材第五、六册的样课试教。对他们为本书所作的努力,我们表示衷心的谢意。

我们还要特别感谢北京语言文化大学出版社社长兼总编辑王建勤教授、王弘宇编辑和王飙编辑,感谢画家杨可千先生,他们为本书的出版作了大量的工作。

本书主编刘珣教授,编者为张凯副教授、刘社会副教授、陈曦副教授、左珊丹女士、施家炜女士和刘珣教授。第一、二册执笔为施家炜、刘珣,第三、四册执笔为刘社会、陈曦,第五、六册执笔为张凯、左珊丹。

我们期待使用本教材的教师和学习者提出宝贵的意见,以便我们对本教材作进一步的修改。

编者

2002 年 1 月

于北京语言文化大学

Preface

New Practical Chinese Reader is a series of Chinese textbooks compiled at the beginning of the new millennium for the purpose of teaching Chinese to native English speakers or those who use English as their principal second language. It aims to develop the learner's communicative ability in Chinese by learning language structures, functions and related cultural knowledge as well as by training their listening, speaking, reading and writing skills. The series consists of seventy lessons in six volumes. The first four volumes, consisting of fifty lessons, are for beginners and pre-intermediate level learners. The last two contain twenty lessons for learners at an intermediate level. This set of textbooks is designed for overseas students who either take Chinese as an elective or major in the language for a period of three years, studying about one lesson a week, or one volume a semester. It can also be used by autonomous learners. Each volume comes equipped with a workbook, an instructor's manual, audiotapes and CD-ROMs.

Why have we named our teaching materials *New Practical Chinese Reader*?

We have given our textbooks this name, because it follows in the footsteps of the highly acclaimed and time-tested *Practical Chinese Reader* (abbreviated PCR below). However, in the meantime, it is an entirely new set of textbooks. PCR has been published in numerous editions since 1981 and has been adopted as a textbook by Chinese language educators and learners worldwide during the last two decades. The characters appearing in the lessons of *PCR* (Palanca, Ding Yun and Gubo, among others), have accompanied two generations of students of different nationalities during their study of beginning Chinese. Now these characters have finally reached middle age, and it is time for their children's generation to learn Chinese and become the principal characters in New Practical Chinese Reader. These include Ding Libo, a Canadian student, who is the son of Gubo and Ding Yun; Ma Dawei, an American student; and Lin Na, a British student. The teaching of Chinese as a second language has changed greatly during the last twenty years as a result of the experience accumulated by the many teachers of the language, both inside and outside China. The new age in which we live requires that we improve our approaches and teaching materials. We hope that this new teaching material will be able to make original contributions to the teaching of Chinese language in a number of areas.

New Teaching Material, New Concepts

More and more Chinese language teachers advocate the idea that the fundamental goal of language teaching is to cultivate the learner's communicative ability in the target language. We believe new teaching materials should be learner-centered. What is taught must be determined by students' needs and must enable them to learn creatively, gradually strengthening their motivation and sense of achievement. We must create a synthesis of all pedagogical schools, ranging from the grammar-translation method to the communicative approach. We should both emphasize the communicative function and also obtain a firm grasp of language structure. We should allow students to gain grounding in the four basic skills by means of a large number of drills and exercises while also mastering the necessary grammatical knowledge and rules for word and sentence formation. The study of pronunciation, vocabulary, sentence patterns, grammar, and speech are the foundation of linguistic communication. The only way that we can make the learning process easier and smoother is by emphasizing the principle of moving from the simple to the complex and from the easy to the difficult, progressing gradually as we constantly review what has come before. Finally, language teaching-materials must help students understand the culture and society of the target language so that they can use the target language more effectively. The above are the basic concepts that guided us while writing *New Practical Chinese Reader*.

Features of *New Practical Chinese Reader*

1. *New Practical Chinese Reader* does not follow the linear structure adopted by earlier Chinese teaching materials, instead adopting a cyclical arrangement with constant review of language structure and function together with important cultural information. The teaching of language structure passes through four cycles in the six volumes. In the first six lessons of Volume One, the focus of which is learning pronunciation, students are exposed to various basic sentence patterns by engaging in simple dialogues, although grammar is not discussed systematically at this stage. The second cycle is found in the twenty lessons that comprise Volume Two and the last eight lessons of Volume One. In this cycle, students learn and practice fundamental sentence patterns. As a result, by the end of the first year of study, they should have an elementary command of basic Chinese language structure. Volumes Three and Four contain the twenty-four lessons of the third cycle, which further consolidate, expand and deepen students' understanding of lexical items and sentence patterns. The fourth cycle is found in the twenty lessons of the last two volumes. Besides introducing more vocabulary items and grammatical points, these lessons concentrate on the teaching of complex sentences and paragraphs not emphasized in earlier Chinese teaching materials. These four large cycles contain smaller ones that interact closely with the unit reviews, not only increasing the students' command of linguistic structures and functions, but also (and more importantly) giving them a sense of accomplishment in communicative abilities at each stage of the learning process.

2. *New Practical Chinese Reader* breaks with the emphasis on structure at the expense of function characteristic of earlier teaching materials. Even in its introduction to phonetics, this new series gives prominence to function, training the students in the most needed functional items, such as greetings and introductions, at the same time as it teaches the phonetics. The first four volumes focus on the teaching of basic functions and topics of conversation, training the students' abilities to use language structures for communication. The last two volumes cultivate students' ability to comprehend and communicate at a higher level, especially in paragraphs. Functional items are included throughout all six volumes in order to constantly improve the learner's listening, speaking, reading and writing. Some pictures and culturally authentic materials such as selections from timetables, menus, advertisements, announcements, newspapers and classical literary pieces are also used.

3. Unlike the vast majority of earlier textbooks, *New Practical Chinese Reader* emphasizes the systematic study of characters. In view of the difficulties encountered by students lacking a background in Chinese characters, the first two volumes stress the fundamental rules of learning the Chinese script, studying easy forms such as basic strokes, character components and single-component characters first before moving on to difficult ones. The first six lessons of Volume One divorce the study of characters from the conversation text. The teaching of characters starts with the introduction of sixty common, easily learnt characters frequently used as components of other characters, along with some character components. The goal of this approach is to allow students to learn multi-component characters by first mastering their

components.

4. Transcending the limits of campus life, *New Practical Chinese Reader* distinguishes itself even at the beginning stage from most previous Chinese textbooks by including a broader range of interesting materials. The first four volumes develop a series of attractive stories, narrating the lives of the three international students mentioned above, including their friendships, love stories and teacher-student relationships with the Chinese students Song Hua, Wang Xiaoyun, the journalist Lu Yuping, the tour guide Xiao Yanzi, as well as several Chinese language teachers. Volumes One and Two interweave campus life with everyday experiences, introducing cultural norms and customs closely associated with speaking and comprehension. The third and fourth volumes concentrate on topics of interest to students, illustrating cultural differences between China and the West. The last two volumes introduce various aspects of Chinese society, highlighting traditional and contemporary cultural life.

5. *New Practical Chinese Reader* abandons the mechanical, monotonous and inflexible formulae of earlier teaching materials and can be adapted to the needs of students beginning at different levels. It increases the amount of vocabulary and exercises, while adopting a module structure that balances the relationship between core material and supplementary contents. By guaranteeing the teaching of core material, it can increase the amount of supplementary contents so that students can learn according to their individual needs, and teachers can use the textbook to suit the differing levels of their students..

The Layout of Volumes One to Four of *New Practical Chinese Reader*

■ Textbook

Text   This section supplies the topics and scenes of each lesson. For the most part, Volumes One and Two use dialogue form (with two paragraphs in each lesson), facilitating audio-lingual practice and providing an overall grounding in the reading and writing of elementary Chinese. The pronunciation section in lessons one to six emphasizes the *pinyin* text, while lessons seven to fourteen focus on Chinese characters, which, however, have *pinyin* written beneath them. In the second volume, *pinyin* disappears, and there are only tone marks. From the third volume onward, tone marks are no longer used. In this way, learners gradually free themselves from pinyin.

New Words   This part of each lesson analyzes the morphemes (characters) that form new words with the aim of improving learners' comprehension and memory. At the same time, students can master the use of new words by practicing them in phrases. Supplementary words can be learned according to the learners' individual abilities.

Notes   For the most part, notes contain explanations of new words, develop grammatical points taught previously, or introduce necessary cultural background. English translations are provided to help students comprehend sentences containing grammar that will be dealt with in later lessons.

Conversation Practice   (included in Lessons 1 – 6), **Drills and Practice** (included in Lessons 7 – 14)
We hope students will thoroughly master the key sentences illustrating the fundamental linguistic structures and functions introduced in the text. By practicing phrases, doing pattern drills, and taking part in di-

alogues and communicative exercises, students can move successfully from mechanical exercises to proficient interaction.

Reading Comprehension and Paraphrasing　Exercises of this kind ensure the review of some of the sentence patterns and lexical items already taught, thereby developing the students' discourse abilities in both oral and written forms. From the second volume on, the contents of reading texts are expanded so as to strengthen the students' reading comprehension.

Phonetics and Pronunciation Drills　(included in Lessons 1 – 6) In view of the peculiarities of Chinese pronunciation and the special difficulties it presents to foreign learners with English as their mother tongue, the text focuses on the principle features of the Chinese pronunciation system, phonetics and spelling rules. Students can gradually achieve a good foundation in pronunciation by doing the exercises for spelling, the four tones, sound discriminations, tone discriminations, tone sandhi, tone combinations, practice on disyllabic and polysyllabic words, and reading classroom expressions.

Grammar　The grammar explanations take into account the special features of the Chinese language and the difficulties encountered by native speakers of English in learning them. They do not attempt to treat Chinese grammar comprehensively but articulate the most important grammatical structures and rules for sentence formation. Each volume has two review lessons that help learners review the grammatical points taught earlier.

Characters　The text first introduces character components, later combining them to form characters. Rules for constructing and writing characters are also given to facilitate the learning of Chinese writing.

Cultural Notes　At first, cultural notes in the English language are provided so that students can gain insight into cultural information related to their language studies. As learners' Chinese proficiency improves, cultural notes are incorporated more and more into the Chinese texts.

■ **Workbook**

The workbook is designed for students to use outside class. In addition to exercises for studying characters, phonetics, sentence patterns and words, it also includes general exercises for speaking, aural comprehension, reading, and writing.

■ **Instructor's Manual**

The Instructor's Manual makes suggestions regarding the goals and methods of teaching and supplies explanations of each lesson's contents. It also supplies the instructors with more knowledge about phonetics, grammar and vocabulary. Unit tests and keys to the tests and exercises are provided.

Acknowledgements

Sponsored by the National Office for Teaching Chinese as a Foreign Language (abbreviated NOTCFL below), this set of teaching materials is one part of a key research project undertaken by the Beijing Language and Culture University. Ms. Yan Meihua, the director-general of the NOTCFL, Professor Jiang Mingbao and Ms. Li Guiling from the NOTCFL were responsible for planning and organizing this project. The president of the Beijing Language and Culture University, Professor Qu Delin, and the chairman of the Council for University Affairs, Researcher Wang Lujiang, guaranteed the smooth implementation of this project undertaken by our university. In order to obtain an understanding of Chinese teaching overseas, we made a study trip to six Canadian universities with Chinese language programs before compiling this set of materials. We are especially grateful to Ms. Xu Lin, Educational Consul of the Chinese Consulate General in Vancouver, whose work helped us establish our partnership with the Asian Studies Department of the University of British Columbia. Our thanks are also due to Mr. Song Yongbo from the Teaching Bureau of the NOTCFL, for the assistance he offered during the whole project.

We are very grateful to McGill University, the University of Montreal, the University of Toronto, the University of British Columbia, Simon Fraser University and the University of Victoria for the great hospitality they offered us during our study trip as well as the valuable suggestions provided by our colleagues from these institutions. Chinese language instructors from Queens University, Huron College of the University of Western Ontario, York University, Langara College, Douglas College, and Comosen College also participated enthusiastically in our forum on Chinese textbooks. It is our pleasant duty to give special thanks to Dr. Robert Shanmu Chen, Chinese Coordinator of the Asian Studies Department of U.B.C., Mr. Zheng Zhining from the same department, Dr. Helen Wu of the University of Toronto, and Mr. Wang Renzhong of McGill University, who agreed to be on the Canadian Consulting Group for our teaching materials.

Dr. Robert S. Chen and Mr. Zheng Zhining were in charge of the Canadian side of this joint project, which would never have succeeded without their continuous organization and coordination. They are also responsible for the final proofreading of both the Chinese and English texts of all six volumes. Dr. Robert S. Chen, Dr. Cheng Maorong, Dr. He Donghui, Dr. Li Tianming, Mr. Zheng Zhining and Ms. Xia Wei, all of U.B.C., spent much time and effort translating the original Chinese text into English. Dr. Cheng Maorong, Dr. He Donghui, Dr. Li Tianming, Dr. Mou Huaichuan, Ms. Lin Huimin, Ms. Lü Mingzhu, Ms. Xia Wei, Ms. Yang Liqiong and Mr. Zheng Zhining participated in the proofreading of the Chinese text. Mr. Allen Haaheim and Mr. Paul Crowe of U.B.C.. edited and proofread the first version of the English translations, while Professor Jerry D. Schmidt proofread the final version of all the English translations. Dr. Cheng Maorong, Dr. He Donghui, Ms. Lin Huimin, Ms. Xia Wei, Ms. Yang Liqiong and Mr. Zheng Zhining did trial teaching of sample lessons from the six volumes at the Asian Studies Department of U.B.C.. We are very grateful to all these people for their professional work.

Special thanks are also due to the director and general editor of the Beijing Language and Culture University Press, Professor Wang Jianqin, editors Wang Hongyu and Wang Biao, and painter Yang Keqian who did much hard work to facilitate the publication of our textbooks.

The chief compiler of this textbook series is Prof. Liu Xun. The other compilers include Associate Prof. Zhang Kai, Associate Prof. Liu Shehui, Associate Prof. Chen Xi, Ms. Zuo Shandan, and Ms. Shi Jiawei. Shi Jiawei and Liu Xun were in charge of writing Volumes One and Two. Volumes Three and Four were largely written by Liu Shehui and Chen Xi, and Volumes Five and Six mainly by Zhang Kai and Zuo Shandan.

We sincerely request teachers and students using our materials to offer their valuable criticisms and suggestions to enable us to improve these textbooks in the future.

Welcome to *New Practical Chinese Reader!*

This textbook features several imaginary characters to make your Chinese learning experience more enjoyable: international students Ding Libo, Lin Na, and Ma Dawei; Chinese teachers Mr. Yang, Ms. Chen, and Professor Zhang; Chinese students Song Hua, and Wang Xiaoyun; and Chinese reporter Lu Yuping. They, together with the help of your instructor, will act as tour guides for your adventure, guiding you and your classmates into the fascinating world of Chinese, the language with the largest number of speakers in the world today. Now let's get to know our companions for this journey:

人物介绍
Introduction to Main Characters in the Text

丁力波 Dīng Lìbō

A Canadian student,
aged 21, male.
Gubo is his father;
Ding Yun is his mother.

马大为 Mǎ Dàwéi

An American student,
aged 22, male.

林娜 Lín Nà

A British student,
aged 19, female.

宋华 Sòng Huá

A Chinese student,
aged 20, male.

王小云 Wáng Xiǎoyún

A Chinese student,
aged 20, female.

陆雨平 Lù Yǔpíng

A Chinese reporter,
aged 26, male.

陈老师 Chén lǎoshī

A Chinese teacher,
aged 30, female.

张教授 Zhāng jiàoshòu

A Chinese professor,
aged 48, male.

杨老师 Yáng lǎoshī

A Chinese teacher,
aged 32, male.

This lesson begins by introducing some sounds unique to the Chinese language, including tones. The Chinese writing system dates back more than four thousand years, and it is especially intriguing to see how Chinese characters developed since their basically pictographic origins in ancient China. By the end of the lesson, you will know eleven Chinese characters and be able to express some everyday greetings in Chinese.

第一课 Lesson 1

Nǐ hǎo
你 好

一. 课文　　Text

（一）

【打招呼】Saying hello

Lù Yǔpíng：　Lìbō, nǐ hǎo.①
陆 雨平：　　力波,你 好。

Lìbō：　　Nǐ hǎo, Lù Yǔpíng.
力波：　　你 好，陆 雨平。

— 3 —

生词 New Words

1. nǐ	Pr	你	you
2. hǎo	A	好	good; well; fine; O.K.
3. Lù Yǔpíng	PN	陆雨平	(name of a Chinese reporter)
4. Lìbō	PN	力波	(name of a Canadian student)

（二）

【问候】Greetings

man/woman. → yin yang.
→ functions as question
→ and you → function as ?

Lìbō: Lín Nà, nǐ hǎo ma? ②

力波：林娜，你好 吗？

Lín Nà: Wǒ hěn hǎo, nǐ ne? ③

林娜：我 很 好，你 呢？

Lìbō: Yě hěn hǎo. ④

力波：也 很 好。

1. ma	QPt	吗	(interrogative particle for question expecting yes-no answer)	
2. wǒ	Pr	我	I; me	
3. hěn	Adv	很	very	
4. ne	MdPt	呢	(a modal particle used for elliptical questions)	
5. yě	Adv	也 [1]	too; also	
6. Lín Nà	PN	林娜	(name of a British student)	

二. 注释　　Notes

① Nǐ hǎo.

"Hello!", "How do you do?"

This is the most common form of greeting in Chinese.　It can be used at any time of day when meeting people for the first time or for people you already know.　The response to this greeting form is also "你好"("Nǐ hǎo").

② Nǐ hǎo ma?

"How are you?"

This is also a form of greeting,　often used after you have not seen someone for some time, and the response is usually "我很好"("Wǒ hěn hǎo") or other similar formulae.

③ Nǐ ne?

"And (how are) you?"

④ Yě hěn hǎo.

"(I am) fine (literally, very good), too."

This is an elliptical sentence, with the subject "我"(wǒ) omitted.　In spoken Chinese, when the context is explicit and there is no ambiguity,　the subject is often omitted.　One may also say "很好"("Hěn hǎo") to answer the question "你好吗？"("Nǐ hǎo ma？").

三. 语音练习　Pronunciation Drills

声母 Initials:	b　p　m　n　l　h
韵母 Finals:	a　o　e　i　u　ü
	ao　en　ie　in　ing　uo

[1] Students are required to master the characters of the purple new words in this lesson.

1. 拼音 Spelling

bā   bō   bī   bū   bīn   bīng

pā   pō   pī   pū   pīn   pīng

mā   mō   mī   mū

nē   nāo   niē

lē   lāo   liē   luō

hē   hāo   huō

2. 四声 The four tones

ā   á   ǎ   à

nī   ní   nǐ   nì

hāo   háo   hǎo   hào   nǐ hǎo

lī   lí   lǐ   lì

bō   bó   bǒ   bò   Lìbō

līn   lín   lǐn   lìn

nā   ná   nǎ   nà   Lín Nà

lū   lú   lǔ   lù

yū   yú   yǔ   yù

pīng   píng   Lù Yǔpíng

wō   wǒ   wò

        hén   hěn   hèn   wǒ hěn hǎo

yē   yé   yě   yè   yě hěn hǎo

3. 辨音 Sound discrimination

bā —— pā   nǚ —— nǔ   wǔ —— hǔ

(eight)   (female)   (five)   (tiger)

bīng —— bīn   piě —— biě   huǒ —— wǒ

(ice)   (left-falling strokes)   (fire)   (I)

4. 辨调 Tone discrimination

mǎ —— mā   mù —— mǔ   yī —— yí

(horse) (mom) (wood)   (one)

yě —— yè   lì —— lǐ   mén —— mèn

(also) (night) (strength) (in)   (door)

5. 三声变调 Third-tone sandhi

nǐ hǎo   hěn hǎo   yě hǎo   yě hěn hǎo

6. 朗读下列课堂用语 Read the following classroom expressions aloud

Nǐ hǎo.

Nǐmen hǎo.

四. 会话练习　　Conversation Practice

> KEY SENTENCES
> 1. Nǐ hǎo.
> 2. Nǐ hǎo ma?
> 3. Wǒ hěn hǎo, nǐ ne?
> 4. Yě hěn hǎo.

（一）【打招呼 Saying hello】

1. 完成下列会话 Complete the following dialogue

Lín Nà：Lìbō，nǐ hǎo!

Lìbō：Nǐ hǎo _____ .

你好

2. 看图会话 Make a dialogue based on the picture

（1）　A：Nǐ hǎo _____ .

　　　B：Nǐ hǎo _____ .

你好

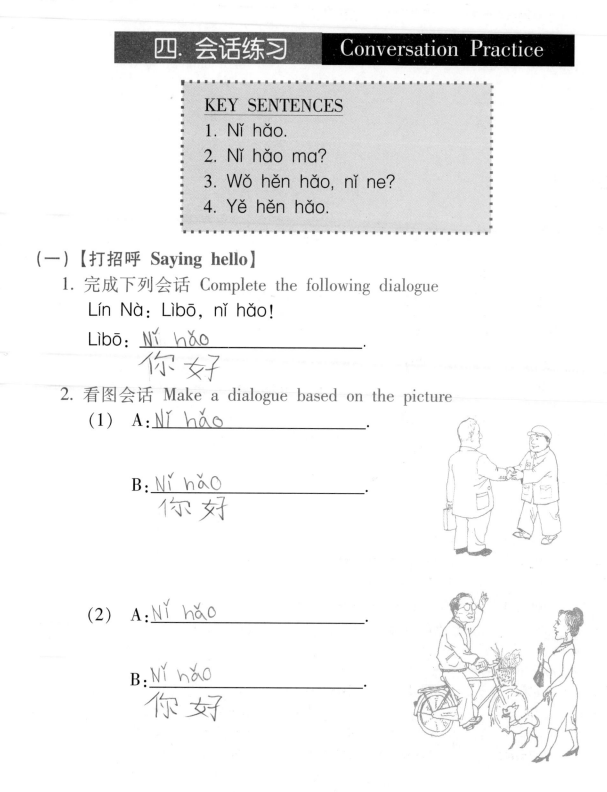

（2）　A：Nǐ hǎo _____ .

　　　B：Nǐ hǎo _____ .

你好

(二) 【问候 Greetings】

1. 完成下列会话 Complete the following dialogue

Mǎ Lì: Nǐ hǎo ma?

Lù Yì: <u>Wǒ hěn hǎo</u>, <u>nǐ ne</u>?

Mǎ Lì: Wǒ yě hěn hǎo.

2. 情景会话 Situational dialogue

You run into a Chinese friend whom you haven't seen for a long time. What will you say to him/her? <u>Name</u>, Nǐ hǎo ma?

(三) 听述 Listen and repeat

你好吗？

我很好，你呢？

我也很好。

五. 语音　　　　Phonetics

1. 声母和韵母 Initials and finals

A syllable in the common speech of modern Chinese usually consists of an initial, which is a consonant that begins the syllable, and a final, which constitutes the rest of the syllable. For example, in the syllable "píng", "p" is the initial and "ing" is the final. A syllable can stand without an initial, such as "yě", but all syllables must have a final. In the common speech of modern Chinese, there are altogether 21 initials and 38 finals.

2. 发音要领 Pronunciation key

Initials: m, n, l, h are pronounced similarly to their counterparts in the English language.

b like "p" in "speak" (unaspirated, voiceless)

p like "p" in "park" (aspirated, voiceless)

Note: Particular attention should be paid to the pronunciation of the aspirated and unaspirated consonants: b-p.

Finals: e like "e" in "her"

ie like "ye" in "yes"

-ng (final) a nasalised sound like the "ng" in "bang" without pronouncing the "g"

Note: The pronunciation of the "e" in a compound final is different from that of the simple final "e".

- 8 -

3. 声调 Tones

Chinese is a tonal language in which the tones convey differences in meaning.

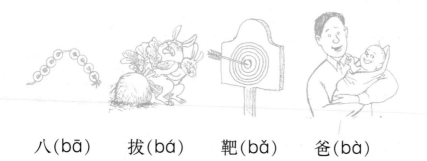

八(bā)　　拔(bá)　　靶(bǎ)　　爸(bà)

In common speech there are four basic tones, represented respectively by the following tone marks：

" ˉ " for the first tone,

" ´ " for the second tone,

" ˇ " for the third tone, and

" ` " for the fourth tone.

When a syllable contains only a single vowel, the tone mark is placed directly above the vowel letter as in "lù" and "hěn". The dot over the vowel "i" should be dropped if the tone mark is placed above it, as in "nǐ", "nín" and "píng". When the final of the syllable is composed of two or more vowels, the tone mark should be placed above the vowel pronounced with the mouth widest open (e.g. hǎo).

The openness of the mouth for the vowels, from widest to smallest is as follows：

a　o　e　i　u　ü

4. 三声变调 Third-tone sandhi

A third tone, when immediately followed by another third tone, should be pronounced in the second tone, but with the tone mark " ˇ " remaining unchanged. For example：

nǐ hǎo　→　ní hǎo　　　　Wǒ hěn hǎo. → Wó hén hǎo.

hěn hǎo → hén hǎo　　　　Yě hěn hǎo. → Yé hén hǎo.

5. 拼写规则 Spelling rules

At the beginning of a syllable, "i" is written as "y" (e.g. iě → yě). "i" is written as "yi" when it forms a syllable all by itself (e.g. ī → yī).

At the beginning of a syllable, "u" is written as "w" (e.g. uǒ → wǒ). "u" is written as "wu" when it forms a syllable all by itself (e.g. ǔ → wǔ).

When "ü" is at the beginning of a syllable or forms a syllable by itself, a "y" is added to it and the two dots over it are omitted (e.g. ǚ → yǔ).

汉语的语序 Word order in Chinese sentences

The main characteristic of Chinese grammar is that it lacks of morphological changes in person, tense, gender, number, and case in the strict sense. The word order, however, is very important to convey different grammatical meanings. The subject of a sentence is usually placed before the predicate. For example：

Subject	Predicate		
你 Nǐ			好。 hǎo.
我 Wǒ		很 hěn	好。 hǎo.
力波 Lìbō	也 yě	很 hěn	好。 hǎo.

七. 汉字　　　　Chinese Characters

Chinese characters originated from pictures. The history of their formation is very long, dating back to remote antiquity. Present-day Chinese characters, which evolved from ancient Chinese characters, are square-shaped. Here are some examples illustrating their long evolution：

Picture	Oracle Bone Inscription	Small Seal Character	Official Script	Complex Character in Regular Script	Simplified Character in Regular Script
	𢒉	馬	馬	馬	马

Brush pen = more effective.

1. 汉字基本笔画 Basic strokes of Chinese characters

Chinese characters are written by combining various kinds of "strokes". These strokes can be divided into "basic" strokes and "combined" strokes.

Basic strokes of Chinese characters

stroke	Name	Example	Way to Write
丶 ↘	diǎn	门	The dot is written from top to bottom-right, as in the first stroke of "门".
一 →	héng	一	The horizontal stroke is written from left to right.
丨 ↓	shù	木	The vertical stroke is written from top downward to bottom, as in the second stroke of "木".
丿 ↙	piě	力	The downward-left stroke is written from top to bottom-left, as in the second stroke of "力".
丶 ↘	nà	八	The downward-right stroke is written from top to bottom-right, as in the second stroke of "八".
╱ ↗	tí	我	The upward stroke is written from bottom-left to top-right, as in the fourth stroke of "我".

2. 认写基本汉字 Learn and write basic Chinese characters

(1) 一　　　一
yī　　one　　　　　1 stroke

(2) 八　　　丿八
bā　　eight　　　　2 strokes

(3) 力　　　𠃌力
lì　　strength　　　2 strokes

(4) 门 (門)　　丶丿门
mén　　door　　　　3 strokes

(5) 也　　　𠃌㇇也
yě　　too; also　　　3 strokes

(6) 马 (馬)　　　フ 马 马

mǎ　　horse　　　　　　3 strokes

Note：“马” is written as “马” on the left side of a character.

(7) 女　　　　　く 女 女

nǚ　　female　　　　　　3 strokes

Note：“女” is written as “女” on the left side of a character.

(8) 五　　　　　一 丁 五 五

wǔ　　five　　　　　　　4 strokes

(9) 木　　　　　一 十 才 木

mù　　wood　　　　　　4 strokes

Note：“木” is written as “才” on the left side of a character.

(10) 火　　　　　丶 丷 少 火

huǒ　　fire　　　　　　　4 strokes

Note：“火” is written as “灬” at the bottom of a character.

3. 认写课文中的汉字 Learn and write the Chinese characters appearing in the texts

林　lín

林 → 木 ＋ 木

| 文化知识 | Cultural Notes |

The Chinese Language (*Hanyu*) and "Common Speech" (*Putonghua*)

Scholars think Chinese writing originated almost four thousand years ago and that the spoken language goes back to remote antiquity, making it one of the world's oldest languages. In spite of its great age, Chinese is now one of the most widely used living languages. The language is spoken in many dialects within China, as well as in many overseas Chinese communities, especially in Southeast Asia, Europe, and the Americas. And there are more than a billion native speakers of Chinese worldwide. It is one of the languages the United Nations uses when conducting official business.

Chinese belongs to the Sino-Tibetan language family. *Hanyu*, literally "language of the *Han*", refers to the standard Chinese language, and is spoken by the *Han*, *Hui*, *Manchu*, and other ethnic groups that constitute 94% of the population of China. There are fifty-six recognized ethnic groups in China, using as many as eighty different languages.

Chinese includes variants from seven main dialect groups. The northern or Mandarin dialect covers three fourths of China's territory and includes two thirds of its population. Standard Chinese is also known by its official designation, *Putonghua*, literally "common speech". *Putonghua* is based on the northern dialect, using the dialect of Beijing as the basis for its pronunciation and modern vernacular literature for its grammatical structure. This is the Chinese that is taught in this textbook.

Have you ever wanted to say hello in Chinese to your friends? By the end of this lesson, you will be able to greet others and express your needs.

第二课 Lesson 2

Nǐ máng ma
你 忙 吗

一. 课文　Text

（一）

【问候别人】Greetings

Lín Nà：　　Lù Yǔpíng, nǐ hǎo ma?
林　娜：　　陆 雨平，你 好 吗？ *Your/my* tpossesme.

Lù Yǔpíng：Wǒ hěn hǎo. Nǐ bàba、māma hǎo ma?①
陆 雨平：　我 很 好。你 爸爸、妈妈 好 吗？

Lín Nà：　　Tāmen dōu hěn hǎo.② Nǐ máng ma?
林　娜：　　他们 都 很 好。你 忙 吗？

Lù Yǔpíng：Wǒ bù máng. Nǐ nán péngyou ne?
陆 雨平：　我 不 忙。你 男 朋友 呢？

Lín Nà：　　Tā hěn máng.
林　娜：　　他 很 忙。

父
巴

heart 心　Angry 怒　忄 vertical heart.　女也 - her. tā
men = plural.　笔

生词 New Words

1. máng	A	忙	busy	
*2. ma	QPt	吗[1]	(a particle used for questions expecting a yes-no answer)	
3. bàba	N	爸爸	dad	
4. māma	N	妈妈	mom	
5. tāmen	Pr	他们	they; them	
tā	Pr	他	he; him	
men	Suf	们	(used after pronouns 我, 你, 他 or certain nouns to denote plural)	
6. dōu	Adv	都	both; all	
7. bù	Adv	不	not; no	
8. nán	A	男	male	
9. péngyou	N	朋友	friend	
*10. ne	MdPt	呢	(a modal particle used for elliptical questions)	

(二)

【问需要】Asking what someone wants

Dīng Lìbō: Gēge, nǐ yào kāfēi ma? ③
丁 力波：哥哥，你 要 咖啡 吗?

Gēge: Wǒ yào kāfēi.
哥哥： 我 要 咖啡。

Family Rules.

Dìdi: Wǒ yě yào kāfēi. ④
弟弟： 我 也 要 咖啡。

Dīng Lìbō: Hǎo, wǒmen dōu hē kāfēi. ⑤
丁 力波： 好, 我们 都 喝 咖啡。

kě 渴
Thirsty

shuǐ 水

---

[1] Words marked by an asterisk have appeared in previous lessons.

Wǒ → only before family members/ response.

生词 New Words

1. gēge	N	哥哥	elder brother
2. yào	V	要	to want
3. kāfēi	N	咖啡	coffee
4. dìdi	N	弟弟	younger brother
5. wǒmen	Pr	我们	we; us
6. hē	V	喝	to drink
7. Dīng	PN	丁	(a surname)

二. 注释　　Notes

① Nǐ bàba、māma hǎo ma?

"How are your mom and dad? "

nǐ bàba —— your dad, nǐ māma —— your mom,

nǐ nán péngyou —— your boyfriend.

② Tāmen dōu hěn hǎo.

"They are both fine (literally, very good)."

③ Nǐ yào kāfēi ma?

"Do you want coffee? "

"你要…吗? "("Nǐ yào … ma? ") is a sentence pattern commonly used when asking what others want, whereas "我要…"("Wǒ yào …") is used to express what "I want".

④ Wǒ yě yào kāfēi.

"I want coffee, too."

⑤ Wǒmen dōu hē kāfēi.

"We all drink coffee."

三. 语音练习　　Pronunciation Drills

声母 Initials:	d	t	g	k	f	*aunny*	*eyou*
韵母 Finals:	ei	ou	an	ang	eng	iao	iou(-iu)

1. 拼音 Spelling

dē	dōu	dān	dāng
tē	tōu	tān	tāng
gē	gōu	gān	gāng
kē	kōu	kān	kāng

bēi	bān	bēng *-uhng*	biāo
pēi	pān	pēng	piāo
fēi	fān	fēng	diū
hēi	hān	hēng	niū

2. 四声 The four tones

tā		tǎ	tà	
mēn	mén		mèn	tāmen
wō		wǒ	wò	wǒmen
nī	ní	nǐ	nì	nǐmen
nān	nán	nǎn	nàn	
pēng	péng	pěng	pèng	
yōu	yóu	yǒu	yòu	nán péngyou
bū	bú	bǔ	bù	
	máng	mǎng		bù máng
gē	gé	gě	gè	gēge
dī	dí	dǐ	dì	dìdi
hē	hé		hè	
kā		kǎ		
fēi	féi	fěi	fèi	hē kāfēi

3. 辨音 Sound discrimination

dà —— tà	kě —— gě	kǒu —— gǒu
(big)	(may)	(mouth) (dog)
dōu —— duō	gēn —— gēng	dīng —— tīng
(all) (many)	(to follow)	(nail) (to listen)

4. 辨调 Tone discrimination

dāo —— dào	tǔ —— tù	yòu —— yǒu
(knife)	(soil)	(again) (to have)
ní —— nǐ	liù —— liú	kàn —— kǎn
(Buddhist nun)	(six)	(to see)

5. 轻声 Neutral tone

bàba　　　māma　　　gēge　　　dìdi

nǐmen　　　wǒmen　　　tāmen

hǎo ma?　　　Nǐ ne?　　　Nǐ nán péngyou ne?

6. 双音节连读 Practice on disyllabic words

yǐnliào (drinks)　　　　　　　yéye (grandpa) _Fathers side._

kělè (coke)　　　　　　　　　mèimei (younger sister)

hànbǎo (hamburger)　　　　　　fāyīn (pronunciation)

píngguǒ (apple)　　　　　　　hēibǎn (blackboard)

7. 朗读下列课堂用语 Read the following classroom expressions aloud

Tīng wǒ fāyīn.　　　(Listen to my pronunciation.)

Kàn hēibǎn.　　　(Look at the blackboard.)

四. 会话练习　　Conversation Practice

> **KEY SENTENCES**
> 1. Tāmen dōu hěn hǎo.
> 2. Nǐ máng ma?
> 3. Wǒ bù máng.
> 4. Nǐ yào kāfēi ma?
> 5. Wǒ yào kāfēi.
> 6. Wǒmen dōu hē kāfēi.　_all._

（一）【问候别人 Greetings】

完成下列会话 Complete the following dialogues

(1) A：Dà Lín, nǐ máng ma?

B：_Wǒ bù máng_. Nǐ ne?

A：_Wǒ hěn máng_.

(2) A：Nǐ bàba māma hǎo ma?

B：_Tāmen dōu hěn hǎo_. Nǐ gēge ne?

A：_Tā hěn hǎo_.

(3) A：Nǐ dìdi hǎo ma?

B：<u>Tā hěn hǎo</u>. Nǐ <u>gēge</u> ne?

nán péngyou

chá 茶

A：<u>Tā hěn máng</u>.

（二）【问需要 Asking what someone wants】

1. 完成下列会话 Complete the following dialogues

(1) A：Nín yào kāfēi ma?

B：Wǒ yào kāfēi.

A：Nǐ ne?

C：<u>Wǒ bù yào kāfēi</u>.

nín (you-polite).

(2) A：Nǐ yào <u>kāfēi</u> ma?

B：<u>wǒ yào kāfēi</u>.

A：Nǐ ne?

C：<u>Wǒ yě yào kāfēi</u>.

kěle (cola).

2. 看图会话 Make a dialogue based on the picture

(1) A：<u>gēge, yào kāfēi ma</u>?

B：<u>Wǒ yào kāfēi</u>.

(2) A：<u>Nǐ yào kāfēi ma</u>?

B：<u>Wǒ bù yào kāfēi</u>.

（三）听述 Listen and repeat

你爸爸妈妈都好吗？

他们都很好。

1. 轻声 Neutral tone

In the common speech of modern Chinese, there are a number of syllables which are unstressed and are pronounced in a "weak" tone. This is known as the neutral tone and is indicated by the absence of a tone mark. For example：

吗 ma　　　呢 ne　　　们 men

2. 发音要领 Pronunciation key

Initials：f　is pronounced similarly to its counterpart in the English language

d　like "t" in "stay" (unaspirated)

t　like "t" in "tag" (aspirated)

g　a soft unaspirated "k" sound

k　like "k" in "kangaroo" (aspirated)

Note：Particular attention should be paid to the pronunciation of the aspirated and unaspirated consonants：d-t, g-k.

Finals：ei　like "ay" in "play" (light)

ou　like "o" in "so"

an　like "an" in "can" (without stressing the "n")

3. 拼写规则 Spelling rules

The compound final "iou" is written as "-iu" when it comes after an initial and the tone mark is placed on "u". For example：liù (six).

1. 形容词谓语句 Sentences with an adjectival predicate

Subject	Predicate		
你 Nǐ			好。 hǎo.
他 Tā		很 hěn	忙。 máng.
我 Wǒ		不 bù	忙。 máng.
他们 Tāmen	都 dōu	很 hěn	好。 hǎo.

yòu before verb

Adjectives in Chinese can function directly as predicates. This kind of sentence is called a sentence with an adjectival predicate. Adjectives in this kind of sentence can be modified by adverbs such as "很", "也", and "都". The negative form of sentences with an adjectival predicate is generated by placing the negative adverb "不" before the adjective that functions as the predicate. For example："我不忙".

Note：Adverbs such as "很", "也", and "都" must be placed before the adjective they modify.

2. 用"吗"的是非问句 "Yes-no" question with "吗"

A declarative sentence can be changed into a "yes-no" question by adding the question particle "吗" at the end of it.

Statement	Question
你好。 Nǐ hǎo. ⟶	你好吗？ Nǐ hǎo ma?
他爸爸、妈妈都好。 Tā bàba、māma dōu hǎo. ⟶	他爸爸、妈妈都好吗？ Tā bàba、māma dōu hǎo ma?
她忙。 Tā máng. ⟶	她忙吗？ Tā máng ma?
你要咖啡。 Nǐ yào kāfēi. ⟶	你要咖啡吗？ Nǐ yào kāfēi ma?

七. 汉字　Chinese Characters

1. 认写基本汉字 Learn and write basic Chinese characters

(1) 丁　一 丁

dīng　nail　2 strokes

Used as family name in modern times.

(2) 刀　フ 刀

dāo　knife　2 strokes

Note："刀" is written as " 刂 " on the right side of a character.

(3) 又　フ 又

yòu　again　2 strokes

Note："又" was originally a pictograph of "the right hand".

(4) 大　一 ナ 大

dà　big　3 strokes

(5) 口 　　丨 冂 口

　　kǒu　　mouth　　　　　　　　　　3 strokes

(6) 土 　　一 十 土

　　tǔ　　earth　　　　　　　　　　3 strokes

Note: "土" is written as "扌" on the left side of a character.

(7) 六 　　丶 亠 六 六

　　liù　　six　　　　　　　　　　4 strokes

(8) 不 　　一 ア 不 不

　　bù　　no, not　　　　　　　　4 strokes

(9) 尼 　　一 コ 尸 尸 尼

　　ní　　Buddhist nun　　　　　　5 strokes

(10) 可 　　一 丨 冂 口 可

　　kě　　can, may　　　　　　　5 strokes

2. 认写课文中的汉字 Learn and write the Chinese characters appearing in the texts

(1) 吗 ma (嗎)

　　吗 → 口 + 马

　　("口" denotes the meaning of speaking, "马" denotes the pronunciation)

(2) 呢 ne

　　呢 → 口 + 尼

　　("口" denotes the meaning of speaking, "尼" denotes the pronunciation)

(3) 妈妈 māma (媽媽)

　　妈 → 女 + 马

　　("女" denotes the meaning of woman, "马" denotes the pronunciation)

(4) 哥哥 gēge

　　哥 → 可 + 可

Chinese Characters and Simplified Script

The Chinese script is the only logographic writing system still in daily use in the world today. Unlike the alphabetic systems used by most languages, Chinese script is made up of characters, the majority of which are "pictophonetic". Most consist of one component indicating the sound of the character, the phonetic, combined with one semantic component, the signific or radical, which shows the category of meaning to which the character belongs.

Chinese characters represent monosyllables, and generally each character represents a single morpheme. The total number of Chinese characters is estimated at over fifty thousand, of which only five to eight thousand are frequently used, while three thousand are normally adequate for everyday situations.

A considerable number of Chinese characters are composed of numerous strokes and are therefore complicated to write. With a view to facilitating writing, modern scholars have made continuous attempts to simplify the writing system. The object of these language reforms has been twofold: to reduce the number of characters by eliminating complex variants, and to reduce the number of strokes in certain characters. What are known as "simplified characters" refer to graphs that have been thus altered; traditional characters, on the other hand, are those that retain their earlier forms.

The use of simplified characters is now official policy in the People's Republic of China, while traditional characters are restricted mainly to academic use or aesthetic purposes. Simplified characters have the advantages of being easier to learn, memorize, read and write. Here are two examples:

妈　mother　(simplified)　　　　媽 mother　(traditional)

门　door　(simplified)　　　　門 door　(traditional)

Simplified characters are used in this textbook, but traditional characters are also supplied for the convenience of the reader.

Now, would you like to use Chinese to learn more about the people you meet? This lesson will show you how to ask a person's occupation and nationality, as well as introduce friends, family and others. In addition, we will create compound words from basic words.

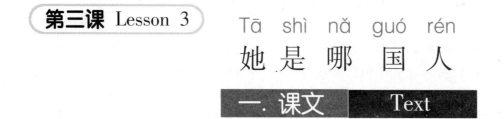

第三课 Lesson 3

Tā shì nǎ guó rén

她 是 哪 国 人

一. 课文 | Text

（一）

Gēge:　　　Lìbō, nà shì shéi?
哥哥：　　　力波，那 是 谁？

【认指人】Identifying people

Dīng Lìbō：Nà shì wǒmen lǎoshī.
丁 力波：　那 是 我们 老师。

【问国籍】Asking someone's nationality

Gēge:　　　Tā shì nǎ guó rén? ①
哥哥：　　　她 是 哪 国 人？

Dīng Lìbō：Tā shì Zhōngguó rén. ② Wǒmen lǎoshī dōu shì Zhōngguó rén.
丁 力波：　她 是 中国 人。　我们 老师 都 是 中国 人。

Wǒ ài nǐ. 爱 下 below.
↳ love. 友 friend.

生词 New Words

1. tā	Pr	她	she; her	
2. shì	V	是	to be 是 → showing existance.	
3. nǎ	QPr	哪 哪	which	讠 speech radical
4. guó	N	国	country, nation	
5. rén	N	人	people, person	
6. nà	Pr	那	that	
7. shéi	QPr	谁 ↗ master.	who; whom (sub.) (obj.)	谁 ≐ 言
8. lǎoshī	N	老师 old	teacher	≐ 言 talk.
*9. dōu	Adv	都	both; all	
10. Zhōngguó	PN	中国 国	China + rén = Chinese → Think 3 times before talking.	

(二)

nǐ shì nǎ guó rén.
lǎo 老 ← dagger.

Dīng Lìbō: Chén lǎoshī, nín hǎo! ③ Zhè shì wǒ yēye, ① tā shì wàiyǔ
丁 力波： 陈 老师，您 好！ 这 是 我 哥哥， 他 是 外语

lǎoshī.
老师。

Chén lǎoshī: Nǐ hǎo.
陈 老师： 你 好。

Dīng Lìbō: Zhè shì wǒ péngyou.
丁 力波： 这 是 我 朋友。

Chén lǎoshī: Nǐ hǎo! Nǐ yě shì lǎoshī ma?
陈 老师： 你 好！你 也 是 老师 吗？

Péngyou: Nín hǎo! Wǒ bú shì lǎoshī, wǒ shì yīshēng.
朋友： 您 好！ 我 不 是 老师， 我 是 医生。

Chén lǎoshī: Lìbō, zhè shì nǐ nǎinai ma?
陈 老师： 力波，这 是 你 奶奶 吗？

她 she, her.

Dīng Lìbō: Bú shì, tā shì wǒ wàipó. ⑤
丁 力波： 不 是， 她 是 我 外婆。

Shi	si	Pronounce
Chi	ci	ū out g
Zhi	zi	Pronounce
ri		ū other vowels.

Chén lǎoshī: Wàipó, nín hǎo!
陈 老师： 外婆， 您 好！

middle kingdom *jade / country.*
Zhōng → guó ↗ rén.
中 国 人

Wáng → heaven → King → earth → hell
王

生词　New Words

1. nín	Pr	您	you (polite form)
2. zhè	Pr	这	this
*3. tā	Pr	他	he; him
4. wàiyǔ	N	外语	foreign language
*5. nǐ	Pr	你	you
6. yīshēng	N	医生	doctor; physician
7. nǎinai	N	奶奶	grandmother on the father's side
8. wàipó	N	外婆	grandmother on the mother's side
9. Chén	PN	陈	(a surname)

二. 注释　Notes

① **Tā shì nǎ guó rén?**

"What's her nationality?"

There are two Chinese characters for the third person singular "tā": one is "他", used for a male; the other "她", refers to a female.

② **Tā shì Zhōngguó rén.**

"She is a Chinese."

To indicate the nationality of an individual, the character "人"(rén) is usually placed after the name of his/her country of origin. For example:

中国(Zhōngguó)——中国人(Zhōngguó rén)

③ **Chén lǎoshī, nín hǎo!**

In China, a person's position or occupation, such as the director of a factory, manager, section head, engineer, movie director, or teacher, is frequently used as a title to address him/her in preference to such expressions as Mr. or Miss. Surnames always precede the titles. It is considered impolite for a student to address a teacher directly by his/her personal name. "Surname + teacher" is the most proper form of address frequently used for a teacher, e.g., "Chén lǎoshī(陈老师)".

"nín(您)" is the polite form of "你", commonly used to refer to an elderly or a senior person during a conversation or to a person of the same generation when speaking on a formal occasion. People in Beijing are quite fond of using this form of address.

④ **Zhè shì wǒ gēge.**

"This is my elder brother."

When introducing someone to a person, we often use the sentence pattern "这是…" ("zhè shì…"). "是"(shì) is pronounced as a weak syllable.

⑤ **Lìbō, zhè shì nǐ nǎinai ma? —— Bú shì, tā shì wǒ wàipó.**

The Chinese language uses many words for referring to individuals in a family so that their specific relationship to other members of the family is made clear. Different words are used depending on whether a relative is on the mother's or wife's side or on the father's or husband's side. Some examples are "yéye" and "nǎinai" used by a child to address the parents of his/her father, differentiated from "wàigōng" and "wàipó" used to address his/her mother's parents.

三. 语音练习　Pronunciation Drills

声母 Initials: zh　ch　sh　r
韵母 Finals: -i [ʅ]
ai　uai　ong

1. 拼音 Spelling

zhā	chā	shā	
zhī	chī	shī	rī
zhē	chē	shē	rēng
zhāi	chāi	shāi	rāng
zhōu	chōu	shōu	
zhuō	chuō	shuō	
zhuāi	chuāi	shuāi	
zhōng	chōng		

2. 四声 The four tones

chā	chá	chǎ	chà	
	rú	rǔ	rù	
zhē	zhé	zhě	zhè	
shī	shí	shǐ	shì	zhè shì

lāo	láo	lǎo	lào	lǎoshī
chēn	chén	chěn	chèn	Chén lǎoshī
wāi		wǎi	wài	
yū	yú	yǔ	yù	wàiyǔ
yī	yí	yǐ	yì	
shēng	shéng	shěng	shèng	yīshēng
zhōng		zhǒng	zhòng	
guō	guó	guǒ	guò	Zhōngguó
	rén	rěn	rèn	Zhōngguó rén

3. 辨音 Sound discrimination

zhōng —— chōng　　shēng —— shāng　　rì —— rè

(middle)　　　　　　(to be born)　　　　　(sun)　　(hot)

bǐ —— pǐ　　　　　dǒng —— tǒng　　　ròu —— ruò

(dagger)　　　　　(to understand)　　　(meat)

4. 辨调 Tone discrimination

shí —— shǐ　　　　zhě —— zhè　　　rén —— rèn

(ten)　　(arrow)　　(person; thing)　(this)　　(person)

pái —— pài　　　　chéng —— chēng　　zhuǎi —— zhuài

　　　　　　　　　(city)

5. 半三声 Half third tone

lǎoshī　　　　　nǎinai　　　　　wǒmen　　　　　nǐmen

wǒ gēge　　　wǒ péngyou　　wǒ nǎinai

nǐ wàipó　　　nǐ bàba　　　　nǎ guó rén

hǎo ma　　　nǐ máng　　　　hěn máng

nǐ yào　　　　wǒ yào　　　　yě yào　　　　　kělè

6. 声调组合 Combination of tones

"ˉ"+"ˉ"　　　"ˉ"+"ˊ"　　　"ˉ"+"ˇ"　　　"ˉ"+"ˋ"　　　"ˉ"+"。"[1]

kāfēi　　　　Zhōngguó　　　hēibǎn　　　　shēngdiào　　　tāmen

　　　　　　　　　　　　　　　　　　　　(tone)

---

[1] " ° " here represents the neutral tone.

yīshēng	hē chá	shēntǐ	chīfàn	zhīdao
	(to drink tea)	(body)	(to eat a meal)	(to know)

"ˊ"+"ˉ"　　"ˊ"+"ˊ"　　"ˊ"+"ˇ"　　"ˊ"+"ˋ"　　"ˊ"+"˚"

túshū	chángcháng	niúnǎi	liúlì	péngyou
(books)	(often)	(milk)	(fluent)	

chénggōng	yínháng	píngguǒ	chídào	yéye
(success)	(bank)	(apple)	(late)	

7. 双音节连读 Practice on disyllabic words

gōngren (worker)　　　　　　Yīngguó (England, UK)

shāngrén (merchant) *(buisness man)*　　Déguó (Germany)

lǜshī (lawyer)　　　　　　Měiguó (America)

gànbu (cadre) *(official (govrn))*　　Fǎguó (France)

chǎngzhǎng (factory manager)　　Éguó (Russia)

nóngmín (peasant) *(farmer)*　　Rìběn (Japan)

8. 朗读下列课堂用语 Read the following classroom expressions aloud

Dǎ kāi shū.　　　(Open the book.)

Gēn wǒ niàn.　　(Read after me.)

Nǐmen niàn.　　　(Read out.)

Dǒng bu dǒng?　(Do you understand?　)

Dǒng le.　　　　(Yes, I/we understand.)

Bù dǒng.　　　　(No, I/we don't understand.)

四. 会话练习　Conversation Practice

KEY SENTENCES

1. Nà shì shéi? *that is who*
2. Nà shì wǒmen lǎoshī. *that is our teacher*
3. Tā shì nǎ guó rén? *she is which country person*
4. Tā shì Zhōngguó rén. *she is Chinese*
5. Zhè shì wǒ péngyou. *this is my friend*
6. Nǐ yě shì lǎoshī ma?
7. Wǒ bú shì lǎoshī, wǒ shì yīshēng. *I am not a teacher / I am a doctor*

（一）【认指人 Identifying people】

看图会话 Make a dialogue based on the picture

(1) A：Nà shì shéi?

B：Nà shì _____.

(2) A：Tā shì shéi?

B：Tā shì _____.

（二）【问国籍 Asking someone's nationality】

1. 完成下列会话 Complete the following dialogues

(1) A：Nín shì nǎ guó rén?

B：_____.

A：Tā ne?

B：_____.

(2) A：Nín shì Yīngguó rén ma?

B：Bú shì, _____. Nín shì nǎ guó rén?

A：_____.

More than 2 syllables no guó to follow.

2. 看图会话 Make a dialogue based on the picture

A：Tā shì nǎ guó rén?

B：_____.

（三）【介绍 **Introducing people**】

1. 完成下列会话 Complete the following dialogues

（1）A：Zhè shì Lín yīshēng. Zhè shì Chén lǎoshī.

B：_____.

C：Nín hǎo, Lín yīshēng.

（2）A：Zhè shì _____. Zhè shì _____.

B：_____.

C：_____.

2. 情景会话 Situational dialogue

Introduce your teacher and classmates.

（四）听述 Listen and repeat

那是谁？那是陈老师。她是中国人。这是我朋友，他不是老师，他是医生。

1. 三声变调 Third-tone sandhi

A third tone, when followed by a first, second or fourth tone, or most neutral tone syllables, usually becomes a half third tone, that is, a tone that only falls but does not rise. The tone mark is unchanged. For example：

nǐ gēge   wǒ yào

nǐ máng ma?

2. "不"的变调 Tone sandhi of "不"

"不" is a fourth tone syllable by itself. But it becomes a second tone when followed by a fourth tone. For example：

bù hē   bù máng   bù hǎo

bú shì   bú yào

3. 发音要领 Pronunciation key

Initials: zh   like "j" in "jerk", but with the tip of the tongue curled farther back, unaspirated.

        ch   like "ch" in "church", but with the tip of the tongue curled farther back, aspirated.

        sh   like "sh" in "ship", but with the tip of the tongue curled farther back.

        r   as in "right" in English, but with lips unrounded, and the tip of the tongue curled farther back. Always pronounce the Chinese /r/ sound with a nice smile! ☺

Finals: ai   like "y" in "sky" (light)

        -i [ʅ]   "-i [ʅ]" in "zhi", "chi", "shi" and "ri" is pronounced differently from the simple final "i [i]". After pronouncing the initials "zh", "ch", "sh" and "r", the tongue does not move. Care must be taken not to pronounce the simple final "i [i]", which is never found after "zh", "ch", "sh" or "r".

六. 汉字   Chinese Characters

1. 认写基本汉字 Learn and write basic Chinese characters

(1) 人   丿 人

rén   people, person   2 strokes

Note：On the left side of a character, "人" is written as "亻".

(2) 十　　一十

shí　　ten　　　　　　　　　　　　　　　　　　2 strokes

(3) 匕　　　ノ匕

bǐ　　　dagger　　　　　　　　　　　　　　2 strokes

(4) 中　　　丨冂口中

zhōng　middle　　　　　　　　　　　　　4 strokes

(5) 日　　　丨冂月日

rì　　　sun　　　　　　　　　　　　　　　4 strokes

(6) 贝(貝)　丨冂贝贝

bèi　　shell (tresure) (baby)　　　　　　4 strokes

(7) 玉　　　一二干王玉

yù　　　jade　　　　　　　　　　　　　　5 strokes

Note: On the left side of a character, "玉" is written as "王".

(8) 矢　　　ノ亠仁矢矢

shǐ　　arrow　　　　　　　　　　　　　　5 strokes

(9) 生　　　ノ亠仁牛生

shēng　to be born; suffix denoting person　　5 strokes

↳ Gender neutral

(10) 者　　一十土耂者者者 (耂 + 日)

zhě　　person; thing　　　　　　　　　　8 strokes

2. 认写课文中已出现的汉字 Learn and write the Chinese characters appearing in the texts

(1) 她 tā　　　　　　　　　　　　mace

她 → 女 + 也　　　　也　men (plural)

(The "female" side, "女", denotes something related to a woman.)

(2) 他 tā

他 → 亻 + 也

(The "standing person" side, "亻", denotes something related to a person.)

(3) 们 men (們)

们 → 亻 + 门

(The meaning side is "亻", and the phonetic side is "门".)

(4) 你 nǐ

你 → 亻 + 尔

(尔: 丿 勹 勺 尔 尔   5 strokes)

(The "standing person" side "亻" denotes something related to a person.)

阝 (yòu'ěrduo) (the "right-ear" side)   ⻖ 阝   2 strokes

月 (nàzìpáng) (the "that" side)   刁 刁 刁 月   4 strokes

(5) 那 nà

那 → 月 + 阝   (that)

(6) 哪 nǎ

哪 → 口 + 那   Which

(The meaning side is "口", and the phonetic side is "那".)

(7) 娜 nà

娜 → 女 + 那   Female elegance.

(The meaning side is "女", and the phonetic side is "那".)

(8) 都 dōu

都 → 者 + 阝   all

耂 (lǎozìtóu) (the "old" top)   一 十 土 耂   4 strokes

巾 (jīnzìr) (the "towel" character)   丨 冂 巾   3 strokes

丿 (shīzìpáng) (the "teacher" side)   丨 丿   2 strokes

(9) 老师 lǎoshī (老師)

老 → 耂 + 匕

师 → 丿 + 一 + 巾

[handwritten: teacher / lǎo — old / shī — master.]

口 (guózìkuàng)(The "country" frame, "口", denotes the boundary of a country.)

丨 冂 口   3 strokes

(10) 中国 Zhōngguó (中國)

国 → 口 + 玉

匚 (yīzìkuàng) (the "doctor" frame) ㇐ 匚   2 strokes

(11) 医生 yīshēng (醫生)

医 → 匚 + 矢

(医：一 丆 丆 乒 乒 医   7 strokes)

疋 (pǐzìdǐ) (the "foot" bottom) 一 丅 下 疋 疋   5 strokes

(12) 是 shì

是 → 日 + 疋

文化知识　Cultural Notes

Scheme for the Chinese Phonetic Alphabet

Chinese differs from alphabetic languages in that its written form is not directly related to its pronunciation. In order to provide phonetic notation for Chinese characters and to facilitate the consultation of dictionaries, phonologists drafted the "Scheme for the Chinese Phonetic Alphabet", and in 1958 the Chinese government passed an act to promote the application of this scheme, commonly known as the *pinyin* ("arranged sounds") system. *Pinyin* adopts the Latin alphabet to transcribe Chinese sounds, and four diacritical tone marks to indicate the different tones of Chinese characters. *Pinyin* is now widely used for the study of Chinese language, and has aided the popularization of standard Chinese (*Putonghua*). The use of *pinyin* in the study of Chinese provides many practical advantages for learning the language.

In this lesson, you will learn how to ask someone's name politely, how to introduce yourself, and how to ask for permission. The pronunciations of the Chinese initials introduced in this lesson are different than similar-sounding initials found in English, and so may seem unfamiliar to you. Don't be discouraged, however, for with daily practice you will surely be able to master them.

第四课 Lesson 4

Rènshi nǐ hěn gāoxìng
认识 你 很 高兴

一. 课文　Text

（一）

【请求允许】Asking for permission

Lǎoshī: Kěyǐ jìnlai ma? ①
老师：可以进来吗?

Lín Nà: Qǐng jìn! ② Yáng lǎoshī, nín hǎo. Zhè shì wǒ péngyou,
林娜：请 进! 杨 老师,您 好。这 是 我 朋友,

tā shì jìzhě.
他 是 记者。

【问姓名】Asking someone's name

Lǎoshī: Qǐngwèn, nín guìxìng? ③
老师：请问, 您 贵姓?

Lù Yǔpíng： Wǒ xìng Lù, jiào Lù Yǔpíng. ④

陆 雨 平： 我 姓 陆， 叫 陆 雨 平。

Lǎoshī： Nǐ hǎo, Lù xiānsheng, rènshi nǐ hěn gāoxìng. ⑤

老师： 你 好， 陆 先生， 认识 你 很 高兴。

Lù Yǔpíng： Yáng lǎoshī, rènshi nín, wǒ yě hěn gāoxìng.

陆 雨 平： 杨 老师， 认识 您， 我 也 很 高兴。

生词 New Words

1. rènshi	V	认识	to know (somebody)
2. gāoxìng	A	高兴	happy; pleased
3. kěyǐ	OpV	可以	may
4. jìnlai	VC	进来	to come in
jìn	V	进	to enter
lái	V	来	to come
5. qǐng	V	请	please
*6. nín	Pr	您	you (polite form)
*7. péngyou	N	朋友	friend
8. jìzhě	N	记者	reporter
9. qǐngwèn	V	请问	May I ask...? (excuse me)
wèn	V	问	to ask
10. guìxìng	IE	贵姓	what's your honorable surname?
xìng	V/N	姓	one's surname is···/surname
11. jiào	V	叫	to be called
12. xiānsheng	N	先生	Mr.
13. Yáng	PN	杨	(a surname)

【自我介绍】
Introducing oneself

(二)

Lín Nà： Wǒ shì Yǔyán Xuéyuàn de xuésheng. ⑥ Wǒ xìng Lín,

林 娜： 我 是 语言 学院 的 学生。 我 姓 林，

jiào Lín Nà. Wǒ shì Yīngguó rén. Nǐ xìng shénme? ⑦

叫 林 娜。 我 是 英国 人。 你 姓 什么？

Mǎ Dàwéi: Wǒ xìng Mǎ, jiào Mǎ Dàwéi.

马 大为： 我 姓 马，叫 马 大为。

Lín Nà: Nǐ shì Jiānádà rén ma?

林 娜： 你 是 加拿大 人 吗？

Mǎ Dàwéi: Wǒ bú shì Jiānádà rén, wǒ shì Měiguó rén, yě shì

马 大为： 我 不是 加拿大人，我 是 美国 人，也 是

Yǔyán Xuéyuàn de xuésheng. Wǒ xuéxí Hànyǔ.

语言 学院 的 学生。 我 学习 汉语。

生词 New Words

1. yǔyán	N	语言	language
2. xuéyuàn	N	学院	institute; college
3. de	Pt	的	(a possessive or modifying particle)
4. xuésheng	N	学生	student
5. shénme	QPr	什么	what
6. xuéxí	V	学习	to learn; to study
7. Hànyǔ	N	汉语	Chinese (language)
8. Yīngguó	PN	英国	Great Britain; England
9. Mǎ Dàwéi	PN	马大为	(name of an American student)
10. Jiānádà	PN	加拿大	Canada
11. Měiguó	PN	美国	the United States; America

二. 注释　　Notes

① Kěyǐ jìnlai ma?

"May I come in? "

② Qǐng jìn!

"Come in, please! "

"Qǐng(请)…" is an expression used for making polite requests.

③ Qǐngwèn, nín guìxìng?

"May I ask what is your (honorable) surname?"

This is a polite way of asking someone's surname. In China, when meeting someone for the first time, it is considered more polite to ask his/her surname rather than his/her full name. Notice that "guì(贵)" can only be used in combination with "nǐ(你)" or "nín(您)", and not with "wǒ(我)" or "tā (他/她)".

"Qǐngwèn(请问)" means "May I ask..." or "Excuse me, but...", and is a polite way of asking a question.

④ Wǒ xìng Lù, jiào Lù Yǔpíng.

"My surname is Lu, and my full name is Lu Yuping."

When answering the question "Nín guìxìng?", one can either give one's surname by saying "Wǒ xìng…", or give one's full name by saying "Wǒ jiào…" or say both "Wǒ xìng …, jiào ….".

Note that in Chinese, one's surname always comes first, and the given name comes last.

⑤ Rènshi nǐ hěn gāoxìng.

"(I'm) glad to meet (literally, know) you."

⑥ Wǒ shì Yǔyán Xuéyuàn de xuésheng.

"I am a student at (literally, of) the Language Institute."

⑦ Nǐ xìng shénme?

"What's your surname?"

This informal way of asking someone's surname is appropriate when an adult is speaking to a child, or when young people are talking with each other.

三. 语音练习　Pronunciation Drills

声母 Initials: j　q　x
韵母 Finals: ia　ian　iang
　　　　　　uei(-ui)　uen(-un)　üe　üan

1. 拼音 Spelling

jī	qī	xī
jiā	qiā	xiā
jiān	qiān	xiān
jiāng	qiāng	xiāng
jīn	qīn	xīn

jīng	qīng	xīng
jū	qū	xū
juē	quē	xuē
juān	quān	xuān
guī	kuī	huī
zhūn	chūn	tūn

2. 四声 The four tones

jī	jí	jǐ	jì	
zhē	zhé	zhě	zhè	jìzhě
qīng	qíng	qǐng	qìng	
jīn		jǐn	jìn	qǐng jìn
guī		guǐ	guì	
xīng	xíng	xǐng	xìng	guìxìng
xiān	xián	xiǎn	xiàn	
shēng	shéng	shěng	shèng	xiānsheng
yū	yú	yǔ	yù	
yān	yán	yǎn	yàn	yǔyán
xuē	xué	xuě	xuè	
yuān	yuán	yuǎn	yuàn	xuéyuàn
xī	xí	xǐ	xì	xuéxí
hān	hán	hǎn	hàn	Hànyǔ
jiā	jiá	jiǎ	jià	Jiānádà

3. 辨音 Sound discrimination

jiāo —— qiāo   yuè —— yè   duì —— tuì

(to teach)   (month)   (night)   (right)

tián —— tíng   yán —— yáng   zhǐ —— chǐ

(field)   (to stop)   (speech)   (sheep)   (only)   (ruler)

4. 辨调 Tone discrimination

shǒu —— shòu   xià —— xiā   shuǐ —— shuì

(hand)   (thin)   (down)   (water)   (to sleep)

xīn —— xìn		bái —— bǎi		xiǎo —— xiào
(heart)	(letter)	(white)	(small)	(to laugh)

5. 声调组合 Combination of tones

" ˇ "+" ¯ "	" ˇ "+" ˊ "	" ˇ "+" ˇ "	" ˇ "+" ˋ "	" ˇ "+" ◦ "
lǎoshī	yǔyán	kěyǐ	qǐng jìn	wǒmen
Běijīng	lǚxíng	yǔfǎ	kǎoshì	jiějie
(Beijing)	(to travel)	(grammar)	(exam)	(elder sister)

" ˋ "+" ¯ "	" ˋ "+" ˊ "	" ˋ "+" ˇ "	" ˋ "+" ˋ "	" ˋ "+" ◦ "
Lìbō	wàipó	Hànyǔ	guìxìng	mèimei
miànbāo	liànxí	bàozhǐ	zhùyì	kèqi
(bread)	(exercise)	(newspaper)	(to pay attention to)	(courtesy)

6. 双音节连读 Practice on disyllabic words

tàitai （Mrs）   Yīngyǔ （English）

xiǎojiě （Miss）   Fǎyǔ （French）

nǚshì （Madam）   Déyǔ （German）

jīnglǐ （manager）   Éyǔ （Russian）

tóngshì （colleague）   Rìyǔ （Japanese）

7. 朗读下列课堂用语 Read the following classroom expressions aloud

Zhùyì fāyīn.   (Pay attention to your pronunciation.)

Zhùyì shēngdiào.   (Pay attention to your tones.)

Duì bu duì?   (Is it right?)

Duì le.   (It's right.)

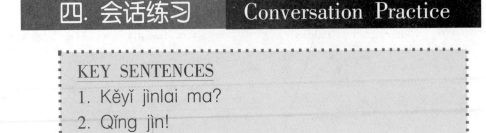

四. 会话练习　Conversation Practice

KEY SENTENCES
1. Kěyǐ jìnlai ma?
2. Qǐng jìn!
3. Nín guìxìng?
4. Wǒ xìng Lù, jiào Lù Yǔpíng.
5. Rènshi nǐ hěn gāoxìng.
6. Wǒ shì Yǔyán Xuéyuàn de xuésheng.
7. Wǒ xuéxí Hànyǔ.

（一）【请求允许 Asking for permission】

看图会话 Make a dialogue based on the picture

A：<u>Kěyǐ jìnlai ma</u>?

B：<u>Qǐng jìn</u>.

（二）【问姓名 Asking someone's name】

完成下列会话 Complete the following dialogues

（1）A：Nín guìxìng?

　　　B：Wǒ xìng <u>Gāo</u>, jiào <u>Gāo Rén jiān</u>.

　　　A：Wǒ jiào <u>Pīng</u>. <u>Rènshi nín</u> wǒ hěn gāoxìng.

　　　B：<u>Wǒ yě hěn gāoxìng</u> Rènshi nín.

（2）A：Nǐ xìng shénme?

　　　B：<u>wǒ xìng Gāo</u>.

（3）A：Tā jiào shénme?

　　　B：<u>Tā jiào Dīng Lìbō</u>.

（4）A：Tā xìng shénme?

　　　B：<u>Tā xìng Dīng</u>.

（三）【自我介绍 Introducing oneself】

情景会话 Situational dialogue

Ask everyone to introduce himself/herself in a meeting by imitating Dialogue II in the text.

（四）听述 Listen and repeat

请进。

您贵姓？

我叫马大为，是语言学院的学生。我学习汉语，杨先生是我们的老师。陆雨平是我朋友，他是记者。认识他，我很高兴。

五. 语音　　　　　Phonetics

1. 发音要领 Pronunciation key

Initials：j is an unaspirated voiceless palatal affricate. To produce this sound, first raise the front of the tongue to the hard palate and press the tip of the tongue against the back of the lower teeth, and then loosen the tongue and let the air squeeze out through the channel thus made. The sound is unaspirated and the vocal cords do not vibrate.

q is an aspirated voiceless palatal affricate. It is produced in the same manner as "j", but it is aspirated.

x is a voiceless palatal fricative. To produce it, first raise the front of the tongue toward (but not touching) the hard palate and then let the air squeeze out. The vocal cords do not vibrate.

Note：The finals that can be combined with "j", "q" and "x" are limited to "i", "ü" and compound finals that start with "i" or "ü".

2. 拼写规则 Spelling rules

（1）When the compound final "uei" is combined with initials, it is simplified to -ui and the tone mark is written over "i". For example：guì.

（2）When the compound final "uen" is combined with initials, it is simplified to -un. For example：lùn.

（3）When "ü" is combined with j, q and x, the two dots over it are omitted. For example：xué. "y" is added to the compound finals which start with "ü" and the two dots over it are omitted. For example：Yǔyán Xuéyuàn.

Note： "J", "q", and "x" are never combined with "u" and "a".

"是"字句(1)　Sentences with "是"(1)

Subject	Predicate			
	Adv	V"是"	N/NP	Pt
他 Tā		是 shì	老师。 lǎoshī.	
马 大为 Mǎ Dàwéi	不 bú	是 shì	老师。 lǎoshī.	
她 Tā		是 shì	学生 xuésheng	吗? ma?

In an "A 是 B" sentence, the verb "是" is used to connect the two parts. Its negative form is made by putting "不" before the verb "是". If the sentence is not particularly emphatic, "是" is read softly.

Note：The adverb "不" must be placed before "是".

七. 汉字　　　　　　Chinese Characters

1. 笔顺规则 Rules of stroke order

Example	Stroke Order	Rule to Write
十	一　十	Horizontal before vertical
人	丿　人	Downward-left before downward-right
妈	女　妈	From left to right
只	口　只	From top to bottom
月	刀　月	From outside to inside
国	冂　国　国	Outside before inside before closing
小	亅　小　小	Middle before two sides

2. 认写基本汉字 Learn and write basic Chinese characters

(1) 七 　　一七

qī　　seven　　　　　　　　　　　2 strokes

(2) 小 　　亅小小

xiǎo　　small, little　　　　　　　3 strokes

(3) 心 　　丶心心心

xīn　　heart　　　　　　　　　　4 strokes

Note：On the left side of a character, "心" is written as "忄", as in "忙".

(4) 水 　　亅水水水

shuǐ　　water　　　　　　　　　　4 strokes

Note：On the left side of a character, "水" is written as "氵", as in "汉".

(5) 月 　　丿刀月月

yuè　　moon　　　　　　　　　　4 strokes

(6) 手 　　一二三手

shǒu　　hand　　　　　　　　　　4 strokes

Note：On the left side of a character, "手" is written as "扌".

(7) 田 　　丨冂日用田

tián　　field　　　　　　　　　　5 strokes

(8) 白 　　丿亻白白白 （一 + 日）

bái　　white　　　　　　　　　　5 strokes

(9) 只 　　丶口口尸只 （口 + 八）

zhǐ　　only　　　　　　　　　　5 strokes

(10) 言 　　丶亠言言言言言

yán　　speech　　　　　　　　　7 strokes

Note：On the left side of a character, "言" is written as "讠", as in "认识".

3. 认写课文中的汉字 Learn and write the Chinese characters appearing in the texts

(1) 认识 rènshi（認識）

认 → 讠 + 人

（"讠", the meaning side plus the phonetic side, "人".)

识 → 讠 + 只

（"讠", the meaning side, denotes language-related behavior.)

(2) 语言 yǔyán（語言）

语 → 讠 + 五 + 口

氵 (sāndiǎnshuǐ)(the "three-drops-of-water" side)　丶丶氵　　3 strokes

(3) 汉语 Hànyǔ（漢語）

汉 → 氵 + 又

(4) 您 nín

您 → 你 + 心

𠂇 (yǒuzìtóu)(the "to have" top)　一𠂇　　2 strokes

(5) 朋友 péngyou

朋 → 月 + 月

友 → 𠂇 + 又

(6) 贵姓 guìxìng（貴姓）

贵 → 中 + 一 + 贝

姓 → 女 + 生

丩 (jiàozìpáng) (the "calling" side)　乚丩　　2 strokes

(7) 叫 jiào

叫 → 口 + 丩

勺 (sháozìpáng) (the "ladle" side) ノ 勹 勺   3 strokes

(8) 的 de

的 → 白 + 勺

How will you be able to find your way around in China? By the end of this lesson, you should be able to ask directions, look for people, express gratitude and regret, and say goodbye in Chinese. Remember to keep practicing your pronunciation and tones every day.

第五课 Lesson 5

Cāntīng zài nǎr
餐厅 在 哪儿

（一）

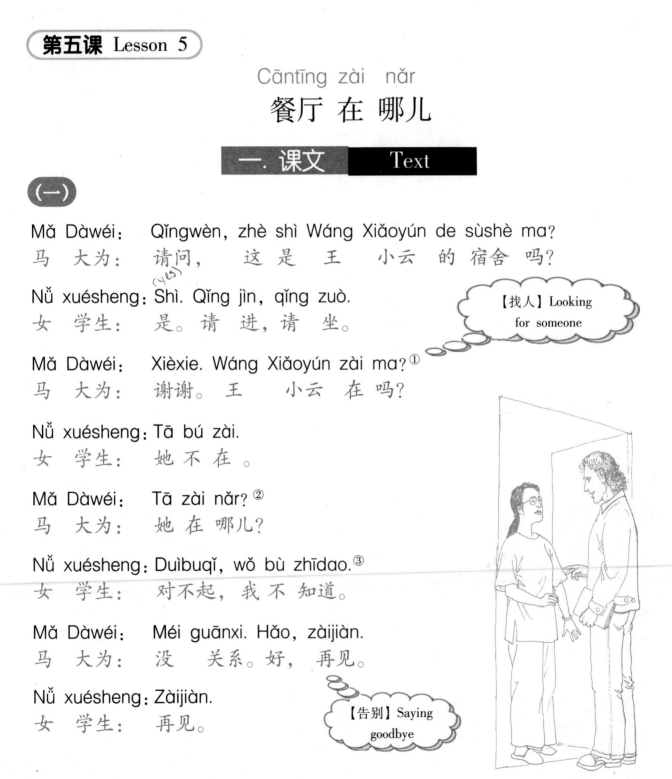

Mǎ Dàwéi: Qǐngwèn, zhè shì Wáng Xiǎoyún de sùshè ma?
马 大为：请问， 这是 王 小云 的 宿舍 吗?

Nǚ xuésheng：Shì. Qǐng jìn, qǐng zuò.
女 学生：是。 请 进，请 坐。

【找人】Looking for someone

Mǎ Dàwéi: Xièxie. Wáng Xiǎoyún zài ma?①
马 大为：谢谢。 王 小云 在 吗?

Nǚ xuésheng：Tā bú zài.
女 学生：她 不 在 。

Mǎ Dàwéi：Tā zài nǎr?②
马 大为：她 在 哪儿?

Nǚ xuésheng：Duìbuqǐ, wǒ bù zhīdao.③
女 学生：对不起，我 不 知道。

Mǎ Dàwéi: Méi guānxi. Hǎo, zàijiàn.
马 大为：没 关系。好，再见。

Nǚ xuésheng：Zàijiàn.
女 学生：再见。

【告别】Saying goodbye

-48-

月月 *(handwritten: moon meat)*

(handwritten: mei → when; "there is" "to have" → yǒu 有)

生词 New Words

1.	cāntīng	N	餐厅	dining room
2.	zài	V	在	to be (here, there); to be (in, on, at)
3.	nǎr	QPr	哪儿	where
*4.	qǐngwèn	V	请问	May I ask...?
	wèn	V	问	to ask
*5.	zhè	Pr	这	this
6.	sùshè	N	宿舍	dormitory
7.	nǔ	A	女	female
*8.	xuésheng	N	学生	student
*9.	jìn	V	进	to enter
10.	zuò	V	坐	to sit
11.	xièxie	V	谢谢	to thank
12.	duìbuqǐ	IE	对不起	I'm sorry
*13.	wǒ	Pr	我	I; me
14.	zhīdao	V	知道	to know
15.	méi guānxi	IE	没关系	never mind; it doesn't matter
*16.	hǎo	A	好	good; well; fine; O.K.
17.	zàijiàn	IE	再见	good-bye
	zài	Adv	再	again
18.	Wáng Xiǎoyún	PN	王小云	(name of a Chinese student)

(handwritten annotations: sù 宿 ? not name (spend night); Zhèr = here; shelter 舍; 宀 - shelter; 厂 long hall; 知道 to know (aware, to know); 身 body; 寸 bowing; → NO (cannot be used instead of bù); 見 → 见)

（二）

【问地点】Asking for directions

Mǎ Dàwéi: Xiǎojiě, qǐngwèn cāntīng zài nǎr? ④
马大为： 小姐， 请问 餐厅 在 哪儿?

Xiǎojiě: Zài èr céng èr líng sì hào. ⑤
小姐： 在 二 层 二 ○ 四 号。

Mǎ Dàwéi: Xièxie.
马大为： 谢谢。

【道谢】Expressing thanks

Xiǎojiě: Búyòng xiè. ⑥
小姐： 不用 谢。

-49-

日 - related to time concept.

Sòng Huá：　　Dàwéi, wǒmen zài zhèr.
宋　华：　　大为，我们 在 这儿。

Mǎ Dàwéi：　　Duìbuqǐ, wǒ lái wǎn le. ⑦
马　大为：　　对不起，我 来 晚 了。

Wáng Xiǎoyún：Méi guānxi.
王　小云：没 关系。

生词 New Words

1. xiǎojiě	N	小姐	Miss；young lady	jiě jiě (old sister)
2. èr	Nu	二	two	
3. céng	M	层	story；floor	T5-
4. líng	Nu	○	zero	
5. sì	Nu	四	four	
6. hào	N	号	number	
7. búyòng	Adv	不用	need not	
8. zhèr	Pr	这儿	here (Beijing)	
9. wǎn	A	晚	late	night/evening (n.)
10. le	Pt	了	(modal partical/aspect partical)	
11. Sòng Huá	PN	宋华	(name of a Chinese student)	

V. + le
↑
depends on an event that already happened

bǎi (100)

百

二. 注释　Notes

① Wáng Xiǎoyún zài ma?

"Is Wang Xiaoyun in?"

② Tā zài nǎr?

"Where is she?"

③ Duìbuqǐ, wǒ bù zhīdao.

"duìbuqǐ(对不起)" is a phrase commonly used in making excuses or apologies, and the response to it is usually "méi guānxi(没关系)".

④ Cāntīng zài nǎr?

"Where is the dining hall?"

⑤ Zài èr céng èr líng sì hào.

"It's in No. 204 on the second floor."

In Chinese the ground floor of a building is considered to be the first floor.

⑥ Búyòng xiè.

"Don't mention it."

This phrase is used as a response to an expression of thanks. One may also say, "Bú xiè(不谢)".

⑦ Duìbuqǐ, wǒ lái wǎn le.

$v = \dfrac{c}{\lambda}$ $E_p = h\nu$

"Sorry, I am late."

三. 语音练习　Pronunciation Drills

声母 Initials: z　c　s
韵母 Finals: -i [ʅ]　er
iong　ua　uan　uang　ün

1. 拼音 Spelling

zā	cā	sā
zī	cī	sī
zū	cū	sū

zuān	cuān	suān
zuī	cuī	suī
zūn	cūn	sūn
zhuāng	chuāng	shuāng
jiōng	qiōng	xiōng
jūn	qūn	xūn
guā	kuā	huā

2. 四声 The four tones

zāi		zǎi	zài	zài
cān	cán	cǎn	càn	
tīng	tíng	tǐng	tìng	cāntīng
sī		sǐ	sì	
cēng	céng		cèng	sì céng
	ér	ěr	èr	èr hào
wēn	wén	wěn	wèn	qǐngwèn
xiē	xié	xiě	xiè	xièxie
jiān		jiǎn	jiàn	zàijiàn
wān	wán	wǎn	wàn	lái wǎn le
yōng	yóng	yǒng	yòng	búyòng
wāng	wáng	wǎng	wàng	
yūn	yún	yǔn	yùn	Wáng Xiǎoyún
sōng	sóng	sǒng	sòng	
huā	huá		huà	Sòng Huá

3. 辨音 Sound discrimination

zǐ —— cǐ   qiě —— jiě   jiàn —— qiàn
(son)   (and)   (to see)

qīng —— jīng   kuài —— kuà   huān —— huāng
(blue-green)   (quick)

4. 辨调 Tone discrimination

sì —— sī   jǐng —— qǐng   èr —— ér

(four)   (well)   (two)   (son)

yǒng —— yòng   wén —— wèn   xióng —— xiōng

                 (written language)   (bear)

5. 韵母er和儿化韵 Final "er" and retroflex ending

èr (two)   zhèr (here)

érzi (son)   nàr (there)

ěrduo (ear)   nǎr (where)

nǚ'ér (daughter)   wánr (to play)

6. 声调组合 Combination of tones

"ˉ"+"ˉ"	"ˉ"+"ˊ"	"ˉ"+"ˇ"	"ˉ"+"ˋ"	"ˉ"+"。"
cāntīng	Yīngguó	jīnglǐ	gāoxìng	xiānsheng
fēijī	shēngcí	qiānbǐ	gōngzuò	xiūxi
(plane)	(new word)	(pencil)	(work)	(rest)
kāichē	huānyíng	kāishǐ	shāngdiàn	qīzi
(to drive a car)	(to welcome)	(to start)	(shop)	(wife)

"ˊ"+"ˉ"	"ˊ"+"ˊ"	"ˊ"+"ˇ"	"ˊ"+"ˋ"	"ˊ"+"。"
míngtiān	xuéxí	yóuyǒng	xuéyuàn	shénme
(tomorrow)		(to swim)		
shíjiān	huídá	píjiǔ	zázhì	míngzi
(time)	(answer)	(beer)	(magazine)	(name)
zuótiān	zúqiú	cídiǎn	cídài	háizi
(yesterday)	(football)	(dictionary)	(audio tape)	(child)

7. 双音节连读 Practice on disyllabic words

jiàoshì (classroom)   Hélán (The Netherlands)

lǐtáng (auditorium)   Āijí (Egypt)

cāochǎng (playground)   Yuènán (Vietnam)

cèsuǒ (toilet)   Tàiguó (Thailand)

yīyuàn (hospital)   Yìndù (India)

8. 多音节连读 Practice on polysyllabic words

túshūguǎn (library)	Xīnjiāpō (Singapore)
shíyànshì	Fēilǜbīn (the Philiphines)
bàngōngshì	Xīnxīlán (New Zealand)
tǐyùguǎn	Àodàlìyà (Australia)
wàishìchù	Mǎláixīyà (Malaysia)
tíngchēchǎng	Yìndùníxīyà (Indonesia)

9. 朗读下列课堂用语 Read the following classroom expressions aloud

Qǐng niàn kèwén. (Please read the text.)

Qǐng niàn shēngcí. (Please read the new words.)

Wǒ shuō, nǐmen tīng. (Listen to me.)

四. 会话练习　Conversation Practice

KEY SENTENCES
1. Qǐng jìn, qǐng zuò.
2. Wǒ bù zhīdao.
3. Zàijiàn.
4. Qǐngwèn, cāntīng zài nǎr?
5. Xièxie.
6. Búyòng xiè.
7. Duìbuqǐ.
8. Méi guānxi.

（一）【问地点 Asking for directions】

　　1. 完成下列会话 Complete the following dialogues

　　　（1）A：Qǐngwèn, cèsuǒ zài nǎr?

　　　　　B：_zài èr céng_.

　　　　　A：Xièxie.

　　　　　B：_Búyòng xiè._

(2) A：Qǐngwèn, jiàoshì zài nǎr? *Classroom*

B：Duìbuqǐ, _Wǒ bú zhīdao._ .

2. 情景会话 Situational dialogues

In an unfamiliar building：

(1) You are looking for the elevator （电梯，diàntī）.

(2) You are looking for Mr. Yang's office.

（二）【找人 Looking for someone】

1. 完成下列会话 Complete the following dialogues

(1) A：Qǐngwèn, Lín Nà zài ma?

              Tā bú zài

B：~~Zài, qǐng jìn.~~ .

A：Tā zài nǎr?

B：Duìbuqǐ, _Wǒ bú zhīdao._ .

A：Méi guānxi. Zàijiàn!

B：_Zàijiàn._ .

                         zài

(2) A：_Qǐngwèn, nǐ dìdi ↓ ma?_

B：Zài. Qǐng jìn.

Chú
厨

2. 看图会话 Make a dialogue based on the picture

(1) Xuésheng：_kéyǐ jìnlai ma_ ?

Yáng lǎoshī：_Qǐng jìn_ .

(2) Lín Nà：Lìbō zài ma ? *Tā bú zài*

Mǎ Dàwéi：_~~Zài~~ ↓_ .

Lín Nà：_Tā zài nǎr_ ?

Mǎ Dàwéi：_Tā zài cāntīng_ .

Lín Nà：_Xièxie, zàijiàn_ .

Mǎ Dàwéi：_Zàijiàn_ .

（三）【道歉 Making an apology】
看图会话 Make a dialogue based on the picture

(1) A：<u>duìbuqǐ, wǒ lái wǎn le</u>.

    B：<u>Méi guānxi, qǐng jìn</u>.

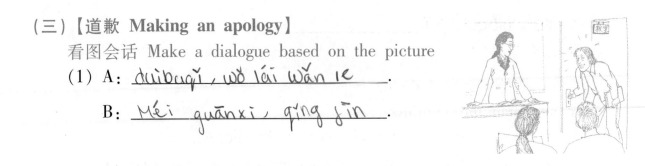

(2) A：<u>duìbuqǐ, wǒ lái wǎn le</u>.

    B：<u>Méi guānxi</u>.

（四）【问职业 Asking about someone's occupation】

1. 完成下列会话 Complete the following dialogues

  (1) A：Nín shì yīshēng ma?

      B：Bú shì, <u>wǒ bú shì / yīshēng</u>, wǒ shì <u>xuésheng</u>.

      A：Nín ne?

      C：Wǒ yě shì xuésheng, wǒ xuéxí Hànyǔ.

  (2) A：<u>Nín péngyou shì lǎoshī ma</u>?

      B：Shì, tā shì wàiyǔ lǎoshī.

      A：Nǐ <u>yě shì wàiyǔ lǎoshī ma</u>?

      B：Wǒ bú shì wàiyǔ lǎoshī. Wǒ shì <u>yīshēng</u>.

（五）听述 Listen and repeat

    请问，他的宿舍在哪儿？

    在三层三一〇号。

    谢谢。

*　　*　　*

请问，您认识陈老师吗？

对不起，我不认识。

没关系。再见。

再见。

五. 语音　　　Phonetics

1. 儿化韵 Retroflex ending (final)

The final "er" sometimes does not form a syllable by itself but is attached to another final to form a retroflex final. A retroflex final is represented by the letter "r" added to the final. In actual writing, "儿" is added to the character in question, as in "nǎr(哪儿)".

2. 发音要领 Pronunciation key

Initials：	z	like "ds" in "beds"
	c	like "ts" in "cats", with aspiration
	s	pronounced as in English, e.g. "s" in "see"
Finals：	-r(final)	like "er" in "sister" (American pronunciation)

六. 语法　　　Grammar

用疑问代词的问句 Questions with an interrogative pronoun

Statement		Question
Nà shì wǒmen lǎoshī.	→	Nà shì shéi?
那　是　我们　老师。		那　是　谁？
Wǒ xìng Mǎ.	→	Nǐ xìng shénme?
我　姓　马。		你　姓　什么？
Cāntīng zài èr céng.	→	Cāntīng zài nǎr?
餐厅　在　二　层。		餐厅　在　哪儿？
Tā shì Zhōngguó rén.	→	Tā shì nǎ guó rén?
她　是　中国　人。		她　是　哪　国　人？

The word order in a question with an interrogative pronoun is the same as that in a declarative sentence. In this kind of sentence, a question pronoun simply replaces the part of the sentence to which the interrogative pronoun corresponds.

nǚ ér
女儿

七. 汉字　　Chinese Characters

1. 汉字复合笔画(1) Combined character strokes (1)

Stroke	Name	Example	Way to Write
乛	hénggōu	你	The horizontal stroke with a hook, is written like the fourth stroke in "你".
㇆	héngzhé	马	The horizontal stroke with a downward turn, is written like the first stroke in "马".
㇇	héngpiě	又	The horizontal stroke with a downward turn to the left, is written like the first stroke in "又".
㇅	héngzhégōu	门	The horizontal stroke with a downward turn and a hook, is written like the third stroke in "门".
乚	héngzhétí	语	The horizontal stroke with a downward turn, and then an upward turn to the right, is written like the second stroke in "语".
亅	shùgōu	丁	The vertical stroke with a hook, is written like the second stroke in "丁".

2. 认写基本汉字 Learn and write basic Chinese characters

(1) 二　　　一 二
　　　èr　two　　　　　　　　　　　2 strokes

(2) 儿(兒)　　丿 儿
　　　ér　son　　　　　　　　　　　2 strokes

(3) 子　　　㇇ 了 子
　　　zǐ　son　　　　　　　　　　　3 strokes

(4) 井　　　一 二 丰 井
　　　jǐng　well　　　　　　　　　　4 strokes

(5) 文　　　丶 亠 ナ 文
　　　wén　written language　　　　4 strokes

(6) 见(見)　丨 冂 贝 见　　　*not* 只

jiàn　　to see　　　　　　　　　　4 strokes

(7) 且　*Male organ*　丨 冂 月 且

qiě　　and　　　　　　　　　　　5 strokes

Note："且" is the original character for "祖"(zǔ, ancestor). When it became a loaned function word, "祖" was substituted for the original character.

(8) 四　　　丨 冂 冈 四 四

sì　　four　　　　　　　　　　　5 strokes

(9) 我　　　ノ 二 于 手 我 我 我

wǒ　　I, me　　　　　　　　　　7 strokes

(10) 青　　　一 二 キ 主 丰 青 青 青

qīng　blue-green (youth)　　　　8 strokes

3. 认写课文中已出现的汉字 Learn and write the Chinese characters appearing in the texts

才 (zàizìtóu) (the "location" top)　一 ナ 才　　3 strokes

(1) 在 zài

在 → 才 + 土

(2) 坐 zuò

坐 → 人 + 人 + 土

(3) 请问 qǐngwèn (請問)

请 → 讠 + 青

(The meaning side is "讠", and the phonetic side is "青".)

问 → 门 + 口

辶 (zǒuzhǐdǐ) (the "hurrying" side)　丶　冫　辶　　　3 strokes

(4) 这 zhè（這）

这 → 文 + 辶

(5) 进 jìn（進）

进 → 井 + 辶

(6) 再见 zàijiàn（再見）

再 → 一 + 冂 + 土

（一 厂 万 万 再 再　　　6 strokes）

⺍ (xuézìtóu) (the "study" top)　丶　丷　⺍　⺍　⺍　　5 strokes

(7) 学生 xuésheng（學生）

学 → ⺍ + 子

(8) 好 hǎo

好 → 女 + 子

(9) 小姐 xiǎojiě

姐 → 女 + 且

冂 (yòngzìkuàng) (the "use" frame)　丿　冂　　　2 strokes

(10) 不用 búyòng

用 → 冂 + 丰

（一 二 丰）

Chinese Dictionaries

Unlike most English dictionaries, in which entries are arranged alphabetically, Chinese dictionaries are organized in a number of different ways. Chinese dictionaries can be compiled alphabetically (using *pinyin* or another romanization system), by the number of strokes used to write the character in question, or by the radical of the character. Many dictionaries published before the 1920s order their entries according to radical, whereas modern dictionaries are often arranged alphabetically and include radical and stroke-number indexes.

The *Xinhua Zidian* (*New Chinese Dictionary*) and *Xiandai Hanyu Cidian* (*Modern Chinese Dictionary*) are among the most widely used dictionaries at present in the People's Republic of China. The first is a pocketsize dictionary, containing some eight thousand entries. It deals mainly with individual characters, their definitions, pronunciations, and tones. The second is a medium-sized dictionary including more than fifty-six thousand entries. It covers single characters, compound words, set phrases, and idiomatic expressions.

The encyclopedic *Cihai* (*Sea of Words*) and the detailed *Ciyuan* (*Sources of Words*) are both large dictionaries, often issued in multi-volume sets. Currently there are also many dictionaries specially designed for international students who want to study Chinese language and culture.

In this lesson, you will be able to learn what to do when you don't understand what another person has said. You will also learn how to make suggestions, how to accept or decline suggestions, and how to make comments. This lesson also provides a review of the pronunciation and tones covered so far.

第六课 Lesson 6 (复习 Review)

Wǒmen qù yóuyǒng, hǎo ma

我们 去 游泳，好 吗

一. 课文　　Text

（一）

【评论】Making comments

Wáng Xiǎoyún： Lín Nà, zuótiān de jīngjù zěnmeyàng? ①
王　小云： 林 娜， 昨天 的 京剧 怎么样？

Lín Nà： Hěn yǒu yìsi. Jīntiān tiānqì hěn hǎo, wǒmen qù
林 娜： 很 有意思。今天 天气 很 好， 我们 去

yóuyǒng, hǎo ma? ②
游泳， 好 吗？

【建议】Making suggestions

Wáng Xiǎoyún： Tài hǎo le! Shénme shíhou qù? ③
王　小云： 太 好 了! 什么 时候 去？

Lín Nà： Xiànzài qù, kěyǐ ma? ④
林 娜： 现在 去, 可以 吗？

Wáng Xiǎoyún： Kěyǐ.
王　小云： 可以。

生词 New Words

1.	qù	V	去	to go
2.	yóuyǒng	VO	游泳	to swim
3.	zuótiān	N	昨天	yesterday
4.	jīngjù	N	京剧	Beijing opera
5.	zěnmeyàng	QPr	怎么样	how is it?
6.	yǒu yìsi	IE	有意思	interesting
7.	jīntiān	N	今天	today
	tiān	N	天	day (SKY / God)
8.	tiānqì	N	天气	weather
9.	tài	Adv	太	too; extremely
*10.	shénme	QPr	什么	what
11.	shíhou	N	时候	time; moment
12.	xiànzài	N	现在	now

(二)

Dīng Lìbō: Yáng lǎoshī, míngtiān nín yǒu shíjiān ma? ⑤
丁 力波: 杨 老师, 明天 您 有 时间 吗?

Yáng lǎoshī: Duìbuqǐ, [qǐng zài shuō yí biàn.] ⑥
杨 老师: 对不起, 请 再 说 一 遍。

【请求重复】Asking someone to repeat something

Dīng Lìbō: Míngtiān nín yǒu shíjiān ma?
丁 力波: 明天 您 有 时间 吗?

Wǒmen qù dǎ qiú, hǎo ma?
我们 去 打球, 好 吗?

Yáng lǎoshī: Hěn bàoqiàn, míngtiān wǒ
杨 老师: 很 抱歉, 明天 我

hěn máng, kǒngpà bù xíng. ⑦
很 忙, 恐怕 不 行。

【婉拒】Refusing or declining politely

Xièxie nǐmen.
谢谢 你们。

生词 New Words

1. míngtiān	N	明天	tomorrow
2. yǒu	V	有	to have
3. shíjiān	N	时间	time
4. shuō	V	说	to say; to speak
5. biàn	M	遍	number of times (of action)
6. dǎ qiú	V O	打球	to play ball
dǎ	V	打	to play
qiú	N	球	ball
7. bàoqiàn	A	抱歉	to feel sorry/sorry
*8. máng	A	忙	busy
9. kǒngpà	Adv	恐怕	to be afraid that; perhaps
10. xíng	V	行	to be O.K.
*11. xièxie	V	谢谢	to thank
12. nǐmen	Pr	你们	you (pl.)

(handwritten annotations: "measure word" pointing to 遍; "serious" / "4 Educated" near 抱歉; "vertical heart radical" pointing to 忙)

二. 注释　　Notes

① Zuótiān de jīngjù zěnmeyàng?

"How was yesterday's Beijing opera?"

"… zěnmeyàng?" is an expression commonly used to ask for someone's opinion.

Among the roughly 300 forms of opera in China, Beijing opera has enjoyed the greatest popularity and has the most extensive influence. As a unique art form representative of Chinese culture, it is loved by many people all over the world.

② Wǒmen qù yóuyǒng, hǎo ma?

"Shall we go swimming?"

"…, hǎo ma?" is a pattern used when making a suggestion.

③ Tài hǎo le! Shénme shíhou qù?

"That's great! When are we going?"

"Tài hǎo le! (太好了!)" is an expression used to show enthusiastic approval. It is also used to express happy agreement with a suggestion. You may also use "hǎo(好)" or "xíng(行)" as a response.

④ Xiànzài qù, kěyǐ ma?

"Is it O.K. to go right now?"

"…, kěyǐ ma?" is another expression used to make a suggestion. If you agree with a suggestion, you may say "kěyǐ(可以)" or "hǎo(好)".

⑤ Míngtiān nín yǒu shíjiān ma?

"Do you have time tomorrow?"

⑥ Qǐng zài shuō yí biàn.

"Pardon? Would you say it again?"

This phrase is used when the speaker's words were not heard clearly and you would like him/her to repeat them.

⑦ Hěn bàoqiàn, míngtiān wǒ hěn máng, kǒngpà bù xíng.

"I'm sorry, but I'll be very busy tomorrow. I'm afraid I can't."

"kǒngpà bù xíng" is a phrase to express a courteous refusal.

三. 语音复习　Pronunciation Review

1. 拼音 Spelling

zhī	chī	zī	cī
jū	qū	gū	kū
bēn	pēng	tān	dāng
zhōng	chōng	gān	kāng
zān	cāng	jīn	qīng
zhā	chā	zū	cū
gē	kē	jī	qī

2. 四声 The four tones

yōu	yóu	yǒu	yòu	
yōng		yǒng	yòng	yóuyǒng
zuō	zuó	zuǒ	zuò	
tiān	tián	tiǎn	tiàn	zuótiān
jīn		jǐn	jìn	jīntiān
	míng	mǐng	mìng	míngtiān
qī	qí	qǐ	qì	tiānqì
xiān	xián	xiǎn	xiàn	xiànzài
jīng		jǐng	jìng	
jū	jú	jǔ	jù	jīngjù
bāo	báo	bǎo	bào	
qiān	qián	qiǎn	qiàn	bàoqiàn
kōng		kǒng	kòng	kǒngpà
xīng	xíng	xǐng	xìng	bù xíng

3. 辨音 Sound discrimination

jiǔ —— xiǔ   sī —— shī   cùn —— zùn
(nine)   (private)   (inch)

qì —— jì   duì —— tuì   guǎn —— juǎn
(air)   (to exchange)

4. 辨调 Tone discrimination

wáng —— wàng   kàn —— kǎn   gōng —— gòng
(to die)   (to see)   (labor)

sān —— sǎn   shēn —— shèn   guāi —— guǎi
(three)   (body)

5. 声调组合 Combination of tones

" ˇ "+"‒"	" ˇ "+" ́ "	" ˇ "+" ˇ "	" ˇ "+" ̀ "	" ˇ "+" ˳ "
lǎoshī	yǔyán	kěyǐ	kǒngpà	jiějie
yǔyīn	dǎ qiú	yǔfǎ	qǐngwèn	zěnme
(pronunciation)		(grammar)		(how)
xiǎoshuō	qǐchuáng	fǔdǎo	nǚshì	yǐzi
(novel)	(to get up)	(coach)	(Madam)	(chair)

" ̀ "+"‒"	" ̀ "+" ́ "	" ̀ "+" ˇ "	" ̀ "+" ̀ "	" ̀ "+" ˳ "
shàngbān	sì céng	wàiyǔ	bàoqiàn	xièxie
(to go to work)				
qìchē	kèwén	diànyǐng	huìhuà	mèimei
(car)	(text)	(movie)	(conversation)	
lùyīn	fùxí	diànnǎo	Hànzì	kèqi
(sound recording)	(review)	(computer)	(Chinese character)	

6. 双音节连读 Practice on disyllabic words

duànliàn (to do physical training)   chànggē (to sing a song)

chīfàn (to eat a meal)   tiàowǔ (to dance)

shàngkè (to have lessons)   xǐzǎo (to take a bath)

xiàkè (class is over)   shuìjiào (to sleep)

7. 多音节连读 Practice on polysyllabic words

shuō Hànyǔ (to speak Chinese)   kàn lùxiàng (to watch video)

niàn shēngcí (to read the new words)   zuò liànxí (to do exercise)

xiě Hànzì (to write Chinese characters)   fānyì jùzi (to translate sentence)

tīng lùyīn (to listen to tape)   yòng diànnǎo (to use computer)

8. 朗读下面的唐诗 Read the following poem aloud

Dēng Guàn Què Lóu
登　　鹳　雀　楼
(Táng) Wáng Zhīhuàn
（唐）　王　　之涣

white → Bái   rì   yī   shān   jìn,   → *mountain*
　　　白　日　依　山　尽，
Huáng Hé   rù   hǎi   liú.   *enter*
　　　黄　河　入　海　流。
Yù   qióng qiān lǐ   mù,   → *eye*
欲　穷　千　里　目。
Gèng shàng yì   céng lóu.
更　上　一　层　楼。

9. 朗读下列课堂用语 Read the following classroom expressions aloud

Qǐng kàn shū.　　　　　(Please look at your books.)

Qǐng xiě Hànzì.　　　　(Please write the characters.)

Qǐng zài niàn yí biàn.　(Please read it again.)

Wǒmen tīngxiě.　　　　(Let's do dictation.)

四. 会话练习　Conversation Practice

KEY SENTENCES

1. Zuótiān de jīngjù zěnmeyàng?

2. Jīntiān tiānqì hěn hǎo, wǒmen qù yóuyǒng, hǎo ma?

3. Tài hǎo le! Shénme shíhou qù?

4. Xiànzài qù, kěyǐ ma?

5. Kěyǐ.

6. Míngtiān nín yǒu shíjiān ma?

7. Duìbuqǐ, qǐng zài shuō yí biàn.

8. Hěn bàoqiàn, kǒngpà bù xíng.

（一）【建议 Making suggestions】

看图会话 Make a dialogue based on the picture

(1) A：<u>wǒmen qu dǎ qiú</u>, hǎo ma?

B：Tài hǎo le! <u>Shénme shíhou ma</u>?

A：<u>Xiànzài qu</u>, kěyǐ ma?

B：<u>kěyǐ</u>.

(2) A：<u>wǒmen qu tiàowǔ</u>, hǎo ma?

B：Shénme shíhou qù?

A：<u>Xiànzài qu</u>, kěyǐ ma?

B：Duìbuqǐ, <u>wǒ hěn máng</u>, <u>kǒngpa bu xíng</u>

A：Méi guānxi.

(Use the word "tiàowǔ"
which means "to dance".)

（二）【请求重复 Asking someone to repeat something】

看图会话 Make a dialogue based on the picture

A：<u>Qǐngwèn, nǐ máng ma.</u>?

B：Duìbuqǐ, <u>qǐng zài shuō yí biàn</u>.

A：<u>Méi guānxi, nǐ máng ma</u>?

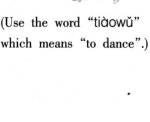

（三）【评论 Making comments】

看图会话 Make a dialogue based on the picture

(1) A：Qǐngwèn, zhè shì shénme?

B：Zhè shì wǔshù.

A：Wǔshù zěnmeyàng?

B：<u>Hěn yǒu yìsi</u>.

(2) A：Zhè shì shénme?

B：Zhè shì (xióngmāo). 熊猫 cat

A：Xióngmāo zěnmeyàng?

B：<u>méi yǒu yìsi</u>.

Kě ài   Loveable
可 爱

（四）模仿下面的会话进行练习 **Imitate the following dialogues**

(1) A：Nín hǎo!

B：Nín hǎo!

A：Qǐngwèn, nín guìxìng?

B：Wǒ xìng Lǐ, jiào Lǐ Mǎlì. Qǐngwèn, nín xìng shénme?

A：Wǒ xìng Sòng, jiào Sòng Huá. Nín shì nǎ guó rén?

B：Wǒ shì Měiguó rén, shì Běijīng Dàxué (university) de

xuésheng.

A：Rènshi nín hěn gāoxìng.

B：Rènshi nín, wǒ yě hěn gāoxìng.

(2) A：Lìbō, nǐ hǎo ma?

B：Wǒ hěn hǎo. Sòng Huá, nǐ ne?

A：Wǒ hěn máng. Nǐ wàipó hǎo ma?

B：Xièxie, tā hěn hǎo. Nǐ bàba、māma dōu hǎo ma?

A：Tāmen dōu hěn hǎo. Mǎlì, zhè shì wǒ péngyou, Dīng Lìbō.

B：Nǐ hǎo.

A：Zhè shì Mǎlì.

C：Nǐ hǎo. Wǒ jiào Mǎlì, shì Běijīng Dàxué de xuésheng. Wǒ

xuéxí Hànyǔ. Qǐngwèn, nǐ shì Měiguó rén ma?

B：Bú shì, wǒ shì Jiānádà rén.

(3) A：Tā shì shéi?

B：Tā shì wǒmen lǎoshī.

A：Tā shì Zhōngguó rén ma?

B：Tā shì Zhōngguó rén. Tā xìng Chén.

A：Nà shì shéi?

B：Tā jiào Lù Yǔpíng.

A：Tā yě shì lǎoshī ma?

B：Tā bú shì lǎoshī. Tā shì jìzhě.

(4) A：Xiānsheng, qǐngwèn, bàngōngshì zài nǎr?

B：Zài wǔ céng.

A：Chén lǎoshī zài ma?

B：Shéi? Duìbuqǐ, qǐng zài shuō yí biàn.

A：Chén Fāngfāng lǎoshī zài ma?

B：Tā zài.

A：Xièxie.

B：Bú xiè.

(5) A：Kěyǐ jìnlai ma?

B：Wáng xiānsheng, nín hǎo. Qǐng jìn, qǐng zuò.

A：Duìbuqǐ, wǒ lái wǎn le.

B：Méi guānxi. Nín yào kāfēi ma?

A：Wǒ bú yào. Xièxie. Míngtiān wǒmen qù kàn jīngjù, hǎo ma?

B：Duìbuqǐ, míngtiān wǒ hěn máng, kǒngpà bù xíng.

（五）听述 Listen and repeat

我没听清楚,请再说一遍。

对不起;明天我没有时间,恐怕不行。

五. 语音　　　　　Phonetics

1. "一"的变调 Tone sandhi of "一"

Normally "一" is pronounced in the first tone when it stands by itself, at the end of a word, phrase or sentence, or is used as an ordinal number. However, "一" is pronounced in the fourth tone when it precedes a first tone, second tone, or third tone syllable. It is read in the second tone when it precedes a fourth tone.

$$
yī + \begin{cases} - \\ ´ \\ ˇ \end{cases} \rightarrow yì + \begin{cases} - & & \text{yì bēi (one cup)} \\ ´ & \text{example：} & \text{yì píng (one bottle)} \\ ˇ & & \text{yì běn (one copy)} \end{cases}
$$

$$
yī + \quad ` \quad \rightarrow yí + \quad ` \quad \text{example：} \quad \text{yí biàn (one time/once)}
$$

2. 普通话声母韵母拼合总表 Table of Combinations of Initials and Finals in Common Speech

There are more than 400 meaningful syllables in the common speech of modern Chinese. If we add the four tones to these, we can distinguish more than 1,200 syllables. The syllables covered from Lesson 1 to Lesson 6 are shown in the table on the next page.

六. 语法 　　　　Grammar

动词谓语句 Sentences with a verbal predicate

The main part of the predicate in a sentence with a verbal predicate is a verb. The object usually follows the verb. One of its negative forms is made by placing the adverb "不" before the verb.

Subject	Predicate			
	Adv	**V**	**O**	**吗? ma?**
你 Nǐ		要 yào	咖啡 kāfēi	吗? ma?
我们 Wǒmen	都 dōu	学习 xuéxí	汉语。 Hànyǔ.	
餐厅 Cāntīng		在 zài	哪儿? nǎr?	
我 Wǒ	不 bù	知道。 zhīdao.		
我 Wǒ		姓 xìng	陆。 Lù.	
她 Tā		叫 jiào	林娜。 Lín Nà.	
您 Nín	明天 míngtiān	有 yǒu	时间 shíjiān	吗? ma?

gōng ren } worker.
工 人 }

xiū } rest.
休 }

七. 汉字　　　Chinese Characters

1. 汉字复合笔画(2) Combined character strokes (2)

Stroke	Name	Example	Way to Write
ㄴ	shùzhé	山	The vertical stroke with a horizontal turn to the right, is written like the second stroke in "山".
ㄴ	shùtí	以	The vertical stroke with an upward turn to the right, is written like the first stroke in "以".
𠃌	shùzhézhégōu	马	The vertical stroke with a horizontal turn to the right, and then a downward turn and a hook, is written like the second stroke in "马".
乙	héngzhéwān gōu	九	The horizontal stroke with a vertical turn, and then a horizontal turn to the right and an upward hook, is written like the second stroke in "九".
ㄥ	piězhé	么	The downward stroke to the left, and then a horizontal turn to the right, is written like the second stroke in "么".
ㄑ	piědiǎn	女	The downward stroke to the left and then an extended dot to the right, is written like the first stroke in "女".

2. 笔画组合 Combination of strokes

The relationship between strokes in a Chinese character can be essential to its meaning.

There are three ways to combine strokes in a character:

(1) Adjacent (not attached) like "八", "儿", "二", "小";

(2) Crossing like "十", "大", "九", "夫";

(3) Connecting like "厂", "丁", "人", "山", "天".

3. 认写基本汉字 Learn and write basic Chinese characters

(1) 九　　丿九

jiǔ　　nine　　　　　　　　2 strokes

(2) 厶　　厶 厶

sī　　private　　　　　　2 strokes

(3) 寸　　一十寸

cùn　　a unit of inch　　3 strokes

(4) 工　　一丁工

gōng　　labour　　　　　3 strokes

(5) 亡　　丶亠亡

wáng　　to die　　　　　3 strokes

(6) 三　　一二三

sān　　three　　　　　　3 strokes

(7) 气(氣)　丿丿气气

qì　　air　　　　　　　　4 strokes

(8) 立　　丶亠立立立

lì　　to stand　　　　　5 strokes

(9) 身　　丿丿冂冃身身身

shēn　　body　　　　　7 strokes

> Note：On the left side or in the middle of a character, "身" is written as "身".

(10) 兑　　丶丷丷屮屮户兑

duì　　to exchange　　　7 strokes

4. 认写课文中的汉字 Learn and write the Chinese characters appearing in the texts

(1) 去 qù

去 → 土 + 厶

(2) 有意思 yǒu yìsi

有 → 𠂇 + 月

意 → 立 + 日 + 心

思 → 田 + 心

(3) 天气 tiānqì (天氣)

天 → 一 + 大

(4) 太 tài

太 → 大 + 丶

(5) 什么 shénme (甚麽)

什 → 亻 + 十

么 → 丿 + 厶

(6) 时候 shíhou (時候)

时 → 日 + 寸

("日", the "sun" side denotes time.)

候 → 亻 + 丨 + 𠃌 + 矢

(丿亻𠂉𠂉𠂋𠋳𠋳𠋳候候   10 strokes)

(7) 现在 xiànzài (现在)

现 → 王 + 见

(8) 明天 míngtiān

明 → 日 + 月

("日", the "sun" side and the "moon" side, "月", denote light.)

普通话声母韵母拼合总表

Table of Combinations of Initials and Finals in *Putonghua*

声母\韵母	a	o	e	-i[1]	-i[2]	er	ai	ei	ao	ou	an	en	ang	eng	ong	i	ia	iao	ie	iu	ian	in	iang	ing	iong	u	ua	uo	uai	ui	uan	un	uang	ueng	ü	üe	üan	ün
	a	o	e			er	ai	ei	ao	ou	an	en	ang	eng		yi	ya	yao	ye	you	yan	yin	yang	ying	yong	wu	wa	wo	wai	wei	wan	wen	wang	weng	yu	yue	yuan	yun
b	ba	bo					bai	bei	bao		ban	ben	bang	beng		bi		biao	bie		bian	bin		bing		bu												
p	pa	po					pai	pei	pao	pou	pan	pen	pang	peng		pi		piao	pie		pian	pin		ping		pu												
m	ma	mo	me				mai	mei	mao	mou	man	men	mang	meng		mi		miao	mie	miu	mian	min		ming		mu												
f	fa	fo						fei		fou	fan	fen	fang	feng												fu												
d	da		de				dai	dei	dao	dou	dan	den	dang	deng	dong	di		diao	die	diu	dian			ding		du		duo		dui	duan	dun						
t	ta		te				tai		tao	tou	tan		tang	teng	tong	ti		tiao	tie		tian			ting		tu		tuo		tui	tuan	tun						
n	na		ne				nai	nei	nao	nou	nan	nen	nang	neng	nong	ni		niao	nie	niu	nian	nin	niang	ning		nu		nuo			nuan				nü	nüe		
l	la		le				lai	lei	lao	lou	lan		lang	leng	long	li	lia	liao	lie	liu	lian	lin	liang	ling		lu		luo			luan	lun			lü	lüe		
z	za		ze	zi			zai	zei	zao	zou	zan	zen	zang	zeng	zong											zu		zuo		zui	zuan	zun						
c	ca		ce	ci			cai		cao	cou	can	cen	cang	ceng	cong											cu		cuo		cui	cuan	cun						
s	sa		se	si			sai		sao	sou	san	sen	sang	seng	song											su		suo		sui	suan	sun						
zh	zha		zhe		zhi		zhai	zhei	zhao	zhou	zhan	zhen	zhang	zheng	zhong											zhu	zhua	zhuo	zhuai	zhui	zhuan	zhun	zhuang					
ch	cha		che		chi		chai		chao	chou	chan	chen	chang	cheng	chong											chu	chua	chuo	chuai	chui	chuan	chun	chuang					
sh	sha		she		shi		shai	shei	shao	shou	shan	shen	shang	sheng												shu	shua	shuo	shuai	shui	shuan	shun	shuang					
r			re		ri				rao	rou	ran	ren	rang	reng	rong											ru	rua	ruo		rui	ruan	run						
j																ji	jia	jiao	jie	jiu	jian	jin	jiang	jing	jiong										ju	jue	juan	jun
q																qi	qia	qiao	qie	qiu	qian	qin	qiang	qing	qiong										qu	que	quan	qun
x																xi	xia	xiao	xie	xiu	xian	xin	xiang	xing	xiong										xu	xue	xuan	xun
g	ga		ge				gai	gei	gao	gou	gan	gen	gang	geng	gong											gu	gua	guo	guai	gui	guan	gun	guang					
k	ka		ke				kai	kei	kao	kou	kan	ken	kang	keng	kong											ku	kua	kuo	kuai	kui	kuan	kun	kuang					
h	ha		he				hai	hei	hao	hou	han	hen	hang	heng	hong											hu	hua	huo	huai	hui	huan	hun	huang					

(9) 时间 shíjiān (時間)

间 → 门 + 日

(10) 说 shuō （说）

说 → 讠 + 兑

忄 (shùxīnpáng)　丶 丶 忄　　　　　　　　　　3 strokes

(On the left side of a character, "心" is written as "忄".)

(11) 忙 máng

忙 → 忄 + 亡

(12) 谢谢 xièxie (謝謝)

谢 → 讠 + 身 + 寸

文化知识　　　Cultural Notes

Beijing Opera

Beijing opera is a branch of traditional Chinese musical drama. It took shape in Beijing about 150 years ago and has been popular ever since. Beijing opera is a theatrical art synthesizing recitation, instrumental music, singing, dancing, acrobatics, and martial arts, and featuring symbolic motions and stage design. The highly formulaic and suggestive movements of the actors are accompanied by the rhythmic beats of gongs and drums, or the haunting melodies of traditional instruments. All contribute to its uniqueness as a performing art. Beijing opera is rooted deeply in Chinese culture and still appeals strongly to many Chinese.

The first six lessons of this textbook provide an overview of the phonetic system of the Chinese language, which consists of twenty-one initials, thirty-eight finals, and the four basic tones. There are only a little over 1,200 ways of combining initials and finals in Chinese. Now that you can use *pinyin*, you should be able to read any Chinese syllable correctly.

A major goal of language learning is to acquire the ability to communicate in that language. For this purpose, you have learned how to respond to a number of basic social situations. In addition, you have met with more than one hundred words and expressions, have learned forty key sentences and have studied twenty-two sentences of classroom Chinese.

So far, you have acquired sixty basic Chinese characters as well as more than fifty new vocabulary items formed from them. You have also learned some rules of stroke order for Chinese characters. This elementary vocabulary will be useful when you start to learn compound words and continue to build your vocabulary.

From this lesson on, apart from continuing to work on improving your Chinese pronunciation, you will learn how to talk about everyday situations using a greater variety of Chinese expressions than before. You will experiment with a larger number of Chinese sentences, and will further explore the culture, customs, and habits of Chinese-speaking peoples.

This lesson will help you with making acquaintances, discussing your studies, and asking questions in a different way than you have previously learned.

kāi
→to start.

第七课 Lesson 7

你 认识 不 认识 他
Nǐ rènshi bu rènshi tā

一. 课文　　Text

（一）

林　娜：　力波， 明天　开学， 我 很　高兴。 你 看，他 是
Lín Nà:　Lìbō, míngtiān kāixué, wǒ hěn gāoxìng. Nǐ kàn, tā shì

不 是 我们　学院　的 老师?
bu shì wǒmen xuéyuàn de lǎoshī?

丁　力波：　我　问 一下。① 请问， 您 是 我们　学院　的
Dīng Lìbō:　Wǒ wèn yíxià. Qǐngwèn, nín shì wǒmen xuéyuàn de

老师　吗? ②
lǎoshī ma?

张　　　教授：是，我是语言学院的老师。
Zhāng jiàoshòu：Shì, wǒ shì Yǔyán Xuéyuàn de lǎoshī.

丁　力波：您贵姓？
Dīng Lìbō：Nín guìxìng？

张　　　教授：我姓张，我们认识一下，这是我的
Zhāng jiàoshòu：Wǒ xìng Zhāng, wǒmen rènshi yíxià, zhè shì wǒ de

名片。
míngpiàn.

【初次见面】 Meeting someone for the first time

丁　力波：谢谢。（看名片）啊，您是张教授。③
Dīng Lìbō：Xièxie.(Kàn míngpiàn) À, nín shì Zhāng jiàoshòu.

我叫丁力波，她叫林娜。我们都是
Wǒ jiào Dīng Lìbō, tā jiào Lín Nà. Wǒmen dōu shì

语言学院的学生。
Yǔyán Xuéyuàn de xuésheng.

林　娜：您是语言学院的教授，认识您，我们
Lín Nà：Nín shì Yǔyán Xuéyuàn de jiàoshòu, rènshi nín, wǒmen

很高兴。
hěn gāoxìng.

张　　　教授：认识你们，我也很高兴。你们都好吗？
Zhāng jiàoshòu：Rènshi nǐmen, wǒ yě hěn gāoxìng. Nǐmen dōu hǎo ma？

林　娜：谢谢，我们都很好。张教授，您忙
Lín Nà：Xièxie, wǒmen dōu hěn hǎo. Zhāng jiàoshòu, nín máng

不忙？
bu máng？

张　　　教授：我很忙。好，你们请坐，再见！
Zhāng jiàoshòu：Wǒ hěn máng. Hǎo, nǐmen qǐng zuò, zàijiàn！

丁力波：
Dīng Lìbō：
　　　　　　　再见！
　　　　　　　Zàijiàn！
林　娜：
Lín Nà：

语言学院经济系
张介元
教授
语言学院 26 楼 301 号　　电话：12345678

生词 New Words

1.	开学	VO	kāixué	to start school	
	开	V	kāi	to open, to start	
*2.	很	Adv	hěn	very 很好，很忙，很有意思	
*3.	高兴	A	gāoxìng	happy, pleased 很高兴	
	高	A	gāo	high, tall	
4.	看	V	kàn	to watch, to look at 看老师，看这儿	
5.	问	V	wèn	to ask 问老师，问朋友	
6.	一下		yíxià	(used after a verb to indicate a short, quick, random, informal action) 介绍一下，认识一下，问一下，看一下	
*7.	学院	N	xuéyuàn	institute 语言学院，汉语学院	
8.	名片	N	míngpiàn	calling card 我的名片，老师的名片	
9.	啊	Int	à	ah, oh	
10.	教授	N	jiàoshòu	professor	
	教	V	jiāo	to teach	
*11.	丁力波	PN	Dīng Lìbō	(name of a Canadian student)	
12.	张	PN	Zhāng	(a surname)	

(Handwritten annotations: "only applied to bu" "paused by" "changes to /" "natural change to soften tone" "bu shì becomes /" "V + V" "/ + V" "→ to give" "lái" "time used after subject" "→ flash (paper)")

(二)

丁 力波： 林 娜，那 是 谁？
Dīng Lìbō： Lín Nà, nà shì shéi?

林 娜： 那 是 马 大为。你 认识 不 认识 他？
Lín Nà： Nà shì Mǎ Dàwéi. Nǐ rènshi bu rènshi tā?

丁 力波： 我 不 认识 他。
Dīng Lìbō： Wǒ bú rènshi tā.

林 娜： 我 来 介绍 一下。你 好，大为，这 是 我 朋友——
Lín Nà： Wǒ lái jièshào yíxià. Nǐ hǎo, Dàwéi, zhè shì wǒ péngyou—

丁 力波： 你 好！我 姓 丁， 叫 丁 力波。请问， 你 叫
Dīng Lìbō： Nǐ hǎo! Wǒ xìng Dīng, jiào Dīng Lìbō. Qǐngwèn, nǐ jiào

什么　　名字？④
shénme míngzi?

马 大 为： 我 的　中文　名字 叫 马 大 为。⑤ 你 是 不 是
Mǎ Dàwéi： Wǒ de Zhōngwén míngzi jiào Mǎ Dàwéi.　　Nǐ shì bu shì

中国　　人？
Zhōngguó rén?

丁 力 波： 我 是 加拿大人。我 妈妈 是　　中国　人，我 爸爸
Dīng Lìbō： Wǒ shì Jiānádà rén. Wǒ māma shì Zhōngguó rén, wǒ bàba

是 加拿大人。你 也 是 加拿大 人 吗？
shì Jiānádà rén. Nǐ yě shì Jiānádà rén ma?

马 大 为： 不 是，我 不 是 加拿大人，我 是 美国 人。你
Mǎ Dàwéi： Bú shì, wǒ bú shì Jiānádà rén, wǒ shì Měiguó rén.　Nǐ

学习 什么　　专业？
xuéxí shénme zhuānyè?

丁 力 波： 我 学习 美术　　专业。你 呢？
Dīng Lìbō： Wǒ xuéxí měishù zhuānyè. Nǐ ne?

【谈专业】Talking about one's major

马 大 为： 我 学习 文学　　专业。 现在 我 学习 汉语。
Mǎ Dàwéi： Wǒ xuéxí wénxué zhuānyè. Xiànzài wǒ xuéxí Hànyǔ.

林　娜： 现在　我们　都 学习 汉语， 也 都 是 汉语 系 的
Lín　Nà： Xiànzài wǒmen dōu xuéxí Hànyǔ, yě dōu shì Hànyǔ xì de

学生。
xuésheng.

生词 New Words

*1. 谁	QPr	shéi	who
*2. 来	V	lái	to come
3. 介绍	V	jièshào	to introduce　介绍林娜，介绍语言学院
4. 名字	N	míngzi	name　你的名字，叫什么名字
5. 中文	N	Zhōngwén	Chinese　中文名字，中文名片
*6. 爸爸	N	bàba	dad

*7. 学习	V	xuéxí	to learn, to study	学习中文，学习汉语	
学	V	xué	to learn, to study	学中文，学汉语，学语言	
8. 专业	N	zhuānyè	major; specialty	中文专业，汉语专业，语言专业	
9. 美术	N	měishù	fine arts	学习美术，美术专业	
美	A	měi	beautiful		
10. 文学	N	wénxué	literature	中国文学，文学专业	
11. 系	N	xì	faculty; department	汉语系，语言系，中文系	
*12. 马大为	PN	Mǎ Dàwéi	(name of an American student)		
*13. 加拿大	PN	Jiānádà	Canada		
14. 美国	PN	Měiguó	the United States		

(handwritten: focus; property; →techniques)

补充生词 Supplementary Words

1. 文化	N	wénhuà	culture	
2. 历史	N	lìshǐ	history	
3. 哲学	N	zhéxué	philosophy	
4. 音乐	N	yīnyuè	music	
5. 经济	N	jīngjì	economy	
6. 数学	N	shùxué	mathematics	
7. 物理	N	wùlǐ	physics	
8. 化学	N	huàxué	chemistry	
9. 教育	N	jiàoyù	education	
10. 选修	V	xuǎnxiū	to take an elective course	

(handwritten: 161 come. 口 吗? ✱don't need for exam.)

二．注释　Notes

① 我问一下。

"一下" is used after a verb to indicate that an action is of short duration, or express the idea "giving something a try". It can soften the tone of an expression so that it sounds less formal. For example: "认识一下"，"介绍一下"，"去一下"，"进来一下"，"说一下"，"坐一下".

"我来介绍一下" and "我们认识一下" are expressions commonly used when people meet each other for the first time.

(handwritten: 张 个 口 只 八 — measure words. flat paper like / 遍 — action measure word)

② 您是我们学院的老师吗？

To indicate the place or organization where one works, plural pronouns are often used as modifiers. For example, the following phrases are used："他们学院"，"你们系"，"我们国家(guójiā, country)"，rather than "他学院"，"你系"，"我国家".

③ 啊，您是张教授。

"啊" is read in the fourth tone, indicating a sudden understanding or expressing admiration.

④ 你叫什么名字？

This is a casual way of asking someone's name, applicable to an adult talking with a child, or used among youngsters. The answer is usually one's full name. For example: "我叫丁力波". You may also answer by giving your surname first, and then your full name. For example: "我姓丁，叫丁力波".

⑤ 我的中文名字叫马大为。

A noun can be placed directly before a noun as its attributive modifier. For example: "中文名字"，"汉语老师"，"中国人".

To render a non-Chinese name into Chinese, we may choose two or three characters based on the pronunciation or meaning of the original name. David March, for example, may be rendered into Chinese as "马大为", and Natalie Lynn as "林娜"；the surname "White" can be translated as "白", and a girl by the name of Amy can be called "爱美".

Both "中文" and "汉语" refer to the Chinese language. "中文" has a broader meaning, referring to the Chinese language in both its written and spoken forms. Originally, "汉语" referred only to the spoken language of the Han people. Today, it is often used to refer to both the written and spoken forms of the Han language. These words are now used interchangeably by most people.

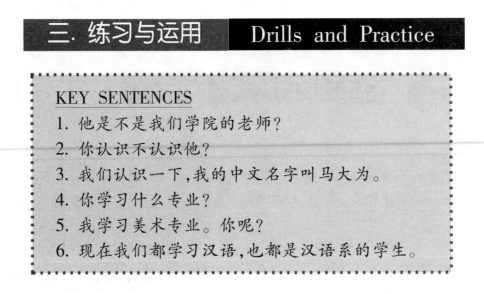

三. 练习与运用　Drills and Practice

KEY SENTENCES
1. 他是不是我们学院的老师？
2. 你认识不认识他？
3. 我们认识一下，我的中文名字叫马大为。
4. 你学习什么专业？
5. 我学习美术专业。你呢？
6. 现在我们都学习汉语，也都是汉语系的学生。

1. 熟读下列词组 Master the following phrases

(1) 看一下　说一下　介绍一下　认识一下　学习一下

(2) 认识不认识　　介绍不介绍　　　学习不学习

　　是不是　看不看　问不问　要不要　在不在　去不去　说不说

(3) 我爸爸　你妈妈　我朋友　她男朋友　我们老师　你们学院

(4) 我的名片　他的名字　我们学院的老师　语言学院的学生　中文系的教授

(5) 中国人　加拿大人　美国人　中国老师　加拿大朋友　美国学生

　　男朋友　女朋友　男老师　女老师　男(学)生　女(学)生

　　男人　女人

2. 句型替换 Pattern drills

(1) A：那是谁?

　　B：那是我朋友。

　　A：他/她姓什么?

　　B：他/她姓马。

她男朋友	张
加拿大学生	丁
英国小姐	林

(2) A：谁是马小姐?

　　B：他/她是马小姐。

　　A：马小姐叫什么名字?

　　B：马小姐叫马玉文。

田医生	田大中
张老师	张青生
Mr. White	白可贝

(3) A：他/她是你们老师吗?

　　B：他/她不是我们老师,他/她是我朋友。

　　A：他/她叫什么名字?

　　B：他/她叫＿＿＿＿＿＿＿＿＿＿。

你妈妈	我们老师
中文老师	美术老师
张教授	马老师

(4) A：你是不是中国人?

　　B：不是,我是加拿大人。

　　A：他也是加拿大人吗?

　　B：是,他也是加拿大人。

老师	学生
美国学生	中国学生
中文系的学生	美术系的学生

(5) A：这是不是你的照片?

　　B：这不是我的照片。

　　A：这是谁的照片?

　　B：这是她的照片。

丁力波	马大为
张教授	田医生
你们老师	他们老师

(6) A: 你认识不认识马大为？

B: 我认识马大为。

A: 他/她是哪国人？

B: 他/她是_____。

> 林小姐
> 田医生
> 白教授

(7) A: 他不是汉语系的学生，她呢？

B: 她也不是汉语系的学生。

A: 谁是汉语系的学生？

B: 张小姐是汉语系的学生。

> 是语言学院的教授
> 忙
> 学习语言

(8) A: 你的专业是不是汉语？

B: 不是。

A: 你学习什么专业？

B: 我学习美术专业，你呢？

A: 我学习文学专业。

> 数学(shùxué)　　历史(lìshǐ)
> 语言　　　　　哲学(zhéxué)
> 音乐(yīnyuè)　　经济(jīngjì)

3. 看图造句 Make sentences according to the pictures

(1)

他是学生，她也是学生。
他们都是学生。

他是老师，她_____老师。
他们_____老师。

他不是美国人，她_____美国人。
他们_____美国人。

他们是中国人，她_____中国人。
他们_____中国人。

(2)

今天天气<u>好不好</u>?　　　　　他＿＿＿＿＿＿?　　　　　他＿＿＿＿＿＿?

今天天气很好。　　　　　　　他很忙。　　　　　　　　他不高兴。

4. 会话练习 Conversation practice

【初次见面 Meeting someone for the first time】

(1) A：请问,您贵姓?

B：我姓＿＿＿＿＿＿,叫＿＿＿＿＿＿＿。您呢?

A：我叫＿＿＿＿＿＿＿＿＿。这是我的名片。

B：谢谢。

(2) A：我们认识一下。我叫＿＿＿＿＿＿＿。你叫什么名字?

B：我叫David March。我的中文名字叫马大为。

(3) A：请问,您是哪国人?

B：我是＿＿＿＿＿＿。你呢?

A：我是＿＿＿＿＿＿。

(4) A：请问,您是不是中国人?

B：我不是＿＿＿＿＿＿,我是＿＿＿＿＿＿。

(5) A：我介绍一下,这是＿＿＿＿＿,他是＿＿＿＿国人,是＿＿＿＿＿。

这是＿＿＿＿＿＿,她是＿＿＿＿＿国人,是＿＿＿＿＿＿。

B：认识你很高兴。

C：＿＿＿＿＿＿＿＿。

(6) 你们好! 我姓丁,叫丁力波,是加拿大人。我的专业是美术。现在我学习
汉语,是语言学院汉语系的学生。认识你们,我很高兴。

【谈专业 Talking about one's major】

(1) A：请问,你是不是汉语系的学生?

B：我是汉语系的学生。

A：你学习什么专业?

B：我学习历史(lìshǐ)专业。你的专业是什么?

A：我的专业是＿＿＿＿＿＿。

（2）A：你们明天开学吗？

　　B：我们明天开学。

　　A：你的专业是不是汉语？

　　B：不是，我的专业是美术。

　　A：你选修(xuǎnxiū)什么？

　　B：我选修中国文化(wénhuà)。

5. 交际练习 Communication exercises

（1）You come across a student whom you don't know. How do you carry out a conversation with him/her in order to know more about him/her?

（2）Two of your friends do not know each other. How do you introduce them to each other?

（3）How do you introduce yourself in a meeting?

（4）How do you ask about your new friend's major?

学生登记表 Student's Registration Form

姓名 name	性别 sex	年龄 age	国籍 nationality	单位 institution
丁力波	男	21	加拿大	语言学院汉语系
林娜	女	19	英国	语言学院汉语系
马大为	男	22	美国	语言学院汉语系

四. 阅读和复述 Reading Comprehension and Paraphrasing

　　他们是不是学生？是，他们都是语言学院的学生。你不认识他们，我介绍一下。他们都有中国姓，有中文名字。这是林娜，她是英国(Yīngguó)人。他是美国人，他姓马，他的中文名字很有意思，叫大为。他叫丁力波，爸爸是加拿大人，妈妈是中国人，他是加拿大人。马大为的专业是文学，丁力波的专业是美术。现在他们都学习汉语。

　　那是语言学院的汉语老师：女老师姓陈，男老师姓杨(Yáng)。他们都是汉语系的老师，也都是中国人。张教授也是语言学院的老师，他很忙。你看，这是张教授的名片。

　　田小姐不是老师，她是语言学院的医生。

1. 表领属关系的定语 Attributives expressing possession

In Chinese, an attributive must be placed before the word it modifies. When a noun or a pronoun is used as an attributive to express possession, the structural particle "的" is usually required.

NP / Pr +	的	+ N
我	的	名片
哥哥	的	咖啡
语言学院	的	老师

When a personal pronoun functions as an attributive and the modified word is a noun referring to a relative or the name of a work unit, the "的" between the attributive and the word it modifies may be omitted. For example:"我妈妈","你爸爸","他们家","我们学院".

2. 正反疑问句 V/A–not–V/A questions

A question can also be formed by juxtaposing the affirmative and negative forms of the main element of the predicate (verb or adjective) in a sentence.

$$V/A \quad + \quad 不 \ V/A \ + \ O$$

Subject	Predicate		
	V/A	**Not V/A**	**O**
你	忙	不　忙?	
你们	认识	不　认识	他?
力波	是	不　是	中国人?

The response to such a question may be a complete sentence (affirmative or negative) or a sentence with its subject or object omitted. One may respond with "是" (affirmative answer) or "不是" (negative answer) at the beginning of an answer to a "是不是" question. For example:

(1) (我)忙。　　　　　(我)不忙。
(2) (我们)认识(他)。　　(我们)不认识(他)。
(3) (力波)是中国人。　　(力波)不是中国人。
　　是,力波是中国人。　不是,力波不是中国人。

3. 用"呢"构成的省略式问句 Abbreviated questions with "呢"

An abbreviated question with "呢" is made by adding "呢" directly after a pronoun or a noun. The meaning of the question, however, must be clearly indicated in the previous sentence.

$$Pr/NP \quad + \quad 呢 ?$$

我很好,你呢? （你呢? ＝ 你好吗? ）

你不忙,你男朋友呢? （你男朋友呢? ＝ 你男朋友忙吗? ）

你是加拿大人,他呢? （他呢? ＝ 他是加拿大人吗? ）

林娜学习汉语,马大为呢? （马大为呢? ＝ 马大为学习汉语吗? ）

4. "也"和"都"的位置 The position of adverbs "也" and "都"

The adverbs "也" and "都" must occur after the subject and before the predicative verb or adjective. For example："他也是加拿大人","他们都是加拿大人". One cannot say "也他是加拿大人","都他们是加拿大人".

If both "也" and "都" modify the predicate, "也" must be put before "都".

$$也/都 \quad + \quad V/A$$

Subject	Predicate	
	Adv	**V/A**
丁力波		是　加拿大人。
丁力波		认识　他。
丁力波	很	忙。
她	也	是　加拿大人。
她	也	认识　他。
她	也很	忙。
他们	都	是　加拿大人。
他们	都	认识　他。
他们	都很	忙。
我们	也都	是　加拿大人。
我们	也都	认识　他。
我们	也都很	忙。

In a negative sentence, "也" must occur before "不". "都" may be put before or after "不", but the meanings of "都 不" and "不 都" are different.

$$也/都 \quad + \quad 不 \quad + \quad V/A$$

Subject	Predicate	
	Adv	**V/A**
她	不	是老师。
你	也不	是老师。
我们	都不	是老师。(none of us)
我们	不都	是老师。(not all of us)

六. 汉字　　Chinese Characters

1. 汉字的部件 Chinese character components

There are three aspects to the structure of a Chinese character: the strokes, the components and the whole character. For example, the character "木" consists of four strokes: "一", "丨", "丿", "丶". It is a basic character and is also used as a component for some other characters. For example, "林" consists of two "木" characters. The components are the core structure of a Chinese character. Chinese characters can be divided into character-parts and non-character-parts. For example, "院" can be divided into the following three parts: "阝", "宀", "元" of which "元" is a character-part, while "阝" and "宀" are the non-character-parts. The key to learning Chinese characters well is to master their components.

2. 认写基本汉字 Learn and write basic Chinese characters

(1) 开 (開)　　一 二 于 开　　

kāi　　to open　　　　　　4 strokes

("开" looks like the bar or the bolt of a door; when the "二" in "开" is removed, the door opens.)

(2) 目　　丨 冂 月 月 目　　

mù　　eye　　　　　　5 strokes

(3) 下　　一 丅 下　　

xià　　below, bottom　　　3 strokes

(in contrast with "上", the "卜" under "一" denotes "bottom" or "beneath")

(4) 元　　一 二 テ 元　　

yuán　　first; primary　　　4 strokes

(5) 片　　丿 丿' 户 片

piàn　　a flat, thin piece; slice　　4 strokes

(6) 皮　　一 厂 广 皮 皮　　

pí　　skin　　　　　　5 strokes

- 89 -

(7) 弓　　　¬ ¬ 弓
gōng　　　an archer's bow　　　　　　3 strokes

(8) 长 (長)　　´ ⌐ ⼟ 长
zhǎng　　to grow　　　　　　　　4 strokes

(9) 来 (來)　　一 ⼏ ⼝ 平 平 来 来
lái　　　to come　　　　　　　　7 strokes

(10) 介　　　丿 人 介 介
jiè　　　be situated between; interpose　　4 strokes

(11) 父　　　´ ハ 分 父
fù　　　father　　　　　　　　　4 strokes

(12) 巴　　　¬ 刀 ⺤ 巴
bā　　　wait anxiously; cling to　　　4 strokes
("巴" stands on the right side or at the bottom of a Chinese character,
and denotes the pronunciation of the character.)

(13) 习 (習)　　丁 丬 习
xí　　　to study　　　　　　　　3 strokes

(14) 专 (專)　　一 二 专 专
zhuān　　special　　　　　　　　4 strokes
(Note that the third stroke of "专" is one stroke, not two strokes.)

(15) 业 (業)　　丨 丬 丬 业 业
yè　　　line of business; trade　　　5 strokes

(16) 羊　　　丶 丷 ⼆ 兰 兰 羊
yáng　　sheep　　　　　　　　　6 strokes

(17) 术 (術)　　一 十 才 木 术
shù　　　art; skill　　　　　　　5 strokes
(Note that "术" has one more dot than "木".)

(18) 系　　　　一　ム　互　玄　号　系　系

xì　　　department；system　　　　　7 strokes

(19) 为 (爲)　　　、ソ为为

wéi　　act；to do　　　　　　4 strokes

3. 认写课文中的汉字 Learn and write the Chinese characters appearing in the texts

彳 (shuānglìrén) ("亻" is called the "single-standing-person" side; "彳" is called the "double-standing-person" side.)　ノク彳　　　3 strokes

艮 gèn　　　フコヨ艮艮艮　　　6 strokes

(1) 很 hěn

很 → 彳 + 艮　　　　9 strokes

亠 (liùzìtóu) (the "six" top)　、亠　　　2 strokes

丷 (xìngzìtóu) (the "excitement" top)　、丷丷丷　　　4 strokes

(2) 高兴 gāoxìng (高興)

高 → 亠 + 口 + 冂 + 口　　　10 strokes

兴 → 丷 + 八　　　6 strokes

𠂇 (kànzìtóu) (In a multi-component character the vertical stroke with a hook "亅" in "手" is written as a downward stroke to the left "丿".)　一二三手　4 strokes

(3) 看 kàn

看 → 𠂇 + 目　　　9 strokes

(Holding a hand "手" above one's eyes "目" to gaze.)

阝 (zuǒ'ěrduo) (the "left-ear" side)　乛阝　　　2 strokes

(4) 学院 xuéyuàn (學院)

院 → 阝 + 宀 + 元　　　9 strokes

(5) 名片 míngpiàn

名 → 夕 + 口   6 strokes

(6) 啊 à

啊 → 口 + 阝 + 可   10 strokes

子 (zǐzìpáng) (the "son" side) (The horizontal stroke in the character "子" is written as an upward stroke, when the character becomes the left side component of another character.)   了子   3 strokes

文 (fǎnwénpáng) (the "tapping" side) (The dot in " 文 " is written as " 丿 ", a downward stroke to the left, when the character becomes the right side component of another character)   丿 亠 夂 文   4 strokes

⺤ (shòuzìtóu) (the "acceptance" top) ⺀ ⺤   4 strokes

冖 (tūbǎogài) (the "bald cover" top) 丶 冖   2 strokes

(7) 教授 jiàoshòu

教 → 耂 + 子 + 文   11 strokes

授 → 扌 + ⺤ + 冖 + 又   11 strokes

(8) 丁力波 Dīng Lìbō

波 → 氵 + 皮   8 strokes

(9) 张 zhāng (張)

张 → 弓 + 长   7 strokes

(The meaning side is "弓", and the phonetic side is "长".)

隹 zhuī 丿 亻 亻 亻 亻 亻 隹 隹   8 strokes

(10) 谁 shéi (誰)

谁 → 讠 + 隹   10 strokes

纟 (jiǎosīpáng) (糹) (the "floss silk" side) ￪ 纟 纟   3 strokes

(11) 介绍 jièshào (介紹)

绍 → 纟 ＋ 刀 ＋ 口   8 strokes

宀 (bǎogàitóu) (the "roof" top) 丶 ￪ 宀   3 strokes

(12) 名字 míngzi

字 → 宀 ＋ 子   6 strokes

(13) 爸爸 bàba

爸 → 父 ＋ 巴   8 strokes

("父" suggests the meaning and "巴" denotes the pronunciation.)

羊 (tūwěiyáng) 丶 丶 丶 ￪ ￪ 羊 羊   6 strokes

(14) 美术 měishù (美術)

美 → 羊 ＋ 大   9 strokes

(15) 加拿大 Jiānádà

加 → 力 ＋ 口   5 strokes

拿 → 人 ＋ 一 ＋ 口 ＋ 手   10 strokes

(Hands joined together to denote the meaning of "taking".)

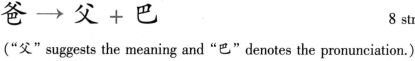

文化知识   Cultural Notes

Personal Names

Like most names in the world, Chinese names are made up of two parts: family names (*xing*) and given names (*ming*). While family names generally come from the father's side (nowadays we also find family names which come from the mother's side), parents choose given names for their children. In contrast to names in most European languages, where the surname usually follows the given name, family names always precede given names in Chinese. In the mainland, women retain their family names after marriage.

There are over a thousand Chinese family names. Zhang, Wang, Li, Chen, and Liu are among the most popular, with about seventy million Zhangs exceeding all others.

The majority of family names in Chinese consist of a single character, but there are some, such as Ouyang and Sima, that have two, and hence are known as disyllabic or double-character family names (*fuxing*). On the other hand, it is common to have single-character or double-character given names, such as in Song Hua and Lu Yuping. Due to the limited number of family names and shortness of given names, it is not unusual for people to have identical names in China.

This lesson will teach you how to describe your family members, and how to talk about your university and department. You will learn how to count to one hundred, and ask questions related to numbers and amount. Finally, we will introduce you to measure words, a grammatical category particularly well-developed in the Chinese language.

× 几 ×× = balanced

第八课 Lesson 8

你们 家 有 几 口 人
Nǐmen jiā yǒu jǐ kǒu rén

一. 课文　　Text

（一）

林 娜：　　这 是 不 是 你们 家 的 照片?
Lín Nà:　　Zhè shì bu shì nǐmen jiā de zhàopiàn?

王 小云：是 啊。①
Wáng Xiǎoyún: Shì a.

【谈家庭】Talking about one's family

林 娜：　　我 看 一下。你们 家 有 几 口 人?
Lín Nà:　　Wǒ kàn yíxià. Nǐmen jiā yǒu jǐ kǒu rén?

王 小云：我们 家 有 四 口 人。这 是 我 爸爸、我 妈妈，
Wáng Xiǎoyún: Wǒmen jiā yǒu sì kǒu rén. Zhè shì wǒ bàba、wǒ māma,

这 是 我 哥哥 和 我。② 你们 家 呢?
zhè shì wǒ gēge hé wǒ.　Nǐmen jiā ne?

- 95 -

林　娜：　　　我 有 妈妈，有 一 个 姐姐 和（两）个 弟弟。③
Lín Nà:　　　Wǒ yǒu māma, yǒu yí ge jiějie hé liǎng ge dìdi.

　　　　　　　我们 家 一共 有 六 口 人。
　　　　　　　Wǒmen jiā yígòng yǒu liù kǒu rén.

王　小云：　　这 是 五 口 人，还 有 谁？④
Wáng Xiǎoyún: Zhè shì wǔ kǒu rén, hái yǒu shéi?

林　娜：　　　还 有 贝贝。
Lín Nà:　　　Hái yǒu Bèibei.

王　小云：　　贝贝 是 你 妹妹 吗？
Wáng Xiǎoyún: Bèibei shì nǐ mèimei ma?

林　娜：　　　不，贝贝 是 我 的 小 狗。
Lín Nà:　　　Bù, Bèibei shì wǒ de xiǎo gǒu.

王　小云：　　小 狗 也 是 一 口 人 吗？
Wáng Xiǎoyún: Xiǎo gǒu yě shì yì kǒu rén ma?

林　娜：　　　贝贝 是 我们 的 好 朋友， 当然 是 我们
Lín Nà:　　　Bèibei shì wǒmen de hǎo péngyou, dāngrán shì wǒmen

　　　　　　　家 的 人。我 有 一 张 贝贝 的 照片， 你 看。
　　　　　　　jiā de rén. Wǒ yǒu yì zhāng Bèibei de zhàopiàn, nǐ kàn.

王　小云：　　真 可爱。
Wáng Xiǎoyún: Zhēn kě'ài.

林　娜：　　　你们 家 有 小 狗 吗？
Lín Nà:　　　Nǐmen jiā yǒu xiǎo gǒu ma?

王　小云：　　我们 家 没有 小 狗。林 娜，你 有 没有 男
Wáng Xiǎoyún: Wǒmen jiā méiyǒu xiǎo gǒu. Lín Nà, nǐ yǒu méiyǒu nán

　　　　　　　朋友？
　　　　　　　péngyou?

林　娜：　　　我 有 男 朋友。
Lín Nà:　　　Wǒ yǒu nán péngyou.

王　小云：　　他 做 什么 工作？
Wáng Xiǎoyún: Tā zuò shénme gōngzuò?

【问职业】Asking about someone's occupation

林　娜：　　　他 是 医生。
Lín Nà:　　　Tā shì yīshēng.

-96-

生词 New Words

犭 (animal)

1. 家	N	jiā	family, home 我们家，你们家，他们家
2. (几)	QPr	jǐ	how many, how much
*3. 口	M	kǒu	(a measure word mainly for the number of people in a family) 几口人，五口人
4. 照片	N	zhàopiàn	picture, photo 我的照片，我们家的照片
5. 和	Conj	hé	and 爸爸和妈妈，哥哥和我，你和他
6. 个	M	gè	(a measure word for general use) 几个弟弟，一个朋友，五个医生，七个学院，九个系
7. 姐姐	N	jiějie	elder sister _↗ two followed by measure word = liǎng_
8. 两	Nu	liǎng	two 两口人，两个姐姐，两个老师，两个系
*9. 弟弟	N	dìdi	younger brother
10. 还	Adv	hái	in addition 还有，还要，还认识，还介绍，还学习
11. 一共	Adv	yígòng	altogether 一共有六口人
12. 妹妹	N	mèimei	younger sister
13. 小	A	xiǎo	little, small 小弟弟，小妹妹 _(may indicate age)_
14. 狗	N	gǒu	dog 小狗，我的小狗
15. 张	M	zhāng	(a measure word for flat objects) 两张照片，一张名片
16. 当然	A	dāngrán	as it should be; only natural that 当然是，当然去
17. 真	A/Adv	zhēn	real/really 真的，真忙，真高兴，真有意思
18. 可爱	A	kě'ài	lovely, cute 真可爱，可爱的贝贝，可爱的照片
爱	V	ài	to love 爱爸爸，爱妈妈，爱弟弟妹妹
19. 没	Adv	méi	not 没有 → _Negates past action. (méi yào)_
*20. 男	A	nán	male 男朋友，男学生，男老师
21. 做	V	zuò	to do; to make
22. 工作	V/N	gōngzuò	to work/work 工作一年，他的工作，做什么工作
23. 王小云	PN	Wáng Xiǎoyún	(name of a Chinese student)
24. 贝贝	PN	Bèibei	(name of a dog)

Xiōng – brothers and sisters.

.describe a family photo.

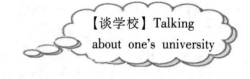

林　娜：　　　语言　学院　大 不 大？
Lín Nà：　　　Yǔyán Xuéyuàn dà bu dà?

王　　小云：不太大。⑤
Wáng Xiǎoyún：Bú tài dà.

林　娜：　　　语言　学院　有　多少　个 系？
Lín Nà：　　　Yǔyán Xuéyuàn yǒu duōshao ge xì?

王　　小云：有　十二 个 系。
Wáng Xiǎoyún：Yǒu shí'èr ge xì.

林　娜：　　　你 喜欢　你们　外语　系 吗？
Lín Nà：　　　Nǐ xǐhuan nǐmen Wàiyǔ xì ma?

王　　小云：我　很 喜欢　外语　系。
Wáng Xiǎoyún：Wǒ hěn xǐhuan Wàiyǔ xì.

林　娜：　　　你们　外语 系 有　多少　老师？
Lín Nà：　　　Nǐmen Wàiyǔ xì yǒu duōshao lǎoshī?

王　　小云：外语　系 有 二十八　个　中国　老师，十一 个
Wáng　Xiǎoyún：Wàiyǔ xì yǒu èrshíbā　ge Zhōngguó lǎoshī, shíyī　ge

　　　　　　　外国　老师。你们　系 呢？
　　　　　　　wàiguó lǎoshī. Nǐmen xì ne?

林　娜：　　　我们　汉语系 很 大。我们　系 的 老师 也 很
Lín Nà：　　　Wǒmen Hànyǔ xì hěn dà. Wǒmen xì de lǎoshī yě hěn

　　　　　　　多，有 一百 个。他们　都 是　中国　人。
　　　　　　　duō, yǒu yìbǎi ge. Tāmen dōu shì Zhōngguó rén.

　　　　　　　我们　系 没有　外国　老师。
　　　　　　　Wǒmen xì méiyǒu wàiguó lǎoshī.

生词 New Words

1. 大	A	dà	big, large　大照片，大学院
2. 多少	QPr	duōshao	how many, how much　多少人，多少教授
多	A	duō	many, much
少	A	shǎo	few, less
3. 喜欢	V	xǐhuan	to like, to prefer　喜欢汉语，喜欢老师

*4. 外语	N	wàiyǔ	foreign language	外语学院，外语老师
外	N	wài	outside	
语	N	yǔ	language	
5. 外国	N	wàiguó	foreign country	外国人，外国朋友，外国学生
6. 百	Nu	bǎi	hundred	一百，二百，三百，四百，八百

补充生词   Supplementary Words

1. 车	N	chē	car; vehicle
2. 词典	N	cídiǎn	dictionary
3. 电脑	N	diànnǎo	computer
4. 孩子	N	háizi	child
5. 爷爷	N	yéye	grandfather on the father's side
6. 外公	N	wàigōng	grandfather on the mother's side
7. 系主任	N	xìzhǔrèn	chairman of the department
8. 助教	N	zhùjiào	teaching assistant
9. 律师	N	lǜshī	lawyer
10. 工程师	N	gōngchéngshī	engineer

二. 注释　　Notes

qiàn 千　1000
wàn 万　10000
bái wàn　1000000

① 是啊。

"啊" is a modal particle expressing affirmation.

② 我哥哥和我

The conjunction "和" is generally used to connect pronouns, nouns, or noun phrases. e.g. "他和她", "哥哥和弟弟", "我们老师和你们老师". "和" cannot be used to connect two clauses, and is seldom used to connect two verbs.

③ 我有一个姐姐和两个弟弟。

When the numeral "2" is used with a measure word in Chinese, the character "两" is used instead of "二". For example："两张照片", "两个人" (we do not say "二张照片", "二个人"). When the numeral "2" is used alone, as in "一，二，三，…", or when it is used in a multi-digit number, we still use "二", even if it is followed by a measure word. For example："十二", "二十二", "九十二个人", "二百".

④ 还有谁？

One of the uses of "还" is to make an additional remark. For example：

我有两个姐姐,还有一个弟弟。

我认识马大为,还认识他朋友。

⑤ 不太大。

The adverb "太" can be used in a negative construction. "不太" means "不很…", so "不太大" means "不很大", and "不太忙" means "不很忙". However, when "太" is used in an affirmative construction, such as "太大(了)", "太小(了)" or "太忙(了)", it often means "too much" or "excessively".

三. 练习与运用　Drills and Practice

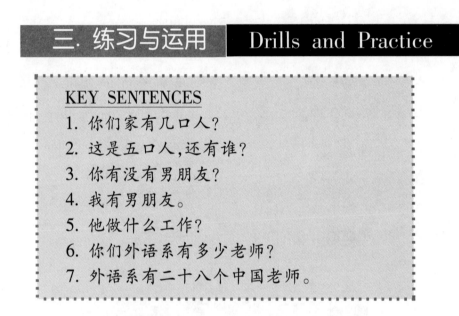

KEY SENTENCES

1. 你们家有几口人？
2. 这是五口人,还有谁？
3. 你有没有男朋友？
4. 我有男朋友。
5. 他做什么工作？
6. 你们外语系有多少老师？
7. 外语系有二十八个中国老师。

1. 熟读下列词组 Master the following phrases

(1) 我们家　我们系　我们学院　我们老师

你们家　你们系　你们学院　你们老师

他们家　他们系　他们学院　他们老师

(2) 我爸爸　我妈妈　我哥哥　我弟弟　我姐姐　我妹妹　我朋友

你爸爸　你妈妈　你哥哥　你弟弟　你姐姐　你妹妹　你朋友

(3) 中国老师　中国学生　中国朋友　中国教授　中国医生　中国人

外国老师　外国学生　外国朋友　外国教授　外国医生　外国人

(4) 我们的名片　我们家的小狗　我们学院的学生　我们系的外国老师

他的照片　他家的照片　他们学院的老师　他们系的中国老师

(5) 我和你　我们系和你们系　我们系的老师和你们系的老师

你们和他们　汉语学院和外语学院　汉语学院的学生和外语学院的学生

(6)　2口人　　　　4口人　　　　　5口人　　　　　8口人

　　12张照片　　　23张照片　　　70张名片　　　100张名片

　　8个学院　　　10个系　　　　26个老师　　　900个学生

　　2个教授　　　4个小姐　　　89个学生　　　37个人

　　几口人　　　　几张照片　　　几个弟弟　　　几个系

　　多少人　　　　多少(张)照片　多少(个)朋友　多少(个)系

2. 句型替换 Pattern drills

(1) A: 你有<u>名片</u>吗?
　　B: 我没有<u>名片</u>。

| 小狗 |
| 照片 |
| 车(chē) |
| 电脑(diànnǎo) |
| 汉语词典(cídiǎn) |

(2) A: 他有没有<u>中国朋友</u>?
　　B: 他有<u>中国朋友</u>。
　　A: 他有几个<u>中国朋友</u>?
　　B: 他有两个<u>中国朋友</u>。

| 弟弟 |
| 姐姐 |
| 孩子(háizi) |

(3) A: 你们系的<u>外国学生</u>多不多?
　　B: 我们系的<u>外国学生</u>不太多。
　　A: 你们系有多少<u>外国学生</u>?
　　B: 我们系有<u>20</u>个<u>外国学生</u>。

教授	3
外国老师	2
助教(zhùjiào)	7
中国学生	15

(4) A: 你们家有几口人?
　　B: 我们家有<u>6</u>口人。
　　A: 你爸爸做什么工作?
　　B: 他是<u>教授</u>。

5	医生
3	记者(jìzhě)
4	律师(lǜshī)

(5) A: 他们有几个孩子(háizi)?
　　B: 他们有<u>2</u>个孩子,都很可爱。
　　A: 都是男孩子吗?
　　B: 不是,他们有<u>1</u>个男孩子和<u>1</u>个女孩子。

3	1	2
4	2	2
5	2	3

3. 与你的同学口头做算术题 Solve the following math problems verbally

(1) E.g.   1+2=?   A：一加(jiā，plus)二是多少？

                                          B：一加二是三。

                 3+7=?

                 28+22=?

                 42+35=?

                 56+12=?

                 68+32=?

(2) E.g.   15−12=?   A：十五减(jiǎn，minus)十二是多少？

                                          B：十五减十二是三。

                 36−16=?

                 47−29=?

                 53−38=?

                 90−69=?

                 100−12=?

(3) E.g.   4×3=?   A：四乘(chéng，times)三是多少？

                                          B：四乘三是十二。

                 4×5=?

                 3×9=?

                 6×7=?

                 8×4=?

                 9×8=?

4. 会话练习 Conversation practice

【谈家庭 Talking about one's family】

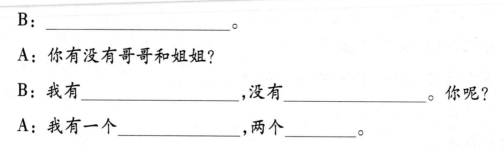

(1) A：你们家有几口人？

      B：_____。

      A：你有没有哥哥和姐姐？

      B：我有_____，没有_____。你呢？

      A：我有一个_____，两个_____。

(2) A：你爸爸、妈妈做什么工作？

B：我爸爸是_____，妈妈是_____。你爸爸、妈妈呢？

A：我爸爸是_____，妈妈不工作。

(3) A：你哥哥做什么工作？

B：他是学生。

A：他学习什么专业？

B：他学习_____。

【谈学校 Talking about one's university】

(1) A：你们学院大不大？

B：_____。

A：你们学院有多少(个)系？

B：_____。

A：你们学院有多少(个)专业？

B：_____。

A：你喜欢你的专业吗？

B：我当然喜欢。

(2) A：你们系的老师多不多？

B：我们系的老师_____。

A：你们系有没有外国老师？

B：我们系有外国老师。

A：你们系的外国老师_____？

B：我们系的外国老师很少。

(3) A：你们汉语系的学生多不多？

B：我们系的学生_____。

A：你们系的男(学)生多吗？

B：我们系的男(学)生很少，女(学)生_____。

A：你喜欢不喜欢你们系？

B：我很喜欢。

5. 交际练习 Communication exercises

（1）Introduce your family to your good friend.

（2）Talk about your friend's family.

（3）One of your friends inquires about your department. How do you answer him/her?

四. 阅读和复述 Reading Comprehension and Paraphrasing

　　丁力波是加拿大学生。他家有五口人：爸爸、妈妈、哥哥、弟弟和他。他妈妈姓丁，叫丁云，是中国人。他爸爸叫古波，是加拿大人。二十年（nián, year）前（qián, ago）古波在加拿大认识丁云，那时候，丁云学习英语（Yīngyǔ, English），古波学习汉语。

　　现在丁云和古波都是汉语教授。他们有三个男孩子（háizi），没有女孩子。现在丁力波和他哥哥、弟弟都在北京（Běijīng）。丁力波是语言学院的学生，他学习汉语。他很喜欢语言学院。语言学院不太大，有十二个系。汉语系有一百个中国老师，学生都是外国人。外语系的学生是中国人，外语系有很多外国老师。丁力波的中国朋友都是外语系的学生。丁力波的哥哥学习历史专业，他弟弟的专业是经济（jīngjì）。

　　他们的外婆（wàipó）也在北京。他们常常（chángcháng, often）去外婆家，他们很爱外婆。

五. 语法 Grammar

1. 11—100的称数法 Numbers from 11 to 100

11 十一	12 十二	13 十三	……	19 十九	20 二十
21 二十一	22 二十二	23 二十三	……	29 二十九	30 三十
31 三十一	32 三十二	33 三十三	……	39 三十九	40 四十
⋮	⋮	⋮		⋮	⋮
81 八十一	82 八十二	83 八十三	……	89 八十九	90 九十
91 九十一	92 九十二	93 九十三	……	99 九十九	100 一百

2. 数量词作定语 Numeral-measure words as attributives

　　In modern Chinese, a numeral alone cannot directly function as an attributive to modify a noun but must be combined with a measure word. All nouns have their own particular measure words.

```
Nu  +  M  +  N
五      口      人
一      个      姐姐
十二    '个      系
二十    张      照片
```

"个" is the most commonly used measure word, applied before nouns referring to people, things, and units. (It is read in the neutral tone). "张" is usually used before nouns of objects with a flat surface such as paper, photographs, and business cards. The measure word "口" is used to express the number of people in a family when it is combined with "人". For example:"五口人". In other cases, "个" should be used. For example:"我们班有二十个人." One cannot say "我们班有二十口人."

3. "有"字句 Sentences with "有"

The sentence taking the verb "有" as the main element of the predicate usually expresses possession. Its negative form is formed by adding the adverb "没" before "有". (Note:"不" cannot be used here.) Its V-not-V form is "有没有".

$$（没)+ 有 + O$$

Subject	Predicate		
	(没)有	O	Pt
我	有	姐姐。	
她	没有	男朋友。	
你	有	名片。	吗？
你	有没有	照片？	
语言学院	有	十二个系。	
我们系	没有	外国老师。	
你们家	有没有	小狗？	

If the subject of a sentence with "有" is a noun indicating a work unit, place or location, this kind of sentence with "有" is similar to the English sentence pattern of "There is / are...".

4. 用"几"或"多少"提问 Questions with "几" or "多少"

The question pronouns "几" and "多少" are used to ask about numbers. "几" is often used to ask about numbers less than 10, and a measure word is needed between it and the noun. "多少" may be used to ask about any number, and the measure word after it is optional.

几 + M + N　　　　　多少（+M）+ N

你们家有几口人？　　你们系有多少(个)学生？

我家有五口人。　　　我们系有五百个学生。

六. 汉字　Chinese Characters

1. 汉字的结构（1）Structure of Chinese characters(1)

Structurally speaking, Chinese characters fall into two categories: The single-component characters and the multi-component characters. All of the basic Chinese characters we have learned so far are simple-component characters, such as "人", "手", "刀", "马", "牛", "羊", "日", "月", "水", "木", "上", "下". The multi-component characters consist of two or more components, such as "爸", "妈", "你", "们", "哪", "语". The order of writing components in a character is similar to the stroke order of writing a character. There are three basic types of configuration for multi-component characters:

The left-right structure ①

a. Equal left-right: (the numbers in the figure indicate the order of writing the components.)

| 1 | 2 | 朋

b. Small left-big right

| 1 | 2 | 汉　　| 1 | 2 / 3 | 语

c. Big left-small right

| 1 / 2 | 3 | 都

2. 认写基本汉字　Learn and write basic Chinese characters

(1) 几(幾)　　丿 几
jǐ　　how many　　2 strokes

(2) 禾　　一 二 千 禾 禾
hé　　standing grain　　5 strokes

(3) 个(個)　　丿 人 个
gè　　(measure word)　　3 strokes

(4) 两　　一 丆 页 丙 丙 两 两
liǎng　　two　　7 strokes

(5) 未 　　 一 二 十 未 未
wèi　have not　　　　　5 strokes

(6) 犬 　　 一 ナ 大 犬
quǎn　dog　　　　　　4 strokes

(7) 云 (雲) 　　 一 二 云 云
yún　clouds　　　　　4 strokes

(8) 少 　　 丨 丷 小 少
shǎo　few; less　　　4 strokes

(9) 士 　　 一 十 士
shì　person　　　　　3 strokes

(10) 欠 　　 丿 𠂉 ケ 欠
qiàn　to owe　　　　 4 strokes

(11) 夕 　　 丿 ク 夕
xī　evening　　　　　3 strokes

(12) 卜 　　 丨 卜
bǔ　divination　　　 2 strokes

(13) 百 　　 (一 + 白)
bǎi　hundred　　　　 6 strokes

3. 认写课文中的汉字 Learn and write the Chinese characters appearing in the texts

豕 shǐ　　 一 丆 丆 豕 豕 豕 豕　　7 strokes

(1) 家 jiā

家 → 宀 + 豕   10 strokes

(The "roof top", "宀", denotes a hut. A hut with a pig
represents a house. The character "家" reflects the history of the ancient Chinese
people advancing from hunting to animal husbandry.)

灬 (sìdiǎndǐ)(The character "火" is written as "灬" at the bottom of a multi-component
character, and is called the "four-dots" bottom.) 丶 丶丶 丶丶丶 丶丶丶丶   4 strokes

(2) 照片 zhàopiàn

照 → 日 + 刀 + 口 + 灬   13 strokes

(The meaning part is "日", and the phonetic part is "召".)

(3) 和 hé

和 → 禾 + 口   8 strokes

ᵔ (dìzìtóu) (the "younger-brother" top) 丶 丶   2 strokes

(4) 弟弟 dìdi

弟 → ᵔ + 弔(乛 ㇕ 弓 弔 弟)   7 strokes

(5) 还 hái (還)

还 → 不 + 辶   7 strokes

(6) 一共 yígòng

共 → 卄 + 八   6 strokes

(7) 妹妹 mèimei

妹 → 女 + 未   8 strokes

(The "female" side "女", indicates the character has a feminine connotation.)

犭 (quǎnzìpáng)(the "dog" side) 丿 犭 犭   3 strokes

勹 (bāozìtóu) (the "wrapping" top) 丿 勹   2 strokes

(8) 狗 gǒu

狗 → 犭 + 勹 + 口   8 strokes

("犬" is the original character for "狗". It is written as "犭" on the left side of
characters indicating animals.)

⺌ (dāngzìtóu) (the "matching" top)   ⼂ ⼃ ⺌   3 strokes

彐 (héngshān)   ⼂ ⼂ 彐   3 strokes

(9) 当然 dāngrán (當然)

当 → ⺌ + 彐   6 strokes

然 → 夕 + 犬 + 灬   12 strokes

(The combination of a "flesh" side, a "dog" side and a "fire" side, indicating "to roast dog meat over the fire", produces the character, "然", which originally meant "burning". Now this character carries other meanings.)

(10) 真 zhēn

真 → ⼗ + 且 + 八   10 strokes

(11) 可爱 kě'ài (可愛)

爱 → ⺮ + ⼍ + 友   10 strokes

殳 shū   ⼃ ⼏ 几 殳   4 strokes

(12) 没 méi

没 → 氵 + 殳   7 strokes

(13) 男 nán

男 → 田 + 力   7 strokes

(14) 做 zuò

做 → 亻 + 古 + 攵   11 strokes

乍 zhà   ⼃ ⼇ 乍 乍 乍   5 strokes

(15) 工作 gōngzuò

作 → 亻 + 乍   7 strokes

(16) 多少 duōshao

多 → 夕 + 夕   6 strokes

(17) 喜欢 xǐhuan (喜歡)

喜 → 士 + 口 + ⸌ + 一 + 口　　12 strokes

欢 → ㄡ + 欠　　6 strokes

(On the left side of a multi-component character, the second stroke of "又" is written as an extended dot.)

(18) 外语 wàiyǔ (外語)

外 → 夕 + 卜　　5 strokes

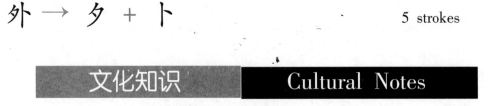

文化知识　　Cultural Notes

Forms of Address for Family and Relatives

While the Chinese words for "mother", "father", "son", and "daughter" are used in ways similar to what we find in English, addressing siblings and relatives is fairly complex in Chinese. Two principles govern how Chinese family members are addressed: 1) relatives on the paternal side are distinguished from those on the mother's side; and 2) age relative to the speaker is taken into consideration.

The English words "grandfather" and "grandmother" can refer to grandparents on either the father's or mother's side. In Chinese, on the other hand, one has to indicate whether they are the father's or the mother's parents. The parents of one's father are *zufu* "grandfather" and *zumu* "grandmother" and are informally called *yeye* "grandpa" and *nainai* "grandma". However, the terms for one's mother's parents are *waizufu* "maternal grandfather" and *waizumu* "maternal grandmother", and in spoken Chinese, *waigong* (or *laoye*), and *waipo* (or *laolao*), meaning literally "maternal grandpa" and "maternal grandma" respectively.

In Chinese special terms indicate whether siblings are older or younger than the speaker. For instance, instead of a term equivalent to the English "brother", Chinese has *gege* "elder brother" and *didi* "younger brother". Similarly, "elder sister" is *jiejie*, and "younger sister" is *meimei*. In Chinese, one must always be sure to differentiate between elder and younger siblings and use the correct term.

Have you ever wondered how Chinese celebrate their birthdays? In this lesson we will talk about birthday customs in China, and you will learn how to ask the age and birthplace of others. You will begin learning the days, weeks, months, and years in Chinese, and look at the Chinese zodiac animals, a remarkable creation of Chinese culture.

第九课 Lesson 9

他 今年 二十 岁
Tā jīnnián èrshí suì

一. 课文　　Text

王　小云：林娜，你 怎么样？①　忙 不 忙？
Wáng Xiǎoyún：Lín Nà, nǐ zěnmeyàng? Máng bu máng? ①

林娜：　　我 今天 很 忙。
Lín Nà：　　Wǒ jīntiān hěn máng.

王　小云：明天　　上午 你 有 没有 课？
Wáng Xiǎoyún：Míngtiān shàngwǔ nǐ yǒu méiyǒu kè?

林娜：　　明天　　是 星期 几？
Lín Nà：　　Míngtiān shì xīngqī jǐ? ②

王　小云：明天　　是 星期四。
Wáng Xiǎoyún：Míngtiān shì xīngqīsì.

林　娜：　　　我　上午、　下午　都　有　课。
Lín Nà：　　Wǒ shàngwǔ、xiàwǔ dōu yǒu kè.

【约会】Making an appointment

王　　小云：　你星期日　有　时间　吗？
Wáng Xiǎoyún　Nǐ xīngqīrì yǒu shíjiān ma?

林　娜：　　　星期日　是　几号？
Lín Nà：　　Xīngqīrì shì jǐ hào?

王　　小云：　星期日　是　十月　二十七号，是　宋华　的　生日。
Wáng Xiǎoyún：Xīngqīrì shì shíyuè èrshíqī hào, shì Sòng Huá de shēngri.

林　娜：　　　是　吗？② 他　今年　多　大？③
Lín Nà：　　Shì ma? Tā jīnnián duō dà?

王　　小云：　宋　　华 一 九 八 二　年　十月　二十七日　出生，
Wáng Xiǎoyún：Sòng Huá yī jiǔ bā èr nián shíyuè èrshíqī rì chūshēng,

属　狗。④ 他　今年　二十　岁。
shǔ gǒu. Tā jīnnián èrshí suì.

【问年龄和出生地】Asking about someone's age and birthplace

林　娜：　　　他　是　哪儿　人？⑤
Lín Nà：　　Tā shì nǎr rén?

王　　小云：　他　是　北京　人。他　爸爸、妈妈　都　在　北京。
Wáng Xiǎoyún：Tā shì Běijīng rén. Tā bàba、māma dōu zài Běijīng.

星期日　下午　我们　有　一个聚会，　祝贺　他　的
Xīngqīrì xiàwǔ wǒmen yǒu yí ge jùhuì, zhùhè tā de

生日。　力波、大为　都　去，你　参加　不　参加？
shēngri. Lìbō、Dàwéi dōu qù, nǐ cānjiā bu cānjiā?

林　娜：　　　太　好　了！我　当然　参加。　中国　人　生日
Lín Nà：　　Tài hǎo le! Wǒ dāngrán cānjiā. Zhōngguó rén shēngri

吃　蛋糕　吗？
chī dàngāo ma?

王　　小云：　吃　蛋糕。
Wáng Xiǎoyún：Chī dàngāo.

林　娜：　　　我　买　一个大　蛋糕，　好　吗？
Lín Nà：　　Wǒ mǎi yí ge dà dàngāo, hǎo ma?

王　　小云：好　啊。我　买　两　　瓶　　红葡萄酒。
Wáng Xiǎoyún：Hǎo a.　Wǒ mǎi liǎng píng hóngpútaojiǔ.

生词 New Words

1. 今年	N	jīnnián	this year	
年	N	nián	year 2002年，2000年，1998年，一年，两年	
2. 岁	M	suì	year (of age) 五岁，十八岁，二十岁，三十六岁	
*3. 怎么样	QPr	zěnmeyàng	how is … 天气怎么样，你怎么样	
*4. 今天	N	jīntiān	today 今天上午，今天下午	
5. 课	N	kè	class；lesson 有课，汉语课，文化课，一课，两课	
6. 星期	N	xīngqī	week 星期一，星期二，星期几，一个星期	
7. 上午	N	shàngwǔ	morning 明天上午，一个上午	
上	N	shàng	above；last 上星期，上星期二，上个月	
8. 下午	N	xiàwǔ	afternoon 明天下午，一个下午	
下	N	xià	below；next 下星期，下星期三，下个月	
9. 星期日	N	xīngqīrì	Sunday 星期日上午，星期日下午	
*10. 号	N	hào	day of the month 五月四号，十月一号	
11. 生日	N	shēngri	birthday 他的生日，二十岁生日	
生	V	shēng	to be born	
12. 多大	IE	duō dà	how old 今年多大	
多	Adv	duō	how	
大	A	dà	old	
13. 出生	V	chūshēng	to be born 1982年出生	
出	V	chū	to go out；to come out	
14. 属	V	shǔ	to be born in the year of 属狗，属马	
15. 聚会	N	jùhuì	get-together；party 生日聚会，有一个聚会	
会	N	huì	meeting	
16. 祝贺	V	zhùhè	to congratulate 祝贺生日	
祝	V	zhù	to wish	

17. 参加	V	cānjiā	to participate；to attend 参加聚会
*18. 了	Pt	le	(modal partical/aspect partical)
19. 吃	V	chī	to eat
20. 蛋糕	N	dàngāo	cake 一个蛋糕，吃蛋糕
蛋	N	dàn	egg
糕	N	gāo	cake
21. 买	V	mǎi	to buy 买蛋糕
22. 瓶	M	píng	bottle 一瓶水
23. 红葡萄酒	N	hóngpútaojiǔ	red wine 一瓶红葡萄酒
红	A	hóng	red
葡萄	N	pútao	grape 吃葡萄，买葡萄
酒	N	jiǔ	wine or liquor
*24. 宋华	PN	Sòng Huá	(name of a Chinese student)
25. 北京	PN	Běijīng	Beijing

(handwritten note near 21: mǎi = sell)

(handwritten note near 23: flower/grass hat)

（二）

林　娜：　　　宋　　华，这是　生日　蛋糕。
Lín Nà:　　　Sòng Huá, zhè shì shēngri dàngāo.

祝　你　生日　快乐！⑥
Zhù nǐ shēngri kuàilè!

【祝贺生日】
Celebrating someone's birthday

宋　华：　谢谢。蛋糕　真　漂亮。你们　来，我　很　高兴。
Sòng Huá：　Xièxie. Dàngāo zhēn piàoliang. Nǐmen lái, wǒ hěn gāoxìng.

马　大为：　今天　我们　吃北京　烤鸭。我　很　喜欢　吃
Mǎ Dàwéi：　Jīntiān wǒmen chī Běijīng kǎoyā. Wǒ hěn xǐhuan chī

烤鸭。⑦
kǎoyā.

丁　力波：　我们　喝　什么　酒？
Dīng Lìbō：　Wǒmen hē shénme jiǔ?

王　　小云：　当然　喝　红葡萄酒，我们　还　吃　寿面。⑧
Wáng Xiǎoyún：Dāngrán hē hóngpútaojiǔ, wǒmen hái chī shòumiàn.

林　娜：　吃　寿面？　真　有意思。
Lín Nà：　Chī shòumiàn? Zhēn yǒu yìsi.

宋　华：　林娜，你的　生日是　哪天？
Sòng Huá：　Lín Nà, nǐ de shēngri shì nǎ tiān?

林　娜：　十一月　十二号。
Lín Nà：　Shíyīyuè shí'èr hào.

宋　华：　好，十一月　十二号　我们　再来吃　寿面。
Sòng Huá：　Hǎo, shíyīyuè shí'èr hào wǒmen zài lái chī shòumiàn.

生词 New Words

1. 快乐	A	kuàilè	happy	生日快乐
2. 漂亮	A	piàoliang	pretty, beautiful; nice	漂亮的小姐，漂亮的照片
3. 烤鸭	N	kǎoyā	roast duck	北京烤鸭，吃烤鸭
鸭	N	yā	duck	
*4. 喝	V	hē	to drink	喝葡萄酒，喝咖啡(kāfēi)
5. 再	Adv	zài	again	再来，再买，再看，再做
6. 寿面	N	shòumiàn	(birthday) longevity noodles	吃寿面
面	N	miàn	noodles	吃面

1. 晚上	N	wǎnshang	evening
2. 中餐	N	zhōngcān	Chinese food
3. 西餐	N	xīcān	Western food
4. 茶	N	chá	tea
5. 可乐	N	kělè	coke
6. 雪碧	PN	Xuěbì	Sprite
7. 啤酒	N	píjiǔ	beer
8. 汉堡	N	hànbǎo	hamburger
9. 热狗	N	règǒu	hotdog
10. 面包	N	miànbāo	bread
11. 牛奶	N	niúnǎi	milk
12. 米饭	N	mǐfàn	(cooked) rice

二. 注释　　Notes

① 你怎么样？

This is also a form of greeting used among acquaintances and friends, and is similar to "你好吗？"

② 是吗？

The phrase "是吗？" does not raise a question here, but expresses mild surprise on the part of the speaker concerning something that he/she does not know. For example：

A：丁力波的哥哥和弟弟都在北京。

B：是吗？

Sometimes it expresses doubt, or modesty when receiving praise. (See Lesson Eleven.)

③ 他今年多大？

Here "多" is an adverb, followed by an adjective. The phrase "多 + A" is used to raise a question, and in this case "大" refers to age.

In asking about age in Chinese, one has to choose different forms for different groups of people. "你今年多大？" can only be used to ask the age of an adult, or people of the same generation as the speaker. When asking the age of a child, we usually say "你今年几岁？", and when asking the age of an elderly person or those older than the speaker, a more polite form has to be used, which will be taught in Lesson Eleven.

④ 宋华一九八二年十月二十七日出生，属狗。

It is customary for the Chinese to designate one's year of birth according to twelve animals, which are arranged in the following order: rat, ox, tiger, rabbit, dragon, snake, horse, ram, monkey, rooster, dog, and pig. These form a twelve-year cycle. For example, the year 1982, 1994 and 2006 are all designated "dog" years. The people who are born in these years are said to "belong to the year of dog", which, in Chinese, is written as "属狗". The years 1988, 2000 and 2012 are dragon years. Those who are born in these years all "属龙".

⑤ 他是哪儿人？

This is an expression usually used to ask someone's place of birth. It can also be said as "他哪儿人？", with "是" omitted; and in answering "哪儿", it is usually necessary to specify a province, city, or county. When asking about nationality, we use the expression "哪国人？"

⑥ 祝你生日快乐！

This is a familiar form of expression used to give greetings to someone on his/her birthday. "祝你…" is used to express good wishes, sometimes with the implication of "congratulating in advance", whereas "祝贺你…" is commonly used to congratulate someone on something that is already known or has already occurred. For example:

    A：我下星期天结婚(jiéhūn, to get married)。
    B：祝贺你!

⑦ 我很喜欢吃烤鸭。

A verb or a verbal phrase can funtion as the object of the predicative verb. For example:

    他喜欢说。
    我喜欢学习汉语。

⑧ 我们还吃寿面。

When celebrating birthdays, a traditional Chinese custom is to eat "longevity noodles". The length of noodles symbolizes "longevity".

```
KEY SENTENCES

1. 他今年多大？
2. 他今年二十岁。
3. 星期日是几号？
4. 星期五上午你有没有课？
5. 他一九八二年十月二十七号出生。
6. 我买一个大蛋糕，好吗？
7. 我很喜欢吃烤鸭。
8. 祝你生日快乐！
```

1. 熟读下列词组 Master the following phrases

(1) 今天上午　　明天下午　　五月八号上午　　上星期 上星期三 上星期三下午
　　星期二上午 星期六下午 九月二十号下午 下星期 下星期日 下星期三上午

(2) 一九七〇年出生　　　　一九八五年学习汉语　　　　一九九〇年工作
　　一九九九年来中国　　　二〇〇〇年认识张教授　　　二〇〇二年到北京

(3) 一个蛋糕　两瓶葡萄酒　五张照片　三个朋友　一个妹妹　一个聚会

(4) 宋华的生日　你的生日　他们的聚会　林娜的蛋糕　王小云的酒

(5) 生日蛋糕　大蛋糕　红葡萄酒　北京烤鸭

2. 句型替换 Pattern drills

(1) A: 今天是(几月)几号？

　　B: 今天是十一月八号。

　　A: 明天是星期几？

　　B: 明天是星期四。

2002		
九月小	27	星期五

2002		
十月大	16	星期三

2002		
十二月大	31	星期二

(2) A: 二月五号是不是星期六？

　　B: 二月五号不是星期六,是星期五。

　　A: 星期五你有没有课？

　　B: 我上午有课,下午没有课。

2月

一	二	三	四	五	六	日
1	2	3	4	5	6	7
8	9	10	11	12	13	14
15	16	17	18	19	20	21
22	23	24	25	26	27	28

(3) A: 星期六是几号？

B: 星期六是十二月十七号。

A: 星期六他做什么？

B: 他去朋友家。

星期五	看京剧(jīngjù)
星期一	参加聚会
星期日	吃烤鸭

(4) A: 你现在忙不忙？

B: 我现在很忙。

A: 你星期几有时间？

B: 我星期五下午有时间。

| 星期日 |
| 星期四上午 |
| 星期二下午 |

(5) A: 你几号来北京？

B: 我下月二号来北京。

A: 下月二号是星期几？

B: 下月二号是星期一。

去	加拿大
来	中国
去	美国

(6) A: 你今年多大？

B: 我今年21岁。

A: 你的生日是哪天？

B: 我的生日是8月31号。

19	1月6日
20	3月12日
22	4月22号

(7) A: 你是哪儿人？

B: 我是北京人。

A: 北京怎么样？

B: 北京很漂亮。

| 上海(Shànghǎi) |
| 温哥华(Wēngēhuá) |
| 多伦多(Duōlúnduō) |
| 纽约(Niǔyuē) |
| 伦敦(Lúndūn) |

(8) A: 你参加明天的聚会吗？

B: 我当然参加。

A: 我买两瓶红葡萄酒，好吗？

B: 好啊，我买一个大蛋糕。

两瓶可乐(kělè)	五个汉堡(hànbǎo)
三瓶雪碧(xuěbì)	八个热狗(règǒu)
六瓶啤酒(píjiǔ)	九个面包(miànbāo)

3. 回答下列问题 Answer the following questions

（1）一年有几个月？

（2）一年有多少个星期？

（3）一个星期有几天？

（4）十一月有多少天？

（5）十一月有几个星期天？

（6）今天几月几号？星期几？

（7）星期天是几号？

（8）星期天你做什么？

（9）你喜欢吃什么？

（10）你喜欢喝茶(chá)吗？

4. 会话练习 Conversation practice

【约会 Making an appointment】

（1）A：你怎么样？忙不忙？

　　B：_____。

　　A：星期五下午你有时间吗？我们去_____,好吗？

　　B：太好了,我当然去。

（2）A：十二号你有时间吗？

　　B：十二号是星期三吗？

　　A：不是,十二号是星期四。我们下午有个聚会,你参加不参加？

　　B：对不起(duìbuqǐ),_____,恐怕(kǒngpà)不行(xíng)。

　　A：没关系(méi guānxi)。

【问年龄和出生地 Asking about someone's age and birthplace】

（1）A：你今年多大？

　　B：我今年二十八(岁)。

　　A：你的生日是哪天？

　　B：今天是我的生日。

　　A：祝你生日快乐！

　　B：谢谢。

(2) A：您是哪儿人？

B：我是上海(Shànghǎi)人。

A：你爸爸妈妈都在上海吗？

B：不，他们现在_____。

A：他们都好吗？

B：谢谢，他们都很好。

(3) A：你哥哥有孩子(háizi)吗？

B：他有一个女孩子。

A：她今年几岁？

B：她_____。

【祝贺生日 Celebrating someone's birthday】

(1) A：下星期五是林娜的生日，我们有个聚会。你来不来？

B：我当然来。_____，好吗？

A：好啊！我买_____。

B：太好了，我们喝葡萄酒，吃蛋糕和寿面。

(2) A：今天是你的生日，祝你生日快乐！

B：谢谢。你们来，我很高兴。

5. 交际练习 Communication exercises

Your friend is trying to make an appointment with you. Please reply according to your schedule for next week：

	星期一	星期二	星期三	星期四	星期五	星期六	星期日
上午	汉语课	文化课	汉语课		汉语课	看朋友	
下午		汉语课		汉语课	打球 dǎ qiú		生日 聚会
晚上 wǎnshang	朋友来		游泳 yóuyǒng			看京剧 jīngjù	

宋华是经济(jīngjì)系的学生,北京人,1982年出生。今年十月二十七日是他二十岁的生日。星期天下午,他的好朋友们有一个聚会,王小云、林娜、丁力波和马大为都来祝贺他的生日。他们在北京烤鸭店(diàn, store)吃烤鸭和寿面,喝红葡萄酒。朋友们祝宋华生日快乐,宋华非常高兴。

林娜的生日是十一月十二号。宋华说那天他们再来吃寿面和烤鸭。

五. 语法　　　　Grammar

1. 年、月、日和星期 Expressing the date and days of the week

In Chinese, the four figures making up the name of a year are read out as four separate numbers and "年" is put at the end. For example:

一九九八年	yī jiǔ jiǔ bā nián
二○○○年	èr líng líng líng nián
二○○二年	èr líng líng èr nián
二○一○年	èr líng yī líng nián

The names of the 12 months are produced by combining the cardinal numbers 1 to 12 with "月". For example:

一月	yīyuè	January	七月	qīyuè	July
二月	èryuè	February	八月	bāyuè	August
三月	sānyuè	March	九月	jiǔyuè	September
四月	sìyuè	April	十月	shíyuè	October
五月	wǔyuè	May	十一月	shíyīyuè	November
六月	liùyuè	June	十二月	shí'èryuè	December

The names of the dates are produced by combining cardinal numbers 1 to 30 （or 31）with "号"（spoken form）or "日"（written form）. For example：

（二月）六号	（èryuè）liù hào	February 6
（十月）十二号	（shíyuè）shí'èr hào	October 12
（十一月）二十二日	（shíyīyuè）èrshí'èr rì	November 22
（十二月）三十一日	（shí'èryuè）sānshíyī rì	December 31

If one mentions a date in the current month, one can omit "月" and simply say "…号".

The cardinal numbers from 1 to 6 follow "星期" to express Monday to Saturday. The name for Sunday is "星期天"（spoken form）or "星期日"（written form）.

星期一	xīngqīyī	Monday	星期五	xīngqīwǔ	Friday
星期二	xīngqī'èr	Tuesday	星期六	xīngqīliù	Saturday
星期三	xīngqīsān	Wednesday	星期日	xīngqīrì	Sunday
星期四	xīngqīsì	Thursday			

The word order for expressing the date and days of the week is：

年 ＋ 月 ＋ 日 ＋ 星期

二〇〇〇年十二月二十五日 星期三

2000年 12月 25日 星期三

2. 表时间的词语作状语 Words expressing time as adverbials

Words expressing time, such as "现在", "今天", "下午", "二月二十号" can function as adverbials to indicate the time of occurrence of an action or a state. Adverbials of time （Time-When）can be placed either（1）after the subject and before the main element of the predicate or（2）before the subject to emphasize the time.

S ＋ TW ＋ VO/A

Subject	Predicate		
	T W	V O ／ A	
你 我 中国人 宋华 我	星期日 上午、下午 生日 1982年10月27日 今天	有　时间 都 有　　课。 　　吃　蛋糕 　　出生。 　　很　　　忙。	吗? 吗?

-123-

TW + S + VO/A

Time words	Subject	Predicate		
		V	**O**	**/ A**
明天上午	你	有没有	课?	
星期日下午	我们	有	一个聚会。	
今天	我们	吃	北京烤鸭。	
11月12号	我们	再 来 吃	寿面。	
今天	我	很		忙。

Note: 1. Adverbials of time (Time–When) can never be placed after the predicative verb. For example, one cannot say "我们吃烤鸭今天".

2. If there is more than one word expressing time in one adverbial, a large unit of time should be put before a smaller unit. For example: "明天上午", "星期日下午".

3. 名词谓语句 Sentences with a nominal predicate

Nouns, noun phrases, and numeral-measure words can function directly as the predicate of a sentence and do not need the verb "是". This kind of sentence is especially used to express age, price (see Lesson 10), and so on. In spoken language, it is also used to express time (see Lesson 11) or birth place.

S + Nu-M

Subject	Predicate	
	Nu-M	
宋华	今年	二十岁。
林娜		十九岁。

4. 用"好吗?"提问 Using "好吗?" to ask a question

Questions with "好吗?" are often used to give a suggestion or to ask for an opinion. The first part of such a question is a declarative sentence, and its last part can also be "可以吗?".

我们买一个大蛋糕,好吗?

我们去游泳(yóuyǒng),好吗?

现在去,可以吗?

Some examples of affirmative answers are: "好啊", "好", "太好了".

六. 汉字   Chinese Characters

1. 汉字的结构(2) Structure of Chinese characters (2)

The left-right structure ②

a. Equal left-middle-right

1	2	3

谢 娜

2. 认写基本汉字 Learn and write basic Chinese characters

(1) 今   ノ 人 人 今

jīn   present day   4 strokes

(2) 年   ノ 仁 仁 仁 生 年

nián   year   6 strokes

(3) 果   丶 口 曰 日 旦 甲 畀 果

guǒ   fruit   8 strokes

(4) 其   一 十 廿 甘 甘 其 其 其

qí   he(his); she(her)   8 strokes

(5) 上   丨 卜 上

shàng   above   3 strokes

(Placing "上" on top of "一" means "above".)

(6) 午   ノ 仁 仁 午

wǔ   noon   4 strokes

(7) 出   乚 屮 屮 出 出

chū   to go/come out   5 strokes

("凵" denotes a cave, and "屮" denotes one foot stepping out of the cave.)

(8) 面 (麵)   一 丆 厂 丙 而 而 面 面 面

miàn   noodles   9 strokes

(9) 尸 　　㇇ コ 尸

shī　　corpse　　3 strokes

("尸" denotes a dead body or a carcass.)

(10) 了 　　㇇ 了

le　　(particle)　　2 strokes

(11) 虫(蟲) 　　丶 冖 口 中 虫 虫

chóng　　insect; worm　　6 strokes

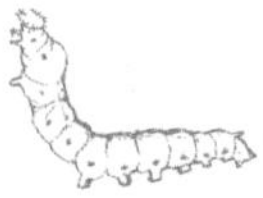

(12) 耳 　　一 厂 丌 开 耳 耳

ěr　　ear　　6 strokes

(13) 乞 　　丿 𠂉 乞

qǐ　　to beg　　3 strokes

(14) 米 　　丶 丷 䒑 半 米 米

mǐ　　rice　　6 strokes

(The four dots in "米" stand for grains of rice.)

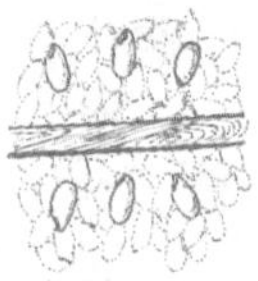

(14) 头(頭) 　　丶 丶 亠 头 头

tóu　　head　　5 strokes

(15) 瓦 　　一 丆 瓦 瓦

wǎ　　tile　　4 strokes

3. 认写课文中的汉字 Learn and write the Chinese characters appearing in the texts

(1) 岁 suì (歲)

岁 → 山 + 夕　　6 strokes

(2) 怎么样 zěnmeyàng (怎麼樣)

怎 → 乍 + 心　　9 strokes

样 → 木 + 羊　　10 strokes

(3) 课 kè（課）

课 → 讠 + 果   10 strokes

(4) 星期 xīngqī

星 → 日 + 生   9 strokes

期 → 其 + 月   12 strokes

丂 (hàozìdǐ) (the "number" bottom)   一 丂   2 strokes

(5) 号 hào（號）

号 → 口 + 丂   5 strokes

(6) 属 shǔ（屬）

属 → 尸 + 一 + 虫 + 冂   12 strokes

氺 (jùzìdǐ)   一 丆 丏 厼 氺 氺   6 strokes

(7) 聚会 jùhuì（聚會）

聚 → 耳 + 又 + 氺   14 strokes

会 → 人 + 云   6 strokes

礻 (shìzìpáng)(the "manifestation" side)   丶 丆 礻 礻   4 strokes

(8) 祝贺 zhùhè（祝賀）

祝 → 礻 + 兄   9 strokes

贺 → 力 + 口 + 贝   9 strokes

(9) 吃 chī

吃 → 口 + 乞   6 strokes

(to use mouth "口" to eat "吃")

疋 (pǐzìtóu) (the "foot" top) 一 丆 疋 疋 疋   5 strokes

(10) 蛋糕 dàngāo

蛋 → 疋 + 虫   11 strokes

糕 → 米 + 羔   16 strokes

(On the left side of a character, the sixth stroke in "米" is written as a dot.)

一 (hénggōu) (a horizontal stroke with a hook)   1 stroke

(11) 买 mǎi (買)

买 → 一 + 头   6 strokes

(12) 瓶 píng

瓶 → 丷 + 开 + 瓦   10 strokes

(13) 红 hóng (紅)

红 → 纟 + 工   6 strokes

艹 (cǎozìtóu) (the "grass" top)   一 十 艹   3 strokes

甫 fǔ   一 丆 万 肙 肙 南 甫   7 strokes

缶 fǒu   丿 乍 仁 午 缶 缶   6 strokes

(14) 葡萄 pútao

葡 → 艹 + 勹 + 甫   12 strokes

萄 → 艹 + 勹 + 缶   11 strokes

酉 yǒu   一 丆 厄 丙 西 酉 酉   7 strokes

(15) 酒 jiǔ

酒 → 氵 + 酉   10 strokes

彡 (sānpiěr) (the "three-downward-strokes-to-the-left" side) 丿 彡 彡   3 strokes

(16) 参加 cānjiā (參加)

参 → 厶 + 大 + 彡   8 strokes

(17) 宋华 Sòng Huá (宋華)

宋 → 宀 + 木   7 strokes

华 → 化 + 十   6 strokes

扌   一 亅 扌   3 strokes

(18) 北京 Běijīng

北 → 扌 + 匕   5 strokes

京 → 亠 + 口 + 小   8 strokes

夬 (juézìpáng)(the "decision" side) ㄱ ㄱ ㅋ 夬   4 strokes

(19) 快乐 kuàilè (快樂)

快 → 忄 + 夬   7 strokes

西 (xīzìtóu) (the "west" top) 一 ㄏ 冂 兀 西 西   6 strokes

(20) 漂亮 piàoliang

漂 → 氵 + 西 + 二 + 小   14 strokes

亮 → 亠 + 口 + 冖 + 几   9 strokes

(21) 烤鸭 kǎoyā (烤鴨)

烤 → 火 + 耂 + 5   10 strokes

(5: 一 5)

鸭 → 甲 + 鸟   10 strokes

(甲: 冂 冂 冃 日 甲; 鸟: ′ ㄅ ㄅ 鸟 鸟)

(22) 喝 hē

喝 → 口 + 日 + 勹 + 人 + 乚   12 strokes

(23) 寿面 shòumiàn (壽麵)

寿 → 耂 + 寸   7 strokes

(耂: 一 二 三 耂)

Bargaining for discounts in China can make shopping quite an experience! This lesson will show you how Chinese currency is used. Now is a chance to talk more about yourself: you will learn how to describe your likes, interests, and hobbies. You will also learn what to do when you can't think of the right thing to say.

第十课 Lesson 10

我 在 这儿 买 光盘
Wǒ zài zhèr mǎi guāngpán

一. 课文   Text

常 cháng → often.

营常 zuó shénme? → you do what often?

跟 gēn

（一）

王小云：　　大为，你 在 这儿 买 什么？
Wáng Xiǎoyún：Dàwéi, nǐ zài zhèr mǎi shénme?

马大为：　　我 买 音乐 光盘。
Mǎ Dàwéi：　　Wǒ mǎi yīnyuè guāngpán.

王小云：　　你 常常 来 这儿 吗？
Wáng Xiǎoyún：Nǐ chángcháng lái zhèr ma?

time can be emphasized

马大为：　　我 不 常 来 这儿。星期天 我 常常 跟
Mǎ Dàwéi：　　Wǒ bù cháng lái zhèr. Xīngqītiān wǒ chángcháng gēn

林 娜 去 小 商场。 这个 商场 很 大。①
Lín Nà qù xiǎo shāngchǎng. Zhè ge shāngchǎng hěn dà.

-130-

王小云： 你 喜欢 什么 音乐？
Wáng Xiǎoyún： Nǐ xǐhuan shénme yīnyuè?

【喜欢不喜欢】
Likes and dislikes

马大为： 我 喜欢 中国 音乐。
Mǎ Dàwéi： Wǒ xǐhuan Zhōngguó yīnyuè.

这 张 光盘 怎么样？
Zhè zhāng guāngpán zěnmeyàng?

王小云： 这 张 很 好， 是《梁 祝》， 很 有名。
Wáng Xiǎoyún： Zhè zhāng hěn hǎo, shì《Liáng Zhù》, hěn yǒumíng.

马大为： 好，我 买 这 张。 这儿 有 没有 书 和 报？
Mǎ Dàwéi： Hǎo, wǒ mǎi zhè zhāng. Zhèr yǒu méiyǒu shū hé bào?

王小云： 这儿 没有 书， 也 没有 报。
Wáng Xiǎoyún： Zhèr méiyǒu shū, yě méiyǒu bào.

马大为： 本子 呢？
Mǎ Dàwéi： Běnzi ne?

王小云： 有， 在 那儿买。 跟 我 来，我 也 买 本子。
Wáng Xiǎoyún： Yǒu, zài nàr mǎi. Gēn wǒ lái, wǒ yě mǎi běnzi.

生词 New Words

*1. 在	Prep	zài	at; in; on	在家, 在学院, 在这儿
2. 光盘	N	guāngpán	CD	一张光盘
3. 音乐	N	yīnyuè	music	音乐光盘, 中国音乐, 外国音乐
4. 商场	N	shāngchǎng	market; bazaar; shopping mall	在商场, 进商场
商	N	shāng	trade; commerce	
5. 常常	Adv	chángcháng	often	常常来, 常常去, 常常看, 常常做
常	Adv	cháng	often	不常
6. 跟	Prep/V	gēn	with/to follow	跟他来, 跟林娜去, 跟我学
7. 有名	A	yǒumíng	famous	有名的教授, 有名的医生
8. 书	N	shū	book	外语书, 汉语书, 有名的书, 看书
9. 报	N	bào	newspaper	买报, 看报
10. 本子	N	běnzi	notebook	一个本子, 买本子
11. 那儿	Pr	nàr	there	去那儿, 在那儿
12. 梁祝	PN	Liáng Zhù	(name of a Chinese violin concerto)	

(二)

师傅：　　　先生，　　您要　什么？②
Shīfu:　　　Xiānsheng, nín yào shénme?

丁　力波：你好，师傅。③请问，　这是　什么？
Dīng Lìbō:　Nǐ hǎo, shīfu.　Qǐngwèn, zhè shì shénme?

师傅：　　　您不认识　吗？这是　　香蕉苹果。
Shīfu:　　　Nín bú rènshi ma? Zhè shì xiāngjiāopíngguǒ.

丁　力波：对不起，我是问：这个　汉语　怎么　说？④
Dīng Lìbō:　Duìbuqǐ, wǒ shì wèn: Zhè ge Hànyǔ zěnme shuō?

师傅：　　　啊，您是　外国　人。您在　哪儿　工作？
Shīfu:　　　À, nín shì wàiguó rén. Nín zài nǎr gōngzuò?

丁　力波：我　在　语言　学院　学习。
Dīng Lìbō:　Wǒ zài Yǔyán Xuéyuàn xuéxí.

师傅：　　　您　学习汉语，是不是？⑤您跟　我　学，很　容易：
Shīfu:　　　Nín xuéxí Hànyǔ, shì bu shì?　Nín gēn wǒ xué, hěn róngyì:

这　叫　香蕉，这叫　　香蕉苹果，　这也是
Zhè jiào xiāngjiāo, zhè jiào xiāngjiāopíngguǒ, zhè yě shì

苹果，　那是　葡萄……
píngguǒ, nà shì pútao…

丁　力波：香蕉、　　苹果、　　香蕉苹果……，一斤　苹果
Dīng Lìbō:　Xiāngjiāo、 píngguǒ、 xiāngjiāopíngguǒ…, yì jīn píngguǒ

多少　钱？⑥
duōshao qián?

【买东西】Shopping

【解决语言困难】
Solving language problems

-132-

师傅： 一斤 三 块 二 毛 钱。⑦ ③
Shīfu: Yì jīn sān (kuài) èr (máo) qián.

丁 力波：您 的 苹果 真 贵。 ④
Dīng Lìbō: Nín de píngguǒ zhēn guì.

师傅： 一斤 三 块 二 不贵。您 看， 我 的 苹果 大。好，
Shīfu: Yì jīn sān kuài èr bú guì. Nín kàn, wǒ de píngguǒ dà. Hǎo,

做 个 朋友， 三 块 钱 一斤。
zuò ge péngyou, sān kuài qián yì jīn.

丁 力波：一斤 香蕉 多少 钱？
Dīng Lìbō: Yì jīn xiāngjiāo duōshao qián?

师傅： 两 块 七 毛 五 分 一斤，五 块 钱 两 斤。
Shīfu: Liǎng (kuài) qī (máo) wǔ (fēn) yì jīn, wǔ (kuài) qián liǎng jīn.

丁 力波：我 买 三 斤 香蕉 和 两 斤 香蕉苹果。
Dīng Lìbō: Wǒ mǎi sān jīn xiāngjiāo hé liǎng jīn xiāngjiāopíngguǒ.

师傅： 一共 十四 块 钱⑤ 再 送 您 一个 苹果。您 还 ⑥
Shīfu: Yígòng shísì kuài qián. Zài sòng nín yí ge píngguǒ. Nín (hái)

要 什么？
yào shénme?

丁力波： 不要 了，谢谢。⑧ 给 你 钱。⑧
Dīng Lìbō: Bú yào le, xièxie. (Gěi) nǐ qián.

师傅： 好， 您 给 我 二十 块 钱， 我 找 您 六 块 钱。
Shīfu: Hǎo, nín gěi wǒ èrshí kuài qián, wǒ zhǎo nín liù kuài qián. ⑨

再见。
Zàijiàn.

丁 力波：再见！
Dīng Lìbō: Zàijiàn!

生词 New Words

*1. 先生	N	xiānsheng	Mr.; sir	张先生， 王先生	
*2. 要	V	yào	to want	要什么，要音乐光盘	
3. 师傅	N	shīfu	master worker	张师傅，王师傅	
4. 香蕉苹果	N	xiāngjiāopíngguǒ	apple with a banana taste	一个香蕉苹果	
香蕉	N	xiāngjiāo	banana	买香蕉	

苹果	N	píngguǒ	apple 一个苹果
*5. 对不起	IE	duìbuqǐ	I'm sorry
6. 怎么	QPr	zěnme	how 怎么说，怎么做，怎么去，怎么介绍
7. 容易	A	róngyì	easy 很容易，不容易，真容易，不太容易
8. 葡萄	N	pútao	grape
9. 钱	N	qián	money 多少钱
10. 斤	M	jīn	(measure word of weight, equal to 500g) 一斤苹果，两斤葡萄
11. 块（钱）	M	kuài(qián)	(measure word of basic Chinese monetary unit, equal to 10 毛)；dollar 两块钱，十二块钱，二十块钱
12. 毛（钱）	M	máo(qián)	(measure word of Chinese monetary unit, equal to 1/10 块)；dime 两毛钱，六毛钱
*13. 贵	A	guì	expensive, precious 很贵，真贵，不太贵，不贵
*14. 做	V	zuò	to be; to make 做个朋友，做好朋友
15. 分（钱）	M	fēn(qián)	(measure word of Chinese monetary unit, equal to 1/100 块)；cent 一分钱，八分钱
16. 送	V	sòng	to give(as a present) 送蛋糕，送葡萄酒
17. 给	V	gěi	to give 给他，给师傅，给我，给香蕉
18. 找（钱）	V	zhǎo(qián)	to give change 找钱

补充生词 Supplementary Words

1. 元	M	yuán	(the same as "块", but used in written language)
2. 笔	N	bǐ	pen
3. 支	M	zhī	(measure word for stick-like things such as pens)
4. 份	M	fèn	(measure word for publications such as newspapers)
5. 本	M	běn	(measure word for books and notebooks)
6. 杯	M	bēi	cup of
7. 售货员	N	shòuhuòyuán	shop assistant; salesperson
8. 作家	N	zuòjiā	writer
9. 便宜	A	piányi	cheap; inexpensive
10. 书店	N	shūdiàn	book store
11. 体育馆	N	tǐyùguǎn	gym
12. 卖	V	mài	to sell

二. 注释　Notes

① 这个商场很大。

When the demonstrative pronoun "这" or "那" is used as an attributive, a measure word is generally inserted between it and the noun it modifies.　For instance: "这张光盘", "那个朋友", "那瓶酒".

② 先生,您要什么?

In addition to being used as a general form of address for a male adult, "先生" can be used as a title of respect to address a senior scholar or specialist,　regardless of sex. Sometimes a woman also uses "我先生" to refer to her husband.

The two expressions "您要什么？", "您还要什么？", are commonly used to ask what someone wants.　Shop clerks or hotel attendants often use these phrases when offering help to customers.

③ 你好,师傅。

"师傅" is a respectful form of address for workers, and people in the service trades.　It may be used to address taxi and bus drivers, ticket sellers, cooks, and hotel staff.　There is a tendency now to increase the range of its usage.　Sometimes the people mentioned above also use it to address people of other trades and professions.

④ 我是问:这个汉语怎么说?

"I am asking how to say this in Chinese.　(What is this in Chinese？)"

"怎么+ VP" is often used to ask about the ways one should act or how one should do something.　"怎么" is an adverbial, modifying verbs.　For example："怎么说？""怎么做？" "怎么去？""怎么介绍？"

⑤ 您学习汉语,是不是?

"…, 是不是？"(or "…, 是吗？") is a sentence pattern we use to express opinion or speculation, with the expectation of a response from the listener.　The affirmative answer to this question is "是啊！", and the negative answer is "不(是)".　For example：

　　A：你喜欢中国音乐,是吗?

　　B：是啊。

⑥ 一斤苹果多少钱?

"How much is one *jin* of apples？"

-135-

"一斤…多少钱?" is a common sentence pattern we use to ask the price of something when shopping. This is a sentence with the noun phrase as the predicate. The predicate "多少钱" is placed immediately after the subject "一斤苹果". Note that the first part (the subject) and the second part (the predicate) can be inverted. We may also say：

A： 多少钱一斤(苹果)?

B： 三块二一斤。

Although the official Chinese system of weights and measures stipulates that "公斤 (gōngjīn, kilo)" is the basic unit, people are still accustomed to using the "斤", which is equivalent to half a kilogram.

In a super market or department store, people do not usually bargain over the price, but when shopping in a free market or at a stall, they frequently bargain.

⑦ 一斤三块二毛钱。

The various monetary units in 人民币 (Rénmínbì), the Chinese currency are： "元 (yuán)", "角 (jiǎo)", and "分 (fēn)". In spoken Chinese, we often use "块 (kuài)" for "元", and "毛 (máo)" for "角". When "毛" or "分" is at the end, "毛钱" and "分钱" can be omitted. For example：

1.75元 —— 一块七毛五(分钱)

4.80元 —— 四块八(毛钱)

Note：When "2毛" is at the beginning of an amount of money, people say "两毛". When "2分" is at the end of an amount of money, the expression "二分" is often used. For example：

0.22元—— 两毛二(分)

⑧ 不要了,谢谢。

"No, thanks."

三. 练习与运用　Drills and Practice

KEY SENTENCES

1. 这个商场很大。
2. 一斤香蕉多少钱?
3. 两块七毛五一斤。
4. 您在哪儿工作?
5. 我常常跟他来这儿。
6. 我送你一个苹果。
7. 您给我二十块钱。
8. 这个汉语怎么说?

1. 熟读下列词组 Master the following phrases

(1) 这张光盘　　这个学生　　这个人　　　这个学院　　这个苹果　　这个蛋糕

那张名片　　那个朋友　　那个小姐　　那个系　　　那个学生　　那瓶酒

哪张照片　　哪个老师　　哪个先生　　哪个专业　　哪个苹果　　哪个本子

(2) 买光盘　送名片　给钱　吃寿面　看书　做工作　认识你　喜欢音乐

买苹果　给照片　找钱　喝酒　　看报　学专业　给他　　学习汉语

(3) 在中国学习　在外国工作　在这儿买书　在那儿看报　　在商场工作

跟我来　　　跟他去　　　跟我学　　跟老师说汉语　　跟朋友去商场

2. 句型替换 Pattern drills

(1) A: 你在哪儿学习?

B: 我在音乐学院学习。

A: 你学习什么专业?

B: 我学习音乐专业。

A: 你忙不忙?

B: 我很忙。

中文系	文学
美术学院	美术
外语学院	外语

(2) A: 你爸爸在哪儿工作?

B: 他在北京工作。

A: 他做什么工作?

B: 他是教授。

A: 他好吗?

B: 谢谢你,他很好。

商场	售货员 (shòuhuòyuán)
北京	作家 (zuòjiā)
学院	医生

(3) A: 星期天你常常去哪儿?

B: 星期天我常常去商场。

A: 你跟谁去商场?

B: 我跟林娜去商场。

书店 (shūdiàn)	我朋友
体育馆 (tǐyùguǎn)	马大为
烤鸭店 (kǎoyādiàn)	我弟弟

(4) A: 他送他朋友什么?

B: 他送他朋友<u>一张光盘</u>。

A: 这张光盘怎么样?

B: 这张光盘很<u>贵</u>。

一个大蛋糕	漂亮
一瓶葡萄酒	便宜(piányi)
一本书	有意思

(5) A: 他给谁<u>二十块钱</u>?

B: 他给<u>师傅</u>二十块钱。

一张名片	力波
一张照片	老师
一个本子	妹妹
一本外语书	弟弟

(6) A: 您买什么?

B: 我买两斤葡萄。一共多少钱?

A: 一共<u>五块</u>钱。

两瓶酒	79.8 元
三支(zhī)笔(bǐ)	7.35 元
一本书和一份(fèn)报	12.60 元

(7) A: <u>这个师傅的葡萄大</u>不大?

B: 这个师傅的葡萄不大,

那个<u>师傅的葡萄</u>大。

外语系的学生	多	汉语系的学生
这课	容易	那课
这儿的烤鸭	贵	那儿的烤鸭
这张照片	漂亮	那张照片

3. 跟你的同学口头作下面的练习 Practice the following exercises verbally with one classmate

A game of giving change

E.g.　A:一共3.24元,我给您5元。　B:我找您<u>1.76</u>元。

　→ A:一共三块两毛四,我给您五块。　B:我找您<u>一块七毛六</u>。

(1) A:一共7.69元,我给您8元。　B:我找您＿＿＿＿。

(2) A:一共13.12元,我给您15元。　B:我找您＿＿＿＿。

(3) A:一共22.78元,我给您30元。　B:我找您＿＿＿＿。

(4) A:一共31.49元,我给您50元。　B:我找您＿＿＿＿。

(5) A:一共84.92元,我给您100元。　B:我找您＿＿＿＿。

4. 根据下列陈述句用疑问代词提问题 Change the following declarative sentences into questions with interrogative pronouns

    (1) 这个商场很有名。(Ask two questions)

    (2) 一斤葡萄两块七毛钱。(Ask three questions)

    (3) 他送我三瓶酒。(Ask four questions)

    (4) 我哥哥在商场卖(mài)光盘。(Ask five questions)

    (5) 林娜常常跟宋华学习汉语。(Ask six questions)

5. 会话练习 Conversation practice

【喜欢不喜欢 Likes and dislikes】

    (1) A：你喜欢什么专业？

        B：我喜欢_____。

        A：你喜欢哪国文学？

        B：我喜欢_____文学。

                _____有很多有名的作家。

    (2) A：你喜欢不喜欢哲学(zhéxué)？

        B：我_____哲学，我喜欢历史。

        A：历史很有意思，我哥哥也学历史专业。

    (3) A：这本书怎么样？

        B：这本书不太好。你喜欢不喜欢？

        A：我也不太喜欢。

【买东西 Shopping】

    (1) A：您买什么？

        B：师傅，有好的葡萄吗？

        A：有，这都是。

        B：_____？

        A：两块五一斤。您要多少？

        B：我要四斤。

        A：_____。 您给我五十，我找_____。

（2）A：小姐，这儿有本子吗？

　　　B：有。您看，都在这儿。

　　　A：多少钱一本？

　　　B：这本＿＿＿＿＿＿＿＿＿，那本＿＿＿＿＿＿＿＿＿。您要哪本？

　　　A：哪个本子好？

　　　B：都很好。

　　　A：好，我都要，买两本。

　　　B：一共＿＿＿＿＿＿＿＿＿。您给我二十，我找您两毛。

（3）A：先生，您要什么？

　　　B：我要一杯(bēi)咖啡(kāfēi)。

　　　A：还要什么？

　　　B：不要了，谢谢。

【解决语言困难 Solving language problems】

（1）A：请问，这个汉语怎么说？

　　　B：对不起，我也不知道。

　　　C：这叫词典(cídiǎn)，汉语词典。

　　　A：谢谢。

（2）A：老师，"cheap" 汉语怎么说？

　　　B：便宜(piányi)，这个本子很便宜。

（3）A：今年是马年，你属什么？

　　　B：对不起，请您再说一遍(yí biàn)。

6. **看图会话** Make a dialogue based on the picture

　　【介绍与认识 Introducing and identifying people】

（1）A：你们认识吗？我来介绍一下。

　　　　这是＿＿＿＿＿＿＿＿＿，

　　　　这是＿＿＿＿＿＿＿＿＿。

　　　B：认识你很高兴。

　　　C：认识你，我也很高兴。

（2）请问您贵姓？

请问您叫什么名字？

我们认识一下：

我姓_____，叫_____。

我的中文名字叫_____。

您是哪国人？

您是哪儿人？

您是我们学院的老师吗？

请问你是不是_____？

【询问 Enquiring】

（1）

那是谁？

他是_____吗？

他是谁？

他是不是_____？

（2）请问学生宿舍在哪儿？

丁力波住几层几号？

丁力波在吗？

他不在。

他现在在哪儿？

他在_____。

7. 交际练习 Communication exercises

（1）Talk to your classmate about what you like or dislike.

（2）Your classmate is a salesperson in a store and you are a customer.

四. 阅读和复述 Reading Comprehension and Paraphrasing

马大为星期天常常跟林娜去商场。那个商场很大，东西(dōngxi, things)也很多。他们在那儿买音乐光盘，王小云也在。马大为喜欢中国音乐。他问王小云，什么音乐光盘好？王小云说《梁祝》很有名，外国朋友也喜欢。马大为很高兴，说："好，我买这张光盘。"马大为还要买书和报，这个商场不卖(mài)书，也不卖报。他跟王小云去买本子和笔(bǐ)。

马大为还常常去书店(shūdiàn)。那个书店也很大，书很多。他在书店买书，也看书。中国书不贵。下月二十号是他弟弟的生日。他弟弟喜欢中国功夫(gōngfu)，马大为要送弟弟一本《中国功夫》。

五. 语法　　　　　　　Grammar

1. 介词词组　Prepositional Phrase

In Lesson 5 the verb "在" was studied. "在" is also a preposition. When combined with words expressing location (usually a noun or phrase), it forms a prepositional phrase. It is used before the predicative verb to indicate the location of an action.

在　＋　PW　＋　V O

Subject	Predicate			
	Prep "在" + N		**V**	**O**
我	在　这儿		买	光盘。
您	在　哪儿		工作?	
他	不　在　语言学院		学习。	

The preposition "跟…" is often combined with a noun or pronoun after it to form a prepositional phrase and used in front of the predicative verb to indicate the manner of an action.

跟　＋　Pr/N (person)　＋　V O

Subject	Predicate			
	Prep "跟" + Pr/N		**V**	**O**
我	跟　力波		来	这儿。
(你)	跟　我		来。	
您	跟　我		学。	

Note：The prepositional phrases "在…" and "跟…" must be placed before the verb. One cannot say "我学习在语言学院"，"你来跟我".

2. 双宾语动词谓语句(1) Sentences with double objects (1):给、送

Some verbs can take two objects, one in front, referring to people; the other, following, referring to things.

$$给/送 \quad + \quad Pr/N \text{ (person)} \quad + \quad NP\text{(thing)}$$

Subject	Predicate		
	V	**Object 1**	**Object 2**
您	给	我	二十块钱。
我	找	您	十块钱。
（我）	送	您	一个苹果。

Note：Not all Chinese verbs can take double objects.

3. 形容词谓语句和副词"很" The adverb "很" in sentences with an adjectival predicate

Many sentences with an adjectival predicate have been studied so far. In this kind of sentence, an adjective follows the subject directly and does not need the verb "是". If there are no other adverbs such as "真", "太" or "不" before the adjective, the adverb "很" is usually placed before it.

S ＋ 很 ＋ A

我很好。

我今天很忙。

这个商场很大。

In this kind of sentence, if the adjective does not have an adverb before it, the sentence has the meaning of comparison. For example：

我忙,他不忙。

我的本子大。（他的本子小。）

The meaning of "很" here is not so obvious. "我很忙" and "我忙" are not much different in degree. In V/A-not-V/A questions, "很" cannot be used. For example："他高兴不高兴？" One cannot say "他很高兴不很高兴？"

六. 汉字　　Chinese Characters

1. 汉字的结构(3) Structure of Chinese characters (3)

The top-bottom structure：

a. Equal top-bottom

1
2

男　是

b. Big top-small bottom

1
2

兴

1	2
3	

然

1	2
	3
	4

您

c. Small top-big bottom

1
2

家

1	
2	3

宿

d. Equal top-middle-bottom

1
2
3

意　贵

2. 认写基本汉字 Learn and write basic Chinese characters

(1) 舟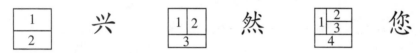
zhōu　　boat　　　　　　　6 strokes

(2) 皿
mǐn　　house hold utensiles　　5 strokes

(3) 乐(樂)
yuè　　music　　　　　　5 strokes

(4) 足
zú　　foot　　　　　　7 strokes

(5) 书(書)
shū　　book　　　　　　4 strokes

(6) 本　　　一 十 才 木 本

běn　　root of a tree　　5 strokes

(The "一" at the bottom of "木" indicates the root.)

(7) 平　　　一 ㇒ 丏 立 平

píng　　flat　　5 strokes

(8) 走　　　一 十 土 キ キ 走 走

zǒu　　to walk　　7 strokes

(The ancient character looks like a person running.)

(9) 已　　　㇇ ㇇ 已

jǐ　　oneself　　3 strokes

(10) 穴　　　丶 丷 宀 宍 穴

xué　　cave　　5 strokes

(11) 勿　　　㇒ 勹 勺 勿

wù　　do not　　4 strokes

(12) 金　　　㇒ 人 스 仒 仐 余 金 金

jīn　　gold　　8 strokes

(13) 斤　　　㇒ 厂 斥 斤

jīn　　(measure word)　　4 strokes

(The ancient character resembles an axe. It is used as a unit of weight now.)

(14) 毛　　　㇒ 二 三 毛

máo　　(dime)　　4 strokes

(15) 戈　　　一 弋 戈 戈

gē　　an ancient weapon　　4 strokes

3. 认写课文中的汉字 Learn and write the Chinese characters appearing in the texts

(1) 光盘 guāngpán (光盤)

光 → 少 + 兀　　　　　6 strokes

盘 → 舟 + 皿　　　　　11 strokes

(2) 音乐 yīnyuè (音樂)

音 → 立 + 日　　　　　9 strokes

土 (tǔzìpáng) (On the left side of a character, the third stroke of "土" is written as an upward stroke. It is called the "earth" side.)　一 十 土　　　　　3 strokes

勿 (chǎngzìbiān) (the "arena" side)　丆 勹 勿　　　　　3 strokes

(3) 商场 shāngchǎng (商場)

商 → 一 + 丶 + 冂 + 八 + 口　　　　　11 strokes

场 → 土 + 勿　　　　　6 strokes

丷 (chángzìtóu) (the "constant" top)　丶 丷 业 丷 丷　　　　　5 strokes

(4) 常常 chángcháng

常 → 丷 + 口 + 巾　　　　　11 strokes

足 (zúzìpáng) (On the left side of a character, the seventh stroke in "足" is written as an upward stroke.)　丶 口 口 甲 甲 足 足　　　　　7 strokes

(5) 跟 gēn

跟 → 足 + 艮　　　　　13 strokes

阝 (dān'ěrduo) (the "single-ear" side)　𠃌 阝　　　　　2 strokes

(6) 报 bào (報)

报 → 扌 + 卩 + 又　　　　　7 strokes

刅 (liángzìjiǎo) (the "millet" corner)　𠃌 刀 刅 刅　　　　　4 strokes

(7) 梁祝 Liáng Zhù

梁 → 氵 + 刅 + 木　　　　　11 strokes

生 (tūwěiniú) (the "tail-less ox" top)　ノ ニ 牛 生　4 strokes

(8) 先生 xiānsheng

先 → 生 + 儿　6 strokes

(9) 要 yào

要 → 西 + 女　9 strokes

(10) 师傅 shīfu (師傅)

傅 (fù) → 亻 + 甫 + 寸　12 strokes

(The meaning side is "亻", and the phonetic side is "甫".)

(11) 香蕉 xiāngjiāo

香 → 禾 + 日　9 strokes

蕉 → 艹 + 隹 + 灬　15 strokes

(12) 苹果 píngguǒ (蘋果)

苹 → 艹 + 平　8 strokes

(The meaning is indicated by "艹", and the pronunciation is indicated by "平".)

(13) 对不起 duìbuqǐ (對不起)

对 → 又 + 寸　5 strokes

起 → 走 + 己　10 strokes

(14) 容易 róngyì

容 → 宀 + 八 + 口　10 strokes

易 → 日 + 勿　8 strokes

钅 (jīnzìpáng) (the "metal" side). (On the left side of a character, "金" is written as "钅".) 丿 𠂆 𠂉 钅 钅   5 strokes

(15) 钱 qián (錢)

钱 → 钅 + 一 + 戈   10 strokes

(16) 块 kuài (塊)

块 → 土 + 夬   7 strokes

(17) 分 fēn

分 → 八 + 刀   4 strokes

(To cut things in half with a knife.)

(18) 送 sòng

送 → 丷 + 天 + 辶   9 strokes

(19) 给 gěi (給)

给 → 纟 + 合   9 strokes

(20) 找 zhǎo

找 → 扌 + 戈   7 strokes

文化知识   Cultural Notes

Currency

The currency of the People's Republic of China is the *renminbi*, literally "people's currency", abbreviated as "RMB". The basic unit of the RMB is the *yuan* or *kuai*. One-tenth of a *yuan* is called a *jiao* or *mao*, and one one-hundredth of a *yuan* equals one *fen*. Chinese money is issued in paper notes as well as coins, in thirteen different denominations:

Bills: 100 *yuan*, 50 *yuan*, 20 *yuan*, 10 *yuan*, 5 *yuan*, 2 *yuan*, 1 *yuan*

5 *jiao*, 2 *jiao*, 1 *jiao*

Coins: 1 *yuan*, 5 *jiao*, 1 *jiao*, 5 *fen*, 2 *fen*, 1 *fen*

By the end of this lesson, you will be able to ask the time, hail a taxi, ask whether something is allowed, and indicate your ability to accomplish tasks. We will pay special attention to how Chinese people respond to compliments.

第十一课 Lesson 11

我　会　说　一点儿　汉语
Wǒ　huì　shuō　yìdiǎnr　Hànyǔ

一. 课文　　Text

（一）

【问时间】Asking about time

司机： 小姐，您 去 哪儿?
Sījī: Xiǎojiě, nín qù nǎr?

林娜： 我 去 语言 学院。师傅，请问 现在 几 点?
Lín Nà: Wǒ qù Yǔyán Xuéyuàn. Shīfu, qǐngwèn xiànzài jǐ diǎn?

司机： 差 一 刻 八 点。您 会 说 汉语 啊!
Sījī: Chà yí kè bā diǎn. Nín huì shuō Hànyǔ a!

林娜： 我 会 说 一点儿 汉语。① 我 是 学生，　现在 回
Lín Nà: Wǒ huì shuō yìdiǎnr Hànyǔ. Wǒ shì xuésheng, xiànzài huí

学院　上课。
xuéyuàn shàngkè.

司机： 你们 几点 上课?
Sījī: Nǐmen jǐ diǎn shàngkè?

-150-

林 娜： 八 点 上课。师傅，我们 八 点 能 到 吗?
Lín Nà： Bā diǎn shàngkè. Shīfu, wǒmen bā diǎn néng dào ma?

司机： 能 到。您 的 汉语 很 好。
Sījī： Néng dào. Nín de Hànyǔ hěn hǎo.

林 娜： 哪里,我 的 汉语 不 太 好。您 会 不 会 说 英语?
Lín Nà： Nǎli, wǒ de Hànyǔ bú tài hǎo. Nín huì bu huì shuō Yīngyǔ?

司机： 我 不 会 说 英语。我 也 喜欢 外语， 常常 在
Sījī： Wǒ bú huì shuō Yīngyǔ. Wǒ yě xǐhuan wàiyǔ, chángcháng zài

家 学 点儿 英语。
jiā xué diǎnr Yīngyǔ.

duo da sui snu? - senior

duo shao sui? - adult

ji sui? - child.

林 娜： 谁 教 您 英语?
Lín Nà： Shéi jiāo nín Yīngyǔ?

司机： 我 孙女儿。
Sījī： Wǒ sūnnür.

林 娜： 真 有 意思。她 今年 几 岁?
Lín Nà： Zhēn yǒu yìsi. Tā jīnnián jǐ suì?

司机： 六 岁。我 的 岁数 太 大 了，学 英语 不 容易。
Sījī： Liù suì. Wǒ de suìshu tài dà le, xué Yīngyǔ bù róngyì.

林 娜： 您 今年 多 大 岁数?
Lín Nà： Nín jīnnián duō dà suìshu?

司机： 我 今年 五十二。语言 学院 到 了。现在 差 五
Sījī： Wǒ jīnnián wǔshí'èr. Yǔyán Xuéyuàn dào le. Xiànzài chà wǔ

分 八 点，您 还 有 五 分钟。
fēn bā diǎn, nín hái yǒu wǔ fēnzhōng.

. Appropriate to ask seniors age.

林 娜： 谢谢， 给 您 钱。
Lín Nà： Xièxie, gěi nín qián.

5.40

司机： 您 给 我 二十， 找 您 五 块 四, OK?
Sījī： Nín gěi wǒ èrshí, zhǎo nín wǔ kuài sì, OK?

↳ give back change

林 娜： 您 会 说 英语!
Lín Nà： Nín huì shuō Yīngyǔ!

司机： 我 也 会 一点儿。拜拜！
Sījī： Wǒ yě huì yìdiǎnr. Báibái!

林 娜： 拜拜！
Lín Nà: Báibái!

handwritten: nǎli nǎli
handwritten: hái méi yǒu hǎo / not ready yet.

生词 New Words

handwritten: used before a noun.

1. 会	OpV	huì	to know how to, can 会说汉语
2. (一)点儿	Nu-M	(yì)diǎnr	a little bit 会说一点儿汉语, 喝一点儿酒
3. 司机	N	sījī	driver
4. 点(钟)	M	diǎn(zhōng)	o'clock 两点(钟), 八点(钟)
5. 差	V	chà	to be short of, lack
6. 刻	M	kè	quarter (of an hour) 一刻(钟), 差一刻八点
7. 回	V	huí	to return 回学院, 回家, 回中国, 回北京
8. 上课	VO	shàngkè	to go to class (both students and teachers)
上	V	shàng	to ascend; to go to 上汉语课, 上文化课
9. 能	OpV	néng	can; be able to 能来上课
10. 到	V	dào	to arrive 到家, 到学院, 到商场, 到北京
11. 哪里	IE	nǎli	no (an expression of modest denial)
12. 教	V	jiāo	to teach 教汉语, 教文学
13. 英语	N	Yīngyǔ	English 会说一点儿英语, 学习英语, 上英语课
14. 孙女儿	N	sūnnǚr	granddaughter on son's side
女儿	N	nǚ'ér	daughter
15. 岁数	N	suìshu	years (of age) 多大岁数
数	N	shù	number
16. 还	Adv	hái	still 还有五分钟
17. 分	M	fēn	minute 八点五分, 差五分八点
18. 拜拜	IE	báibái	bye-bye (transliteration)

handwritten margin notes: not circumstantial / ability; used before Vo.; condition / unable / to / allowed.; → clock.; → to reach a certain spot.; + can be 'where'; → sooner bù; wǒ dào le / I have arrived; → no meaning love; (senior) → 'age #'; ('additional'); 差五分八点

（二）

丁 力波： 陈 老师，马 大为 今天 不 能 来 上课。
Dīng lìbō: Chén lǎoshī, Mǎ Dàwéi jīntiān bù néng lái shàngkè. ①

陈 老师：他 为什么 不 能 来 上课？
Chén lǎoshī: Tā wèishénme bù néng lái shàngkè? ②

handwritten: → before sentence

丁　力波：　昨天　　是　星期日，他　　上午　去　　商场　　买
Dīng Lìbō：　Zuótiān shì (xīngqīrì) tā (shàngwǔ) qù shāngchǎng mǎi

东西，　　下午　去　　朋友　家　玩儿。他　晚上　　　十一
dōngxi, (xiàwǔ) qù péngyou jiā wánr. Tā wǎnshang (shíyī

点　半　回　学院，　十二　点　写　汉字，两　　点
diǎn bàn) huí xuéyuàn, (shí'èr) diǎn xiě Hànzì, liǎng diǎn-

钟　　睡觉。　现在　他　还　没有　起床。③
zhōng shuìjiào. Xiànzài tā hái méiyǒu qǐchuáng.

后 hòu

陈　老师：他　应该　来　　上课。④
Chén lǎoshī：Tā yīnggāi lái shàngkè.

丁　力波：　老师，　我　能　不　能　问　您　一　个　问题？
Dīng Lìbō：　Lǎoshī, wǒ néng bu néng wèn nín yí ge wèntí? ⑥

陈　老师：可以。→ permission (néng)
Chén lǎoshī：Kěyǐ. → between Location / activities.

【表示允许或禁止】
Expressing permission
or prohibition

丁　力波：　我们　　为什么　八　点　　上课？
Dīng Lìbō：　Wǒmen wèishénme bā diǎn shàngkè?

hòu 2 times
after
(day/week
/year).

生词 New Words

1. 为什么	Qpr	wèishénme	why · can be used before whole sentence.	
为	Prep	wèi	for	
2. 昨天	N	zuótiān	yesterday	昨天上午，昨天下午
3. 东西	N	dōngxi	things; objects	买东西, 吃东西, 送东西
4. 玩儿	V	wánr	to have fun, to play	去朋友家玩儿, 跟朋友玩儿
		↳ not pronounced		
*5. 晚上	N	wǎnshang	evening, night	昨天晚上, 星期六晚上, 五号晚上
晚	A	wǎn	late	来晚了
6. 半	Nu	bàn	half	九点半, 半天, 半年, 半个星期, 半个月, 半个苹果, 半斤葡萄
7. 写	V	xiě	to write	
8. 汉字	N	Hànzì	Chinese character	写汉字, 一个汉字
字	N	zì	character	
9. 睡觉	VO	shuìjiào	to sleep	十一点睡觉, 还没有睡觉
睡	V	shuì	to sleep	

xiǎng – im thinking...

10.	起床	VO	qǐchuáng	to get up 六点起床，还没有起床
	起	V	qǐ	to get up,to rise
	床	N	chuáng	bed 一张床
11.	应该	OpV	yīnggāi	should;ought to 应该来，应该看，应该祝贺
	该	OpV	gāi	should;ought to
12.	问题	N	wèntí	question 一个问题，问问题，有问题，没问题
13.	可以	OpV	kěyǐ	may 可以进来，可以问问题，可以去
14.	陈	PN	Chén	(a surname)

↳ requiring permission

补充生词　Supplementary Words

1.	下课	VO	xiàkè	to get out of class；to finish class
2.	吃饭	VO	chīfàn	to eat (a meal)
3.	开车	VO	kāichē	to drive a car
4.	唱歌	VO	chànggē	to sing(a song)
5.	跳舞	VO	tiàowǔ	to dance
6.	回答	V	huídá	to answer
7.	礼物	N	lǐwù	gift；present
8.	打球	V O	dǎ qiú	to play ball
9.	打的	VO	dǎdī	to take a taxi
10.	吸烟	VO	xīyān	to smoke
11.	表	N	biǎo	watch
12.	难	A	nán	difficult

二. 注释　Notes

① 我会说一点儿汉语。

"一点儿" is an indefinite measure word expressing the idea of a small amount, and is used to modify a noun. When the context allows of no ambiguity, the noun it modifies can be omitted. For example：

A：您会说汉语啊！

B：我会说一点儿(汉语)。

yuàn yì
↳ I do, willing

I just wanted to

When "一点儿" is not at the beginning of a sentence, "一" may be omitted. For example："吃（一）点儿烤鸭","喝（一）点儿酒","看（一）点儿书".

② 哪里，我的汉语不太好。

"哪里" is actually an interrogative pronoun, and has the same meaning as "哪儿", but "哪里" here has a negative connotation. It is often used to express modesty when responding to praise. We can also use "是吗？" to express doubt. For example："是吗？ 我的汉语不太好." Whether we use a word expressing negation or doubt, the purpose is to show a modest attitude toward other people's compliments. In Chinese culture this is regarded as an appropriate response.

③ 学英语不容易。

"It is not easy to learn English."

④ 您今年多大岁数?

This is a courteous way of asking the age of an elderly or senior person.

⑤ 语言学院到了。

"Here we are at the Language Institute."

⑥ 您还有五分钟。

"You still have five minutes."

One of the senses of "还" already learned is to make an additional remark. Another use of "还" is to express the continuation of a state or action. For example：

晚上十一点他还工作。 (He is still working at eleven o'clock at night.)
他现在还不能看中文报。 (He is still unable to read Chinese newspapers.)
他还没有起床。 (He still hasn't got out of bed. /He is still in bed.)

三. 练习与运用　Drills and Practice

KEY SENTENCES
1. 请问,现在几点?
2. 现在差五分八点,他还没有起床。
3. 你们几点上课?
4. 他昨天下午两点去朋友家玩儿。
5. 我会说一点儿汉语。
6. 他为什么不能来上课?
7. 他应该来。
8. 可以问您一个问题吗?

1. 熟读下列词语 Master the following phrases

(1) 会说汉语　会说英语　会写汉字　不会问问题　　不会学习　不会工作

(2) 能来学院　能到商场　能回家　不能看中文书　不能上课　不能喝酒

(3) 可以进来　　　可以坐　　　　　可以认识一下

　　不可以看　　　不可以说英语　　不可以问问题

(4) 应该起床　　　应该睡觉　　　　应该工作　　　　应该玩儿

　　不应该说　　　不应该问　　　　不应该喝酒　　　不应该来

(5) 还没有起床　　还没有睡觉　　　还没有写汉字

　　还不会说汉语　还不能看中文书　还不认识他

(6) 说点儿英语　吃点儿蛋糕　　喝点儿葡萄酒

　　买点儿东西　看点儿书　　　有点儿时间

2. 句型替换 Pattern drills

(1) 现在几点？

　　现在<u>七点四十</u>。

8:30	9:58
10:05	12:15
3:28	5:45

(2) 你几点<u>起床</u>？

　　我<u>六点十分</u><u>起床</u>。

下课(xiàkè)	11:50
吃饭(fàn)	12:15
写汉字	8:20
睡觉	10:50

(3) 你现在去哪儿？

　　我现在<u>回学院</u>。

　　你<u>回学院</u>做什么？

　　我<u>回学院</u><u>上课</u>。

去商场	买东西
去朋友家	玩儿
回家	看爸爸妈妈

(4) 你今天下午有没有课？

　　有课。

　　你有什么课？

　　我有<u>汉语</u>课。

　　谁教你们<u>汉语</u>？

　　<u>陈老师</u>教我们<u>汉语</u>。

文化(wénhuà)	张教授
文学	王先生
美术	马老师
音乐	丁小姐

（5）你会游泳（yóuyǒng）吗？

我会游泳。

你今天能游泳吗？

对不起，我今天不能游泳。

开车（kāichē）
打球（dǎ qiú）
跳舞（tiàowǔ）
唱歌（chànggē）

（6）你能不能看中文报？

我现在还不能看中文报。

你为什么不能看中文报？

我的汉语还不太好。

学	中国历史
教	汉语
回答（huídá）	他的问题

（7）现在可以问问题吗？

可以。

说	英语
回	家
看	书
坐	你的车（chē）

（8）明天是不是林娜的生日？

是她的生日。

我们应该买点儿苹果。

吃	寿面
喝	葡萄酒
送	礼物（lǐwù）

3. 根据画线部分提出问题 Ask a question concerning the underlined words in each of the following sentences

（1）现在七点三十八分。

（2）他五点一刻回家。

（3）二月二十二号是他的生日。

（4）明天晚上八点他们有一个聚会。

4. 会话练习 Conversation practice

【问时间 Asking about time】

（1）A：请问，您的表（biǎo）现在几点？

B：＿＿＿＿＿＿＿＿＿，我的表快（kuài, fast）一点儿。

A：谢谢。

（2）A：今天晚上你有没有时间？

B：我有时间。

A：你来我家玩儿，好吗？

B：好啊。几点去？

A：＿＿＿＿＿＿＿＿＿，怎么样？

B：晚一点儿，＿＿＿＿＿＿＿好吗？

A：好。

【表示能力 Expressing one's ability】

（1）A：你会不会＿＿＿＿＿＿＿＿？

B：我会一点儿。

A：你能教我吗？

B：好，有时间我们去体育馆(tǐyùguǎn)练习。

（2）A：这个汉字怎么写？

B：对不起，我也不会。

（3）A：你现在能不能选修(xuǎnxiū)哲学(zhéxué)课？

B：我现在还＿＿＿＿＿＿＿＿。

A：为什么？

B：我的汉语还不太好。

【表示允许或禁止 Expressing permission or prohibition】

（1）A：可以进来吗？

B：对不起，请等(děng, to wait)一下。

（2）A：可以吸烟(xīyān)吗？

B：对不起，这儿不可以＿＿＿＿＿＿＿。

（3）A：老师，今天的课很难(nán)，我有问题，能不能问您？

B：可以。明天下午我有时间，你四点来，好吗？

A：好，谢谢。

5. 交际练习 Communication exercises

(1) Your classmate is a taxi driver, and you want to go to somewhere by taxi. How do you converse with the taxi driver?

(2) Your watch has stopped. How do you ask a passerby the time?

(3) You are talking about families with your friend. How do you ask him/her about the ages of his/her parents and about the children of his/her brothers and sisters?

(4) You are visiting somewhere and you want to find out whether or not you can take pictures (拍照, pāizhào) or smoke (吸烟, xīyān). How do you ask?

便条 (biàntiáo, note)

小云，你好！

今天下午我来找你，你不在。明天晚上你有时间吗？我们有一个聚会，你能不能参加？七点我们去，好吗？再见。

林娜　十月四日

四. 阅读和复述　Reading Comprehension and Paraphrasing

星期日林娜到一个英国朋友家玩儿。星期一八点她有课，七点三刻她打的(dǎdī)回学院上课。这个司机今年五十二岁，他有一个孙女儿，今年六岁。他说林娜的汉语很好。他也喜欢外语，现在跟他孙女儿学英语。他们八点差五分到学院。

马大为星期天很忙。他上午去商场买东西，下午去朋友家玩儿，晚上很晚回学院。他十二点写汉字，两点钟睡觉。星期一八点上课，他八点十分还没有起床。陈老师很不高兴，她问丁力波：马大为在哪儿？丁力波说马大为现在还没有起床，他不能来上课。

五. 语法　　　　Grammar

1. 钟点　Telling time

These words are used to tell time in Chinese："点(钟)"，"刻" and "分".

When telling someone the time the following rules apply:

2:00　两点(钟)　　(The "钟" in "点钟" can be omitted.)

2:05　两点(〇)五分　(When "分" is a number less than ten, "〇" may be added before it.)

2:10　两点十分

2:12　两点十二(分)　(When "分" is more than 10, "分" may be omitted.)

2:15　两点一刻 or 两点十五(分)

2:30　两点半 or 两点三十(分)

2:45　两点三刻 or 差一刻三点 or 两点四十五(分)

2:55　差五分三点 or 两点五十五(分)

The order of time expressions and expressions of date is:

年 ＋ 月 ＋ 日 ＋ 上午/下午/晚上 ＋ 钟点

二〇〇二年　十二月　一日 星期日　晚上　　八点二十五分

2000年　　12月　　1日 星期日　晚上　　　8:25

2. 能愿动词谓语句(1) Sentences with the optative verbs (1)："会"，"能"，"可以"，"应该"

Optative verbs such as "会"，"能"，"可以"，"应该"，and "要" are often placed before verbs to express ability, possibility, or willingness.

Optative verbs such as "会"，"能"，and "可以" indicate the ability to do something and can be translated with the English word "can; be able to".

It should be noted, though, that "会" emphasizes skills acquired through learning, while "能" and "可以" express the possession of skills in general.

(不) ＋ OpV ＋ V O

Subject	Predicate			
	TW	OpV	V	O
你		会不会	说	汉语？
他		不会	打	球。
我		会	写	这个汉字。
谁		会	游泳？	
他孙女儿		能	教	他英语吗？
马大为	今天	能不能	学习？	
你朋友		能	喝	多少酒？
你		可以不可以	介绍一下	你们系？

"能" and "可以" are also be used to express permission or prohibition under specific circumstances. For example：

Subject	Predicate			
	TW	OpV	V	O
我们	八点	能不能	到	那儿？
我	明天	不能	上	课。
（我）		可以	进来	吗？
这儿		不可以	吃	东西。

The optative verb "应该" is used to express needs arising from moral or factual necessity.

Subject	Predicate		
	OpV	V	O
他	应该	来 上	课。
你	不应该	去	那儿。

Note：1. In a sentence with an optative verb, the affirmative-negative form (V/A-not-V/A) is formed by juxtaposing the affirmative and negative forms of the optative verb, that is OpV-not-OpV.

OpV	+	不	+	OpV	+	V	O
会		不		会		说	汉语
能		不		能		去	
可以		不		可以		介绍	

2. The negative form of "能" and "可以" is usually "不能". "不可以" is only used to express prohibition. For example："不可以吸烟 (xīyān, smoke)". If the answer to the question "你可以不可以介绍一下你们系？" is negative, it should be "我不能介绍我们系." One cannot say "我不可以介绍我们系."

3. To answer briefly, one may use only the optative verb. For example：

你会说汉语吗？———不会。

可以进来吗？———可以。

4. Some of the optative verbs are also general verbs. For example：

他会英语。

我要咖啡。

3. 连动句(1)：表示目的 Sentences with serial verb phrases (1)：Purpose

In a sentence with a verbal predicate, the subject may take two consecutive verbs or verb phrases. The order of these verb phrases is fixed. In the sentences with serial verb phrases introduced in this chapter, the second verb indicates the purpose of the action denoted by the first verb.

S + V₁ O + V₂ O

Subject	Predicate				
	TW	**V₁**	**O**	**V₂**	**O**
我	现在	回	学院	上	课。
他	下午	去不去	朋友家	玩儿?	
他	下午	不去	朋友家	玩儿。	

4. 双宾语动词谓语(2) Sentences with double objects (2)："教"，"问"

Such verbs as "教" and "问" can take double objects.

Subject	Predicate		
	V	**Object 1**	**Object 2**
他孙女儿	教	他	英语。
哪个老师	教	你们	中国文化?
他	问	我	一个问题。
他	问	你	什么?

六. 汉字　　Chinese Characters

1. 汉字的结构(4) Structure of Chinese characters (4)

The enclosure structure ①

a. Four-side enclosure

 国　回

b. Left-top-right enclosure

 用　问

c. Top-left enclosure

应　属

d. Top-left-bottom enclosure

 医

e. Top-right enclosure

 可　司

2. 认写基本汉字 Learn and write basic Chinese characters

(1) 占　　`丨 卜 上 占 占`

　　zhàn　　to occupy　　　　　　　　5 strokes

(2) 里(裏)　`丨 口 曰 日 甲 里 里`

　　lǐ　　inside　　　　　　　　7 strokes

(3) 至　　`一 工 云 至 至 至`

　　zhì　　to　　　　　　　　6 strokes

(4) 央　　`丶 口 卩 央 央`

　　yāng　　center　　　　　　　　5 strokes

(5) 东(東)　`一 𠃋 车 东 东`

　　dōng　　east　　　　　　　　5 strokes

(6) 西　　`一 厂 冂 丙 西 西`

　　xī　　west　　　　　　　　6 strokes

(7) 免　　`丿 𠂉 𠂆 𠃊 色 免 免`

　　miǎn　　be excused from　　　　7 strokes

(8) 半　　`丶 丷 ⺊ 兰 半`

　　bàn　　half　　　　　　　　5 strokes

(9) 与(與)　`一 ヒ 与`

　　yǔ　　and　　　　　　　　3 strokes

　　(Please differentiate "与" from "马".)

(10) 页(頁)　`一 丆 丆 页 页 页`

　　yè　　page　　　　　　　　6 strokes

(11) 以　　`ㄥ 𠄌 以 以`

　　yǐ　　to use　　　　　　　　4 strokes

3. 认写课文中的汉字 Learn and write the Chinese characters appearing in the texts

(1) 司机 sījī（司機）

司 → 刁 + 一 + 口　　　　5 strokes

机 → 木 + 几　　　　6 strokes

(2) 点钟 diǎnzhōng（點鐘）

点 → 占 + 灬　　　　9 strokes

钟 → 钅 + 中　　　　9 strokes

羊 (piěwěiyáng)(the "slanting-tailed-goat" top)　(On the top of a character, the vertical stroke in "羊" is written as a downward stroke to the left "丿".)

丶 丷 亚 兰 兰 羊　　　　6 strokes

(3) 差 chà

差 → 羊 + 工　　　　9 strokes

刂 (lìdāopáng)(On the right side of a multi-component character, "刀" is written as "刂". It is called the "standing knife" side.)　丨 刂　　2 strokes

亥 hài　丶 亠 亥 亥 亥 亥　　　　6 strokes

(4) 刻 kè

刻 → 亥 + 刂　　8 strokes

(5) 回 huí

回 → 囗 + 口　　6 strokes

(6) 能 néng

能 → 厶 + 月 + 匕 + 匕　　10 strokes

(7) 到 dào

到 → 至 + 刂　　　　8 strokes

(8) 英语 Yīngyǔ (英語)

英 → 艹 + 央　　　　　　　　　　　　8 strokes

(9) 孙女儿 sūnnür (孫女兒)

孙 → 子 + 小　　　　　　　　　　　　6 strokes

(10) 岁数 suìshu (歲數)

数 → 米 + 女 + 攵　　　　　　　　　13 strokes

手 (piěshǒu) (the "slanting-hand" side) (On the left side of a character, the fourth stroke in "手" is written as "丿".) 丿 二 三 手　　4 strokes

(11) 拜拜 báibái

拜 → 手 + 一 + 丰　　　　　　　　　9 strokes

(12) 昨天 zuótiān

昨 → 日 + 乍　　　　　　　　　　　　9 strokes

(The "sun" side, "日", shows the character has a temporal connotation.)

(13) 玩儿 wánr (玩兒)

玩 → 王 + 元　　　　　　　　　　　　8 strokes

(14) 写 xiě (寫)

写 → 冖 + 与　　　　　　　　　　　　5 strokes

(15) 晚上 wǎnshang

晚 → 日 + 免　　　　　　　　　　　11 strokes

(The "sun" side, "日", shows the character has a temporal connotation.)

垂 chuí (千 + 艹 + 二) 丿 二 三 三 丘 丢 垂 垂　　8 strokes

(16) 睡觉 shuìjiào (睡覺)

睡 → 目 + 垂　　　　　　　　　　　13 strokes

(Please note the left side of the character is the "eye" side "目", not the "sun" side "日". "Sleeping" is related to the "eyes".)

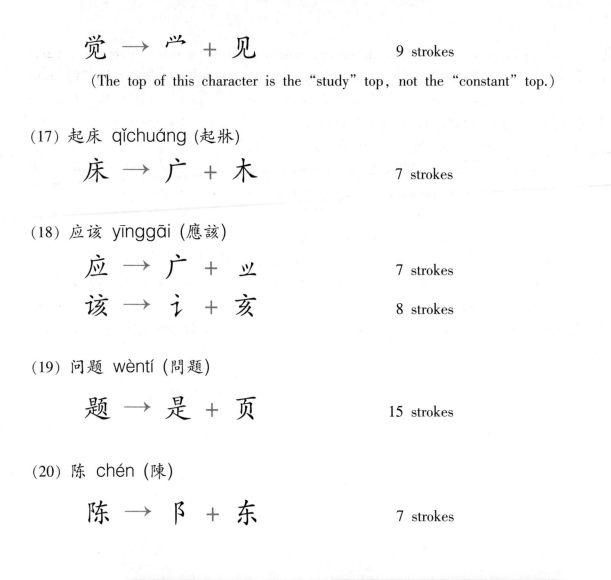

觉 → 丷 + 见   9 strokes

(The top of this character is the "study" top, not the "constant" top.)

(17) 起床 qǐchuáng (起牀)

床 → 广 + 木   7 strokes

(18) 应该 yīnggāi (應該)

应 → 广 + 丷   7 strokes

该 → 讠 + 亥   8 strokes

(19) 问题 wèntí (問題)

题 → 是 + 页   15 strokes

(20) 陈 chén (陳)

陈 → 阝 + 东   7 strokes

<hr>

文化知识	Cultural Notes

Loanwords

Like other languages, Chinese also borrows words from foreign languages. Most loanwords in Chinese come from English, French, Japanese, or Russian. They generally fall into five groups: First are interpretative translations or semantic equivalents. Both terms refer to using Chinese words to translate imported concepts. Words of this category usually do not appear noticeably foreign. One example is the word 电视 *dianshi* "television", in which 电 *dian* (originally "lightning", later "electricity") is freely adapted to correspond to the prefix "tele" (originally from the ancient Greek word meaning "far"), and 视 *shi* literally translates as "vision". The words 电话 *dianhua* "telephone", and 电报 *dianbao* "telegram" fall under the same category.

Second are transliterations, renditions that imitate the sound of the source word. The non-native origin stands out in this group of words, for example: 沙发 *shafa* "sofa", 咖啡 *kafei* "coffee", 可口可乐 *kekoukele* for "coca cola", and 夹克 *jiake* "jacket".

Third is a combination of the first and second modes described above: partly free paraphrasing/semantic matching, and partly transliteration. Examples can be found with 啤酒 *pijiu* "beer", 摩托车 *motuoche* "motorcycle", and 坦克车 *tankeche* "tank". While 啤 *pi* is the transliteration for "beer", 摩托 *motuo* for "motor", and 坦克 *tanke* for "tank"; 酒 *jiu* "alcoholic drink" and 车 *che* "vehicle" are translations.

Fourth are roman letters plus Chinese words, such as AA 制 *zhi* "go Dutch", BP 机 *ji* "pager", and B 超 *chao* "ultrasound". Fifth is the use of roman letters only, in a direct borrowing of acronyms, for example: "CD", "DVD", "CPU", and "DNA".

As a rule, loanwords are added to the Chinese lexicon only in cases where available Chinese expressions are inadequate to describe new concepts, situations, or other phenomena that arise when Chinese and foreign cultures interact. However, words like 拜拜 *baibai* "bye-bye" and "OK" do not represent new concepts and can be replaced by words of Chinese origin. Yet many people, especially the young, love such expressions precisely for their foreign flavour.

In China, what should you do if you don't feel well? Here you will learn how to describe health problems to a doctor. You will also learn how to express volition, indicate necessity, and learn a new way of asking questions.

第十二课 Lesson 12

我 全身 都 不 舒服
Wǒ quánshēn dōu bù shūfu

一. 课文　**Text**

（一）

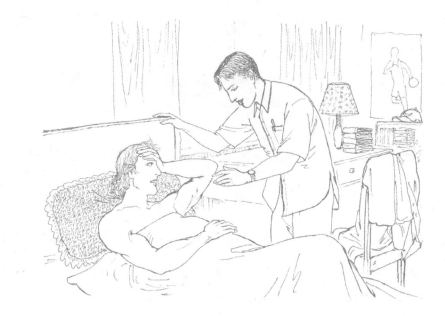

丁　力波：大为， 你 每 天 都 六点 起床 去 锻炼，[①]
Dīng Lìbō： Dàwéi, nǐ měi tiān dōu liù diǎn "qǐchuáng qù duànliàn",

　　　　现在 九点 一刻， 你 怎么 还 不 起床？ [②]
　　　　xiànzài jiǔ diǎn yí kè, nǐ zěnme hái bù qǐchuáng?

马　大为：我 头 疼。
Mǎ Dàwéi： Wǒ tóu téng.

-168-

丁力波： 你 嗓子 怎么样？
Dīng Lìbō： Nǐ sǎngzi zěnmeyàng?

【谈身体状况】
Talking about one's health

马大为： 我 嗓子 也 疼。
Mǎ Dàwéi： Wǒ sǎngzi yě téng. ③

丁力波： 我 想， 你 应该 去 医院 看病。③
Dīng Lìbō： Wǒ xiǎng, Nǐ yīnggāi qù yīyuàn kànbìng.

马大为： 我 身体 没 问题，④ 不用 去 看病。
Mǎ Dàwéi： Wǒ shēntǐ méi wèntí, búyòng qù kànbìng.
no problem

【表示意愿】
Expressing one's desire

我 要 睡觉， 不想 去 医院。
Wǒ yào shuìjiào, bù xiǎng qù yīyuàn.

Nín shēntǐ hǎo ma?
ask senior - polite.

丁力波： 你 不 去 看病， 明天 你 还 不 能 上课。
Dīng Lìbō： Nǐ bú qù kànbìng, míngtiān nǐ hái bù néng shàngkè.

马大为： 好 吧。我 去 医院。⑤ 现在 去 还是 下午 去？
Mǎ Dàwéi： Hǎo ba. Wǒ qù yīyuàn. Xiànzài qù háishi xiàwǔ qù?
soften tone

丁力波： 当然 现在 去，我 跟 你 一起 去。⑥ 今天 天气 很
Dīng Lìbō： Dāngrán xiànzài qù, wǒ gēn nǐ yìqǐ qù. Jīntiān tiānqì hěn
manner of action

冷，你 要 多 穿 点儿 衣服。
lěng, nǐ yào duō chuān diǎnr yīfu.
wear a little bit more clothes.

Wǒ míngtiān dōu Yīngāi xué hànyǔ

【表示必要】Expressing
need or necessity

měi—dōu
everyday

生词 New Words

1.	全身	N	quánshēn	all over (the body)	全身疼，全身不舒服
	全	A	quán	whole	
	身	N	shēn	body	
2.	舒服	A	shūfu	comfortable	不舒服，很舒服，舒服不舒服
3.	每	Pr	měi	every; each	每天，每年，每个学生，每瓶酒
4.	锻炼	V	duànliàn	to do physical exercise	去锻炼 √
5.	头	N	tóu	head	
6.	疼	A	téng	painful	头疼，手疼 √
7.	嗓子	N	sǎngzi	throat	嗓子疼，嗓子不舒服 √

metal radical
to spread.
Creepin'
voice
no more a 2 syllable

8. 想	V/OpV	xiǎng	to think/to want to do sth.　想睡觉，想喝水
9. 医院	N	yīyuàn	hospital　去医院，有一个医院
10. 看病	VO	kànbìng	to see a doctor　去看病，去医院看病
病	N/V	bìng	illness/to get sick　看病，有病，没有病
11. 身体	N	shēntǐ	body, health　身体好，锻炼身体
*12. 要	OpV	yào	must, to want to do something　要看病，要锻炼
13. 吧	MdPt	ba	(modal particle)
14. 还是	Conj	háishi	or　现在还是晚上，睡觉还是起床
15. 一起	Adv	yìqǐ	together　跟他一起，一起去，一起锻炼
16. 冷	A	lěng	cold　天气很冷
17. 穿	V	chuān	to wear
18. 衣服	N	yīfu	clothes　穿衣服，买衣服，做衣服

(14. 还是 annotation: always make a question)

（二）

丁　力波：你在这儿休息一下，我去给你挂号。⑦
Dīng Lìbō：Nǐ zài zhèr xiūxi yíxià, wǒ qù gěi nǐ guàhào.

马　大为：好。
Mǎ Dàwéi：Hǎo.

医生：8 号，8 号是谁？
Yīshēng：Bā hào, bā hào shì shéi?

丁　力波：我是 8 号。
Dīng Lìbō：Wǒ shì bā hào.

医生：你看病　还是他看病？
Yīshēng：Nǐ kànbìng háishi tā kànbìng?

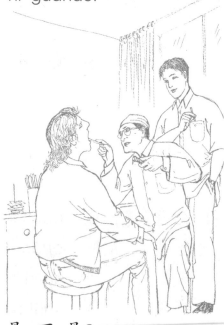

丁力波：他看病。
Dīng Lìbō：Tā kànbìng.

医生：请坐吧。你叫马大为，是不是？
Yīshēng：Qǐng zuò ba. Nǐ jiào Mǎ Dàwéi, shì bu shì?

马大为：是，我叫马大为。
Mǎ Dàwéi：Shì, wǒ jiào Mǎ Dàwéi.

医生：你今年多大？
Yīshēng：Nǐ jīnnián duō dà?

马 大为： 我 今年 二十二 岁。
Mǎ Dàwéi： Wǒ jīnnián èrshí'èr suì.

【看病】Going
to see a doctor

医生： 你 哪儿 不 舒服？ ⑧
Yīshēng： Nǐ nǎr bù shūfu?

马 大为： 我 头疼， 全身 都 不 舒服。③
Mǎ Dàwéi： Wǒ tóu téng, quánshēn dōu bù shūfu.

医生： 我 看 一下。 你 嗓子 有点儿 发炎，⑨ 还 有点儿
Yīshēng： Wǒ kàn yíxià. Nǐ sǎngzi yǒudiǎnr fāyán, hái yǒudiǎnr

发烧， 是 感冒。
fāshāo, shì gǎnmào.

yīdiǎnr followed by noun.

丁 力波： 他 要 不 要 住院？
Dīng Lìbō： Tā yào bu yào zhùyuàn?

医生： 不用。 你 要 多 喝 水， 还 要 吃 点儿 药。 你
Yīshēng： Búyòng. Nǐ yào duō hē shuǐ, hái yào chī diǎnr yào. Nǐ
No need

愿意 吃 中药 还是 愿意 吃 西药？
yuànyì chī zhōngyào háishi yuànyì chī xīyào?

马 大为： 我 愿意 吃 中药。
Mǎ Dàwéi： Wǒ yuànyì chī zhōngyào.

医生： 好， 你 吃 一点儿 中药， 下 星期一 再 来。
Yīshēng： Hǎo, nǐ chī yìdiǎnr zhōngyào, xià xīngqīyī zài lái.

给 + sub. + verb.

生词 New Words

1. 休息	V	xiūxi	to take a rest	休息一下，应该休息
*2. 给	Prep	gěi	to; for	给他买，给他介绍，给我们上课
3. 挂号	VO	guàhào	to register (at a hospital, etc.)	给他挂号
号	N	hào	number	八号，四九二号
4. 有点儿	Adv	yǒudiǎnr	somewhat; rather; a bit	有点儿疼，有点儿不舒服
5. 发炎	VO	fāyán	to become inflamed	有点儿发炎
6. 发烧	VO	fāshāo	to have a fever	有点儿发烧
烧	V	shāo	to burn	
7. 感冒	V/N	gǎnmào	to have a cold/cold	有点儿感冒
8. 住院	VO	zhùyuàn	to be in hospital; to be hospitalized	

verb. (to give)

only ab hospital

followed by situation → negative (adj).

9. 水	N	shuǐ	water 喝水
10. 药	N	yào	medicine 吃药，买药
11. 愿意	OpV	yuànyì	to be willing to do sth. 愿意学习，愿意上课，不愿意
12. 中药	N	zhōngyào	traditional Chinese medicine
13. 西药	N	xīyào	Western medicine
西	N	xī	west

补充生词　　Supplementary　Words

1. 牙	N	yá	tooth
2. 肚子	N	dùzi	abdomen；stomach
3. 开刀	VO	kāidāo	to have an operation
4. 化验	V	huàyàn	to have a medical test
5. 血	N	xiě	blood
6. 大便	N	dàbiàn	stool
7. 小便	N	xiǎobiàn	urine
8. 打针	VO	dǎzhēn	to have an injection
9. 热	A	rè	hot
10. 凉快	A	liángkuai	cool
11. 生活	N	shēnghuó	life
12. 英文	N	Yīngwén	English

二. 注释　　Notes

① 你每天都六点起床去锻炼。

When the pronoun "每" modifies a noun, a measure word should be used before the noun it modifies as in the following examples: "每个学生", "每斤苹果". However, before the nouns "天" and "年" a measure word cannot be used, and measure words are optional before "月". For example, we say "每天", "每年", and say cither "每月" or "每个月". "每" is often used in combination with "都". For example：

他每天都来学院。

我每月都回家。

② 你怎么还不起床？

"Why are you still in bed？"

"怎么" can also be used to ask about the cause of something, and the difference between "怎么" and "为什么" is that the former indicates a sense of surprise on the part of the speaker. For example：

八点上课,你怎么八点半来?

今天天气很好,你怎么不去锻炼?

Note："怎么" and "怎么样" are both interrogative pronouns, but "怎么" is often used as an adverbial in a sentence, whereas "怎么样" usually functions as the predicate as in "你怎么样?". When asking the reason for something, "怎么样" cannot be used and so one could not say "你怎么样还不起床?"

③ 我想，你应该去医院看病。

"I think you must go to see a doctor."

In this sentence "想" is a common verb.

④ 我身体没问题。

"No problem with my health."

"身体" means "body", but it may also mean "health". "你身体怎么样?" is also a form of greeting among friends and acquaintances. The phrase "没问题" means "no problem" and it is often used in spoken Chinese to indicate an affirmative, confident attitude. For example：

A：明天你能来吗?

B：没问题! 我能来。

⑤ 好吧。我去医院。

The modal particle "吧" has many uses. It is used to soften the tone of speech here and it may also be used in sentences expressing requests, commands, persuasion and consultation. For example：

请吧。 请坐吧。 我问一下吧。

⑥ 我跟你一起去。

"I'll go with you."

When the prepositional phrase "跟+Pr/NP" is placed before a verb as an adverbial modifier, it is generally used with the adverb "一起"; together they form the phrase "跟+Pr/NP+一起". For example：

他跟他朋友一起做练习。

他跟宋华一起锻炼。

⑦ 我去给你挂号。

"给" is a verb (see Lesson Ten), but it can also function as a preposition. When used as a preposition, "给" and the noun or noun phrase that follows it (usually the receiver of the action's benefit) form a prepositional phrase, which is placed before the predicative verb indicating that the object of "给" is indirectly affected by the activity of the predicate.

⑧ 你哪儿不舒服？

"What's wrong with you？"

This is an everyday expression used by doctors when talking to their patients.

⑨ 你嗓子有点儿发炎。

The phrase "有（一）点儿"（with "一" often omitted）is used before certain adjectives or verbs as an adverbial modifier, indicating moderation. When used before an adjective, it often implies dissatisfaction or negation. For example：

有点儿不高兴　有点儿贵　有点儿晚　有点儿发烧

Note：There is some difference between "有一点儿" and "一点儿"."有一点儿" is used adverbially, modifying the adjective or verb that follows it, whereas "一点儿" is used as an attributive, modifying a noun. For example：

一点儿东西　　一点儿钱　　一点儿书

The construction "一点儿 + N" is usually placed after a verb as its object. For example：

我去买一点儿东西。

It is not permissible to replace "有一点儿" with "一点儿". For example：

他有点儿不高兴。　（We cannot say "他一点儿不高兴".）

我有点儿发烧。　（We cannot say "我一点儿发烧".）

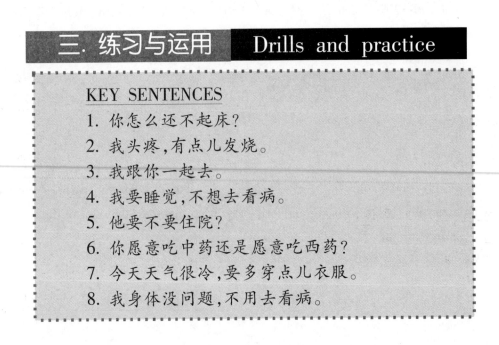

三. 练习与运用　Drills and practice

KEY SENTENCES

1. 你怎么还不起床？
2. 我头疼，有点儿发烧。
3. 我跟你一起去。
4. 我要睡觉，不想去看病。
5. 他要不要住院？
6. 你愿意吃中药还是愿意吃西药？
7. 今天天气很冷，要多穿点儿衣服。
8. 我身体没问题，不用去看病。

1. 熟读下列词组 Master the following phrases

(1) 头疼　手疼　全身疼　学习很好　身体不太好　天气很冷

(2) 下午还是晚上　　　　今天还是明天　　　　　两点还是三点

　　你还是我　　　　　他们还是她们　　　　　老师还是学生

　　睡觉还是起床　　　工作还是休息　　　　　学习还是玩儿

　　认识还是不认识　　买衣服还是买本子　　　吃中药还是吃西药

　　要香蕉还是要苹果　学习语言还是学习文学　喜欢香蕉还是喜欢苹果

(3) 要喝水　　　　　　　要回家　　　　想认识他

　　想看京剧(jīngjù)　　不想吃　　　不想学美术

(4) 愿意参加　　　　　愿意写汉字　　　　愿意学习汉语

　　不愿意喝酒　　　不愿意住院　　　　不愿意起床

(5) 要看病　要挂号　要锻炼　要不要吃药　不用介绍　不用找钱

2. 句型替换 Pattern drills

(1) A：你想不想学习 音乐？

　　B：我很想学习音乐。

去	加拿大
认识	陈老师
看	京剧(jīngjù)

(2) A：现在五点,你要学习还是

　　　要锻炼？

　　B：我要锻炼。

　　A：我不想锻炼,我要学习。

回家	去商场
看书	写汉字
去买衣服	去买苹果
看中文报	看英文(Yīngwén)报

(3) A：你愿意吃中药还是愿意吃西药？

　　B：我愿意吃中药。你呢？

　　A：我愿意吃西药。

吃蛋糕	吃寿面
学习语言	学习文学
去游泳(yóuyǒng)	去打球(dǎ qiú)
今天去	明天去
两点来	两点半来

(4) A：医生,他要不要住院？

　　B：不用。

开刀(kāidāo)	不用
化验(huàyàn)血(xiě)	要
化验(huàyàn)大便(dàbiàn)	不用
化验(huàyàn)小便(xiǎobiàn)	要

(5) A: 现在是<u>八点一刻</u>,你怎么还不<u>起床</u>?

     B: 我不太舒服。

     A: 你哪儿不舒服?

     B: 我<u>头</u>有点儿疼。

9:30	去上课	嗓子
4:20	锻炼	牙(yá)
11:45	睡觉	肚子(dùzi)

(6) A: 你常常去看你朋友吗?

     B: 我常常去看他。

     A: 他<u>身体</u>怎么样?

     B: 他<u>身体</u> 没问题。

工作	有点儿忙
学习	不太好
生活(shēnghuó)	很快乐

(7) A: 他跟谁一起去?

     B: 他跟<u>力波</u>一起去。

住	他朋友
锻炼	老师
说汉语	中国朋友

(8) A: 你每天<u>晚上</u>都做什么?

     B: 我每天晚上都<u>写汉字</u>。

晚上	看书
下午	锻炼身体
上午	上课

3. 看图造句 Make up sentences according to the pictures

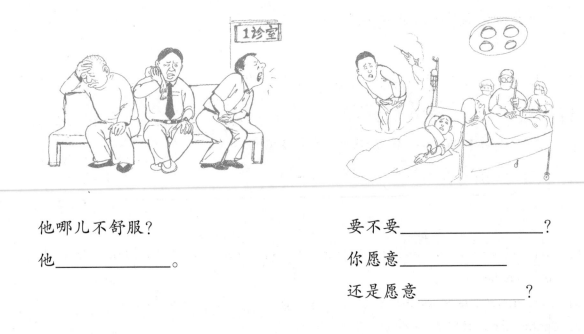

他哪儿不舒服?

他＿＿＿＿＿＿＿。

要不要＿＿＿＿＿＿＿＿?

你愿意＿＿＿＿＿＿?

还是愿意＿＿＿＿＿＿?

4. 会话练习 Conversation practice

【谈论身体状况 Talking about one's health】

(1) A：你怎么样？不太舒服吗？

　　B：我_____有点儿疼。

　　A：要不要去医院？

　　B：不用，我想休息一下。

(2) A：我今天怎么全身不舒服？

　　B：啊，你有点儿发烧。你现在不能去上课，要休息一下。

　　A：你跟陈老师说一下，好吗？

　　B：没问题。

(3) A：你身体真好。

　　B：是啊，我很少去医院。

　　A：你每天都锻炼身体吗？

　　B：我每天下午都锻炼。

【表达意愿与必要 Expressing one's desire or need】

(1) A：明天是星期天，你想做什么？

　　B：我不想做什么，我想在家休息。你想去哪儿？

　　A：我要去市场买点儿东西。

(2) A：你明天有时间吗？我们去打球(dǎ qiú)，好吗？

　　B：对不起，我明天要去学太极拳(tàijíquán, taiji boxing)。你会打(dǎ)

　　　太极拳(tàijíquán)吗？

　　A：我会一点儿。

　　B：太好了！我想学，你能教我吗？

(3) A：你为什么要学习汉语？

　　B：我喜欢汉语。我想做一个汉语老师。

　　A：我也喜欢教孩子(háizi)们汉语。

5. 交际练习 Communication exercises

(1) You feel sick while reading together with your classmate in the library. How do you tell him/her ?

(2) Your friend has a toothache (牙疼，yá téng). How do you help him/her tell the doctor about it?

(3) You want to go to China to study Chinese and to visit the city of Shanghai, but your friend thinks that in order to study Chinese well you should go to Beijing. How do you talk to him/her about this?

请假条(qǐngjiàtiáo, note requesting leave)

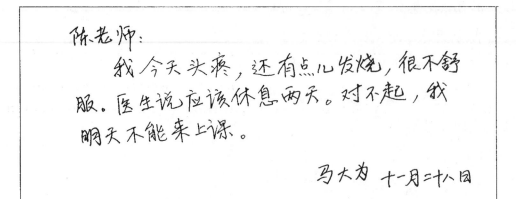

陈老师：
　我今天头疼，还有点儿发烧，很不舒服。医生说应该休息两天。对不起，我明天不能来上课。

　　　　　马大为　十一月二十八日

四. 阅读和复述　Reading Comprehension and Paraphrasing

大为，你怎么还不起床？什么？你头疼？你全身都不舒服？你要睡觉，不想起床？你应该去看病。你要睡觉，不愿意去医院？大为，你不能睡觉，你应该去医院，你得去看病。我跟你一起去医院。现在去还是下午去？当然现在去。我们应该现在去。

医生，他是8号，他的中文名字叫马大为，今年22岁。他头疼，全身都不舒服。您给他看一下。您说他发烧，嗓子还有点儿发炎。是感冒！他要不要住院？不用住院，要吃药。大为，你愿意吃中药还是愿意吃西药？你可以吃西药。什么？你不愿意吃西药？你愿意吃中药？好吧，医生，您给他一点儿中药。

五. 语法　　　Grammar

1. 主谓谓语句 Sentences with a subject-predicate phrase as predicate

The main element of the predicate in this kind of sentence is a subject-predicate phrase. In many cases the person or thing that the subject of the subject-predicate phrase (subject 2) denotes is a part of the person or thing denoted by the subject of the whole sentence (subject 1).

Subject 1	Predicate 1	
	Subject 2	Predicate 2
马大为	头	疼。
他	全身	都 不 舒服。
你	身体	好 吗?
宋华	学习	怎么样?
今天	天气	冷 不 冷?

The negative adverb "不" is usually placed before the predicate of the subject-predicate phrase (predicate 2). Its A/V-not-A/V form is produced by juxtaposing the affirmative and negative forms of predicate 2.

2. 选择疑问句 Alternative questions

An alternative question is created when two possible situations, A and B, are connected by the conjunction "还是". The person to whom the question is addressed is expected to choose one of the alternatives.

Question			Answer
Alternative A	还是	Alternative B	
现在去	还是	下午去?	现在去。(Alternative A)
你看病	还是	他看病?	他看病。(Alternative B)
你愿意吃中药	还是	愿意吃西药?	我愿意吃中药。(Alternative A)
你是老师	还是	学生?	我是学生。(Alternative B)

3. 能愿动词谓语句(2) Sentences with an optative verb (2):要,想,愿意

The optative verbs "要" and "想" both express subjective intention and desire. They are basically the same in meaning. Sometimes "要" emphasizes intent or a demand, while "想" places more emphasis on intention or hope. For example:

我要吃烤鸭。

我想去北京吃烤鸭。

The negative form for both "想" and "要" (denoting desire) is "不想".

"愿意" is also used to express one's wishes. It means a willingness to do something or a hope that something will occur according to the wishes of the person denoted by the subject.

Subject	Predicate	
	OpV	**V O**
马大为	要	睡觉。
丁力波	想	学习　美术。
他	不　想	去　　医院。
她	愿意　不愿意	参加　聚会？

The optative verb "要" is also used to express need. Its negative form is "不用". For example：

他要不要住院？

明天天气怎么样？要多穿衣服吗？

明天不用多穿衣服。

六. 汉字　　Chinese Characters

1. 汉字的结构（5）Structure of Chinese characters（5）

The enclosure structure ②

a. Left-bottom-right enclosure

出　　画

b. Left-bottom enclosure

这　起　题

2. 认写基本汉字 Learn and write basic Chinese characters

(1) 予　　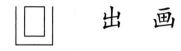

yǔ　　to give　　　　　4 strokes

(2) 母　　乚凸母母母

mǔ　　mother　　　　　5 strokes

(3) 冬　　ノ夂夂冬冬

dōng　　winter　　　　　5 strokes

(4) 令　　ノ人亼今令

lìng　　order　　　　　5 strokes

(5) 牙　　ー 匚 于 牙
yá　　tooth　　　　　　　　　　4 strokes

(6) 衣　　丶 亠 亡 亣 衣 衣
yī　　clothes　　　　　　　　　6 strokes

(7) 自　　（丿+目）
zì　　self　　　　　　　　　　6 strokes

(8) 发(發)　ー ナ 屮 发 发
fā　　to send out　　　　　　5 strokes

(9) 主　　（丶+王）
zhǔ　　host　　　　　　　　　5 strokes

(10) 厂(厰)　ー 厂
chǎng　factory　　　　　　　2 strokes

3. 认写课文中的汉字 Learn and write the Chinese characters appearing in the texts

(1) 全身 quánshēn

全 → 人 + 王　　　　　6 strokes

(2) 舒服 shūfu

舒 → 人 + 舌 + 予　　12 strokes

服 → 月 + 卩 + 又　　8 strokes

亠 (měizìtóu)　　丿 乚　　2 strokes

(3) 每 měi

每 → 亠 + 母　　　　7 strokes

疒 (bìngzìpáng)(the "illness" side, denoting disease or ailment.)

　　　　丶 一 广 广 疒　　5 strokes

(4) 疼 téng

疼 → 疒 + 冬   10 strokes

(The "illness" side denotes the meaning, "冬" indicates the pronunciation.)

(5) 嗓子 sǎngzi

嗓 → 口 + 又 + 又 + 又 + 木   13 strokes

东 jiǎn   一 七 车 东 东   5 strokes

火 (huǒzìpáng, on the left side of a multi-component character, the fourth stroke in "火" is written as a dot. It is called the "fire" side.)   丶 丷 火 火   4 strokes

(6) 锻炼 duànliàn (鍛煉)

锻 → 钅 + 段   14 strokes

(The meaning side is "钅", and the phonetic side is "段".)

炼 → 火 + 东   9 strokes

(7) 想 xiǎng

想 → 木 + 目 + 心   13 strokes

(The meaning part is "心", and the phonetic part is "相".)

(8) 病 bìng

病 → 疒 + 丙   10 strokes

(The meaning side is "疒", and the phonetic side is "丙".)

(9) 身体 shēntǐ (身體)

体 → 亻 + 本   7 strokes

(10) 吧 ba

吧 → 口 + 巴   7 strokes

(The meaning side is "口", and the phonetic side is "巴".)

冫 (liǎngdiǎnshuǐ) (the "two-drops-of-water" side)   丶 冫   2 strokes

(11) 冷 lěng

冷 → 冫 + 令   7 strokes

(12) 穿 chuān

穿 → 穴 + 牙　　　　　　　　　9 strokes

(13) 休息 xiūxi

休 → 亻 + 木　　　　　　　　　6 strokes

息 → 自 + 心　　　　　　　　　10 strokes

(14) 挂号 guàhào (掛號)

挂 → 扌 + 土 + 土　　　　　　9 strokes

(15) 发炎 fāyán (發炎)

炎 → 火 + 火　　　　　　　　　8 strokes

尧 (yáozìtóu)　　　　一 弋 尧　　　　　　3 strokes

(the "eminent" top)　(Please differentiate from "戈".)

(16) 发烧 fāshāo (發燒)

烧 → 火 + 尧 + 兀　　　　　　10 strokes

(17) 感冒 gǎnmào

感 → 戊 + 一 + 口 + 心　　　13 strokes

冒 → 曰 + 目　　　　　　　　　9 strokes

(18) 住院 zhùyuàn

住 → 亻 + 主　　　　　　　　　7 strokes

(The meaning side is "亻", and the phonetic side is "主".)

(19) 中药 zhōngyào (中藥)

药 → 艹 + 纟 + 勺　　　　　　9 strokes

(20) 愿意 yuànyì (願意)

愿 → 厂 + 白 + 小 + 心　　　14 strokes

Chinese Herbal Medicine

Chinese herbal medicine is used in traditional Chinese medical practice, which has a history of thousands of years. According to tradition, a sage-emperor of remote antiquity called Shennong ("Holy Farmer") experimented with many types of herbs in order to find cures for his subjects. Traditional Chinese herbal medicine differs from modern Western medicine in that basically it does not use artificially created chemicals but is extracted directly from natural substances.

Traditional Chinese remedies can be divided into three categories, according to their sources. First is medicine from vegetable sources, such as the roots, stems, leaves, and fruits of plants. Second is medicine from animals, including their organs and secretions such as bezoar (cow gallstones), snake venom, and deer musk. Third are medicines from mineral sources, including gypsum and others.

Traditional Chinese medicine can be effective in treating many frequently occurring health problems like the common cold and fevers. Most doctors agree that side effects from the majority of herbal medicines are relatively mild. Currently, doctors in China, be they practitioners trained in Chinese or Western medicine, are exploring ways to combine the two traditions for use in treatment as well as prevention therapies.

Ma Dawei recently met a new female friend. In this lesson, he will show us how to make phone calls, rent lodgings, ask for help, and invite people for a visit.

第十三课 Lesson 13

我 认识 了一 个 漂亮 的 姑娘

Wǒ rènshi le yí ge piàoliang de gūniang

一. 课文 Text

（一）

宋　华： 大为， 听说 你 得 了 感冒， 现在 你 身体
Sòng Huá： Dàwéi, tīngshuō nǐ dé le gǎnmào, xiànzài nǐ shēntǐ

怎么样?
zěnmeyàng?

马　大为： 我 去 了 医院， 吃 了 很 多 中药。① 现在 我 头
Mǎ Dàwéi： Wǒ qù le yīyuàn, chī le hěn duō zhōngyào. Xiànzài wǒ tóu

还 有点儿 疼。
hái yǒudiǎnr téng.

宋　华：你 还　应该　多 休息。
Sòng Huá：Nǐ hái yīnggāi duō xiūxi.

马　大为：宋　华，我 想　告诉 你一 件 事儿。
Mǎ Dàwéi：Sòng Huá, wǒ xiǎng gàosu nǐ yí jiàn shìr.

宋　华：什么　事儿？
Sòng Huá：Shénme shìr?

【谈已经发生的事】Talking about something that has happened

马　大为：我 认识 了一个 漂亮　的 姑娘，　她 愿意 做我
Mǎ Dàwéi：Wǒ rènshi le yí ge piàoliang de gūniang, tā yuànyì zuò wǒ

女 朋友。　我们　常常　一起 散步，一起 看
nǚ péngyou. Wǒmen chángcháng yìqǐ sànbù, yìqǐ kàn

电影、　喝 咖啡，一起 听 音乐。
diànyǐng、 hē kāfēi, yìqǐ tīng yīnyuè.

宋　华：祝贺 你！ 这 是 好 事 啊。
Sòng Huá：Zhùhè nǐ! Zhè shì hǎo shì a.

马　大为：谢谢。是 好 事，可是 我 的 宿舍 太 小，她 不 能
Mǎ Dàwéi：Xièxie. Shì hǎo shì, kěshì wǒ de sùshè tài xiǎo, tā bù néng

常　来我 这儿。② 我 想　找 一 间 房子。
cháng lái wǒ zhèr. Wǒ xiǎng zhǎo yì jiān fángzi.

宋　华：你 想 租 房子？③
Sòng Huá：Nǐ xiǎng zū fángzi?

【租房】Renting a house

马　大为：是 啊，我 想 租一 间 有 厨房　和 厕所 的 房子，④
Mǎ Dàwéi：Shì a, wǒ xiǎng zū yì jiān yǒu chúfáng hé cèsuǒ de fángzi,

房租 不 能 太 贵。
fángzū bù néng tài guì.

宋　华：星期六 我 跟 你一起去 租 房　公司，好 吗？
Sòng Huá：Xīngqīliù wǒ gēn nǐ yìqǐ qù zū fáng gōngsī, hǎo ma?

马大为：太 好 了。
Mǎ Dàwéi：Tài hǎo le.

生词 New Words

1.	姑娘	N	gūniang	girl 漂亮的姑娘，小姑娘
2.	听说	V	tīngshuō	to be told
	听	V	tīng	to listen
3.	得	V	dé	to have, to get 得感冒，得病
4.	告诉	V	gàosu	to tell
5.	件	M	jiàn	(a measure word) piece 一件工作
6.	事儿	N	shìr	matter; affair; thing 一件事儿，什么事儿
7.	散步	VO	sànbù	to take a walk; to walk 一起散步
	步	N	bù	step
8.	电影	N	diànyǐng	movie 看电影，中国电影
	电	N	diàn	electricity
	影	N	yǐng	shadow
*9.	咖啡	N	kāfēi	coffee 喝咖啡
10.	可是	Conj	kěshì	but
*11.	宿舍	N	sùshè	dormitory 学生宿舍，回宿舍
*12.	找	V	zhǎo	to look for 找房子，找人，找东西
13.	房子	N	fángzi	house 住房子，没有房子，买房子
14.	租	V	zū	to rent 租房子，租光盘
15.	间	M	jiān	(a measure word for room, house, etc) 一间房子
16.	厨房	N	chúfáng	kitchen 一间厨房
17.	厕所	N	cèsuǒ	toilet 一间厕所，男厕所，女厕所
18.	房租	N	fángzū	rent (for a house, flat, etc)
19.	公司	N	gōngsī	company 小公司，大公司，租房公司

（二）

【征求建议】
Asking for suggestions

（宋华与马大为在家美租房公司。）

马　大为：那　间　房子　房租　太贵，你　说，我　应该　怎么　办？⑤
Mǎ Dàwéi： Nà jiān fángzi fángzū tài guì, nǐ shuō, wǒ yīnggāi zěnme bàn?

宋　华：你 想 租 还是 不 想 租?
Sòng Huá：Nǐ xiǎng zū háishi bù xiǎng zū?

马 大为：当然 想 租。
Mǎ Dàwéi：Dāngrán xiǎng zū.

宋　华：我 给 陆 雨平 打 个 电话， 让 他 来 帮助
Sòng Huá：Wǒ gěi Lù Yǔpíng dǎ ge diànhuà, ràng tā lái bāngzhù

　　　　我们。
　　　　wǒmen.

马 大为：他 很 忙， 会 来 吗?
Mǎ Dàwéi：Tā hěn máng, huì lái ma?

宋　华：他 会 来。
Sòng Huá：Tā huì lái.

（宋华给陆雨平打电话。）

陆 雨平：喂， 哪 一 位 啊? ⑥
Lù Yǔpíng：Wèi, nǎ yí wèi a?

【打电话】Making a phone call

宋　华：我 是 宋 华，我 和 大为 现在 在 家美 租 房
Sòng Huá：Wǒ shì Sòng Huá, wǒ hé Dàwéi xiànzài zài Jiāměi Zū Fáng

　　　　公司。
　　　　Gōngsī.

陆 雨平：你们 怎么 在 那儿?
Lù Yǔpíng：Nǐmen zěnme zài nàr?

宋　华：大为 要 租 房子。
Sòng Huá：Dàwéi yào zū fángzi.

陆 雨平：你们 看 没 看 房子?
Lù Yǔpíng：Nǐmen kàn méi kàn fángzi?

宋　华：我们 看 了 一间 房子。那 间 房子 很 好，可是
Sòng Huá：Wǒmen kàn le yì jiān fángzi. Nà jiān fángzi hěn hǎo, kěshì

　　　　房租 有点儿 贵。
　　　　fángzū yǒudiǎnr guì.

陆 雨平：你们 找 了经理 没有? ⑦
Lù Yǔpíng：Nǐmen zhǎo le jīnglǐ méiyǒu?

宋　华：　我们　　没有　找　经理。
Sòng Huá：Wǒmen méiyǒu zhǎo jīnglǐ.

陆 雨平：宋　华，这个　公司　的 经理 是 我　朋友，我　跟
Lù Yǔpíng：Sòng Huá, zhè ge gōngsī de jīnglǐ shì wǒ péngyou, wǒ gēn

他 说　一下，请 他　帮助　你们，我　想　可能
tā shuō yíxià, qǐng tā bāngzhù nǐmen, wǒ xiǎng kěnéng

没有　问题。
méiyǒu wèntí.

【邀请】
Invitations

宋　华：　好 啊。晚上　　我们　　请 你 和 你　朋友　吃饭。⑧
Sòng Huá：Hǎo a. Wǎnshang wǒmen qǐng nǐ hé nǐ péngyou chīfàn.

陆 雨平：好，你们　在　公司　等　我，再见。
Lù Yǔpíng：Hǎo, nǐmen zài gōngsī děng wǒ, zàijiàn.

宋　华：　再见。
Sòng Huá：Zàijiàn.

生词 New Words

1. 办	V	bàn	to do	怎么办
2. 打电话	V O	dǎ diànhuà	to make a phone call	给她打电话
电话	N	diànhuà	telephone; phone call	一个电话，你的电话
3. 让	V	ràng	to let; to allow; to make	
4. 帮助	V	bāngzhù	to help	
5. 喂	Int	wèi	hello; hey	
6. 位	M	wèi	(a polite measure word for person)	
			一位小姐，一位老师，一位医生，哪一位	
7. 经理	N	jīnglǐ	manager	
8. 可能	OpV	kěnéng	maybe	可能来，可能感冒，可能住院
9. 吃饭	VO	chīfàn	to eat (a meal)	
饭	N	fàn	meal	中国饭
10. 等	V	děng	to wait	等人，等他们，等一下
11. 家美	PN	Jiāměi	(name of a house rental agency)	

1. 客厅	N	kètīng	living room
2. 卧室	N	wòshì	bedroom
3. 书房	N	shūfáng	a study
4. 套	M	tào	suite
5. 方便	A	fāngbiàn	convenient
6. 巧	A	qiǎo	coincidental
7. 合适	A	héshì	suitable
8. 热心	A	rèxīn	enthusiastic
9. 包括	V	bāokuò	to include
10. 水电费	N	shuǐdiànfèi	utility
11. 新	A	xīn	new
12. 回信	N/VO	huíxìn	reply/to reply

二. 注释　Notes

① 我吃了很多中药。

When the adjectives "多" and "少" are used as attributive modifiers, we must put adverbs such as "很" before them. For example："很多中药" or "很多学生", and not "多中药", "多学生". "的" may be left out after "很多".

② 她不能常来我这儿。

"She cannot come to my place very often."

The objects of the verbs "来,去,到,在" and the preposition "在" are generally words of place or location; if they are not, then "这儿" and "那儿" must be added to them. For example："来我这儿","去力波那儿","到我朋友那儿","在老师这儿".

We cannot say "来我" or "在老师".

Generally, "常常" and "常" are used interchangeably.

③ 你想租房子?

A declarative sentence can be turned into a question by reading it with the same intonation as an interrogative sentence.

④ 我想租一间有厨房和厕所的房子。

"I want to rent a house with a kitchen and a bathroom."

We must add "的" to a verb or verbal phrase to turn it into an adjective modifier. For example：

　　有厨房的房子

　　给她的蛋糕 (the cake given to her)

　　今天来的人(the people who come today)

As has been said previously, the attributive must be placed before the words it modifies.

⑤ 你说，我应该怎么办？

"What do you think I should do？"

"你说" (or "你看") is used here to solicit the listener's opinion.

⑥ 喂，哪一位啊？

"Hello, who is speaking？"

"喂" is an interjection often used in phone calls as a form of greeting or response. For example：

　　喂，是丁力波吗？

　　喂，我是马大为，请问您找谁？

　　喂，您好，我想找一下王小云。

The measure word "位" applies to persons only and is a more polite and respectful form than the measure word "个". For example：

　　这位先生　　二十位老师　　两位教授

⑦ 你们找了经理没有？

"Have you (found and) talked to the manager？"

"找经理" here means "talk to the manager".

⑧ 晚上我们请你和你朋友吃饭。

"We'll invite you and your friend to dinner this evening."

"吃饭" means "to eat (a meal)". "请…吃饭" means "to invite someone to dinner (or lunch)".

三. 练习与运用　　Drills and practice

KEY SENTENCES

1. 你们看没看房子?
2. 我们看了一间房子。
3. 你们找了经理没有?
4. 我们没有找经理。
5. 我给陆雨平打个电话,让他来帮助我们。
6. 晚上我们请你和你朋友吃饭。
7. 他会来吗?
8. 她不能常来我这儿。
9. 我想租一间有厨房和厕所的房子。

1. 熟读下列词组 Master the following phrases

(1) 看了一间房子　认识了一位教授　买了两斤香蕉　找了两块钱　　说了一件事
　　送了一张光盘　参加了一个聚会　写了十个汉字　吃了一个蛋糕　喝了红葡萄酒

(2) 找没找　租没租　等没等　买没买　看没看　问没问　来没来　送没送
　　上课没上课　休息没休息　起床没起床　锻炼没锻炼　帮助没帮助

(3) 这儿　他那儿　老师那儿　医生那儿　我朋友那儿　我哥哥这儿　王经理那儿

(4) 可能来　可能去　可能做　不可能等　不可能租　不可能帮助　可能不可能得

(5) 一件事儿　　一件工作　　这件衣服　　　那间厨房　　　这间宿舍
　　这位小姐　　那位医生　　一位朋友　　　一位经理　　　一位记者

(6) 让他帮助你　　　　　　让他去那儿　·　　　　　让他写汉字
　　请他们吃饭　　　　　　请小姐喝咖啡　　　　　请我朋友教我

2. 句型替换 Pattern drills

(1) 我想告诉你一件事儿。

　　什么事儿?

　　我认识了一个姑娘。

　　好啊。

看	一个中国电影
买	一件衣服
参加	一个聚会
写	二十个汉字

(2) 他们看没看 房子？
　　他们看了一间房子。
　　你呢？
　　我没有看。

买	苹果	五斤
吃	蛋糕	很多
喝	葡萄酒	一瓶

(3) 你去了租房公司没有？
　　我去了租房公司。
　　租房公司怎么样？
　　租房公司很好。

吃	生日蛋糕
买	那本中文书
听	那张光盘
租	那间房子

(4) 你给大为打个电话，好吗？
　　什么事儿？
　　让他去 租房公司。
　　没有问题。

来	我这儿
去	老师那儿
等	他女朋友
找	张教授

(5) 你请他做什么？
　　我请他吃饭。
　　他会来吗？
　　他会来。

看电影	去
散步	来
喝咖啡	去
介绍中国文化(wénhuà)	来

(6) 喂，哪一位啊？
　　我是马大为。
　　我现在在租房公司。
　　你怎么在那儿？
　　我要租房子。

王小云	丁力波宿舍	帮助他学习
宋华	汉语系	找陈老师
陆雨平	宋华家	祝贺他的生日
丁力波	医院	看病

3. 看图造句 Make up sentences according to the pictures

他想买什么？

他_____。

他买了什么？

他_____。

他要什么？

他_____。

他要了咖啡还是要了酒？

他_____。

4. 会话练习 Conversation practice

【打电话 Making a phone call】

(1) B：喂，哪一位啊？

A：我是_____。

B：是你啊。你怎么样？有什么事儿？

A：_____。

(2) B：喂，你好，请问您找谁？

A：我找丁力波，我是他朋友。

B：好，请等一下。

C：喂，我是丁力波。

A：你好，力波，我想告诉你一件事儿。

(3) A：喂，是403号宿舍吗？

B：是啊，您找谁？

A：王小云在吗？

B：她不在。

A：请问，她家的电话号码是多少？

B：82305647。

A：谢谢。

【租房 Renting a house】

(1) A：我想租一间房子。

B：你的宿舍不好吗？

A：我的宿舍＿＿＿＿＿＿＿＿，想＿＿＿＿＿＿＿＿＿。

B：好，我跟你一起去租房公司。

(2) A：您想租房子吗？

B：是，我想租一间有＿＿＿＿＿＿、＿＿＿＿＿＿的房子。

A：我们家美租房公司有很多好房子。

B：房租贵不贵？

A：不贵，每月＿＿＿＿＿＿＿＿元。

B：包括(bāokuò)水电费(shuǐdiànfèi)吗？

A：不包括。

B：可以看一下吗？

A：当然可以。

【征求建议 Asking for suggestions】

(1) A：明天是我姐姐的生日。你说，我应该给她买什么？

B：你可以买＿＿＿＿＿。

A：我应该在哪儿买＿＿＿＿＿＿？

B：＿＿＿＿＿＿＿。

(2) A：我想跟你说一件事儿。

B：什么事儿？

A：星期日是我女朋友的生日，可是宋华让我参加一个聚会。你说，我应该怎么办？

B：＿＿＿＿＿＿＿＿＿＿＿。

【邀请 An invitation】

(1) A：星期天你有时间吗？

B：我＿＿＿＿＿＿＿＿。

A：我想请你＿＿＿＿＿＿＿＿＿。

B：＿＿＿＿＿＿＿＿＿＿＿。

(2) A：白小姐，晚上我请你＿＿＿＿＿＿＿，好吗？

B：对不起，我＿＿＿＿＿＿＿。

A：你什么时候有时间？

B：＿＿＿＿＿＿＿＿＿＿＿。

5. 交际练习 Communication exercises

(1) Make a phone call from the university dormitory to a friend of yours to tell him/her something that has happened recently in your life or studies.

(2) Your mother and father are coming to China to see you, and you want to rent a house for them. Your request to the rental company is for a large house with a kitchen and a bathroom. Your parents want to live in it for one week.

(3) Thanksgiving Day(感恩节, Gǎn'ēn Jié) is coming and you are inviting a few good friends to dinner. Some of them can come and some cannot.

(4) You are buying things to make Thanksgiving dinner in a super market. How would you ask the salesperson for help?

Sing a song.

康定情歌
Kāngdìng Qínggē

稍慢　饱满地　　　　　　　　　　　　　　　　　　　四川民歌

跑马　溜溜的　　山上　　　一朵　溜溜的　　云哟
Pǎomǎ　liūliū de　shān shàng　　yì duǒ　liūliū de　yún yo

李家　溜溜的　　大姐　　　人才　溜溜的　　好哟
Lǐjiā　liūliū de　dàjiě　　réncái　liūliū de　hǎo yo

一来　溜溜的　　看上　　　人才　溜溜的　　好哟
Yī lái　liūliū de　kàn shàng　　réncái　liūliū de　hǎo yo

世间　溜溜的　　女子　　　任我　溜溜的　　爱哟
Shìjiān　liūliū de　nǚzǐ　　rèn wǒ　liūliū de　ài yo

端端　溜溜的　　照在　　　康定　溜溜的　　城哟
Duānduān liūliū de　zhào zài　　Kāngdìng　liūliū de　chéng yo

张家　溜溜的　　大哥　　　看上　溜溜的　　她哟
Zhāngjiā　liūliū de　dàgē　　kànshàng　liūliū de　tā yo

二来　溜溜的　　看上　　　会当　溜溜的　　家哟
Èr lái　liūliū de　kàn shàng　　huì dāng　liūliū de　jiā yo

世间　溜溜的　　男子　　　任你　溜溜的　　求哟
Shìjiān　liūliū de　nánzǐ　　rèn nǐ　liūliū de　qiú yo

月亮　弯　弯　　　康定　溜溜的　城哟
Yuèliàng　wān　wān　　Kāngdìng　liūliūde chéng yo

月亮　弯　弯　　　看上　溜溜的　她哟
Yuèliàng　wān　wān　　kàn shàng liūliūde tā yo

月亮　弯　弯　　　会当　溜溜的　家哟
Yuèliàng　wān　wān　　huì dāng　liūliūde jiā yo

月亮　弯　弯　　　任你　溜溜的　求哟
Yuèliàng　wān　wān　　rèn nǐ　liūliūde qiú yo

马大为给女朋友小燕子(Xiǎoyànzi)的一封信

亲爱(qīn'ài, dear)的小燕子：

　　你好吗？我很想(xiǎng, miss)你。

　　星期三我得了感冒，头疼，嗓子有点儿发炎，还有点儿发烧。可是现在我好了。

　　我想跟你说一件事儿。小燕子，我很喜欢你。我想让你常常来看我，跟我一起听音乐，喝咖啡。可是我住的宿舍太小，也不方便(fāngbiàn)。我想租一间房子，有厨房，有厕所，房租不能太贵。我请宋华帮助我找房子。

　　星期六我和宋华一起去了家美租房公司，我们看了一间房子，房子很好，很大，有厨房、厕所，可是房租太贵。宋华给陆雨平打了一个电话，问他我们应该怎么办。真巧(qiǎo)，家美租房公司的经理是陆雨平的朋友，陆雨平请他帮助我们。这位经理很热心(rèxīn)，他让我们看了很多房子。我租了一间很合适(héshì)的房子，房租不太贵。晚上我们请陆雨平和经理去吃了北京烤鸭。我真高兴。

　　小燕子，我想请你来看一下我的新(xīn)房子。你说，什么时候合适？

　　我等你的回信(huíxìn)。

你的大为

12月10日

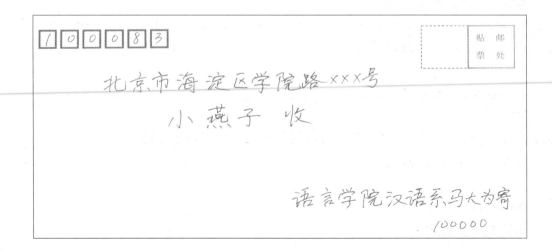

五. 语法　　　　　　Grammar

1. 助词"了"(1)　The Particle "了"(1)

　　The particle "了" can be used after a verb to indicate realization or completion of an action. For example：

你买了几个苹果？　　　***Compare***：　　你买几个苹果？
(How many apples have you bought？)　　(How many apples are you going to buy?
　　　　　　　　　　　　　　　　　　　　　How many apples will you buy？)

我买了五个苹果。　　　　　　　　　　我买五个苹果。
(I have bought five apples.)　　　　　(I'm going to buy five apples.
　　　　　　　　　　　　　　　　　　　I will buy five apples.)

　　If the verb with a "了" takes an object, this object usually has an attributive, which, in many cases, is a numeral-measure word, an adjective, or a pronoun.

$$V + 了 + Nu—M / A /Pr + O$$

Subject	Predicate			
	Verb	**了**	**Nu– M　/ Pr /A**	**Object**
我们	看	了	一间	房子。
王小云	买	了	两瓶	酒。
马大为	认识	了	一个　　　　漂亮的	姑娘。
大为	吃	了	很多	中药。
我	介绍	了	那位	教授。
他	看	了	有名的	京剧。
她朋友	租	了	她的	房子。

　　If the object does not have an attributive (eg："他买了苹果" or "大为得了感冒"), other elements are needed in the predicate to form a complete sentence. For example：

　　　　听说你得了感冒,现在你身体怎么样？
　　　　我去了医院,也吃了很多中药。

　　The negative form of this kind of sentence is made by placing "没" or "没有" before the verb and dropping "了" after the verb.

　　　　没有 + V + O
　　　　我们没有找经理。
　　　　他没买酒。

Note：One can never use "不" to negate this kind of sentence.
The V/A–not–V/A form is "V+没(有)+V" or "V+了没有".

　　　　V + 没(有)V + O
　　　　你们看没看房子？
　　　　你们找没找经理？

V ＋ 了 ＋ O ＋ 没有

你们看了房子没有？

你们找了经理没有？

Note：“了” indicates only the stage of the realization or completion of an action, but not the time at which this action occurs (which may be in the past, present, or future). In this kind of sentence the action, in many cases, has already happened. It is also possible, though, that the completion of the action will occur in the future. For example：

明天下午我买了本子去吃饭。

(Tomorrow afternoon I'll have supper after I have bought the notebooks.)

Not all past actions need the particle “了”. If an action occurs frequently or a sentence describes an action in the past but does not emphasize the completion of the action, “了” is not used. For example：

过去(guòqù, in the past)他常常来看我。

去年(qùnián, last year)我在美术学院学习美术。

2. 兼语句 Pivotal sentences

The pivotal sentence is also a sentence with a verbal predicate. Its predicate is composed of two verbal phrases. The object of the first verb is simultaneously the subject of the second verb. The first verb in a pivotal sentence should be a verb with a meaning of "making" or "ordering" somebody to do something, such as “请” or “让”.

Both “请” and “让” have the meaning of requiring others to do something. “请” is used in a formal situation and sounds polite. “请” also has the meaning of "to invite". For example：

晚上我们请你和你朋友吃饭。

| Subject | Predicate | | | |
	Verb 1	Object 1 (Subject 2)	Verb 2	Object 2
宋华	让	陆雨平	来帮助	他们。
陆雨平	请	经理	帮助	马大为。
妈妈	不让	她	喝	咖啡。

3. 能愿动词谓语句(3) Sentences with an optative verb (3)：“可能”，“会”

The optative verb “可能” expresses possibility. Besides expressing ability, “会” is also used to express possibility. For example：

今年八月他可能去上海。

现在八点,他不可能睡觉。

明天他会不会来上课？

他得了感冒,明天不会来上课。

六. 汉字　　　Chinese Characters

1. 部首查字法 Consulting a Chinese dictionary using radicals

Many Chinese character dictionaries are organized according to the order of the characters' "radicals". Radicals are common components, located on the top, bottom, left, right, or outer part of characters, which usually indicate the class of meaning to which a character belongs. For example, "好", "她", "妈", "姐", "妹", "姓", and "娜" are grouped under the radical "女", which is the common component on the left side of these characters. However, "意", "思", "想", "您", and "愿" are grouped under the radical "心", which is the common component at the bottom of these characters.

In the radical index of a dictionary, radicals are listed in order according to the number of their strokes. In the index of entries, characters of the same radical are arranged in groups according to the number of their strokes exceeding those of the radical.

Therefore, after determining the radical of a character, you should count the number of strokes in the radical and consult the radical index to obtain the page number where the radical entry can be found in the index of entries. Then, count the number of strokes in the character excluding the radical and consult the corresponding group to find the character and its page number in the dictionary. For example, the character "锻" will be found under the "钅" radical and in the section containing characters with 9 strokes more than those of the radical.

2. 认写基本汉字 Learn and write basic Chinese characters

(1) 古　　　（十+口）
　　gǔ　　ancient　　　　　　　　　　5 strokes

(2) 良　　　（丶+艮）
　　liáng　good　　　　　　　　　　7 strokes

(3) 斥　　　´ 厂 斤 斥 斥
　　chì　　scold　　　　　　　　　　5 strokes

(4) 事　　　一 丆 亐 写 写 写 事
　　shì　　matter　　　　　　　　　8 strokes

(5) 步　　　丨 ト ⺊ ⺊ 步 步 步
　　bù　　step　　　　　　　　　　7 strokes
(The ancient character depicts two feet walking.)

(6) 电(電)　　（日+ 乚）

diàn　　electricity　　　　　　　　　5 strokes

(The ancient character depicts lightning.)

(7) 户　　　（丶+尸）

hù　　door　　　　　　　　　　4 strokes

(The ancient character looks like a door with a single leaf.)

(8) 方　　　（丶+万）

fāng　　square　　　　　　　　　4 strokes

(9) 豆　　　一 厂 厂 丏 丏 豆 豆

dòu　　bean　　　　　　　　　　7 strokes

(The ancient character looks like a long-stemmed wine cup.)

(10) 办(辦)　　フ 力 办 办

bàn　　to do　　　　　　　　　4 strokes

(11) 竹　　　丿 丆 丿 亇 牪 竹

zhú　　bamboo　　　　　　　　6 strokes

(The ancient character resembles bamboo leaves.)

(12) 反　　　一 厂 反 反

fǎn　　reverse　　　　　　　　　4 strokes

3. 认写课文中的汉字 Learn and write the Chinese characters appearing in the texts

(1) 姑娘 gūniang

姑 → 女 + 古　　　　　　8 strokes

(The meaning side is "女", and the phonetic side is "古".)

娘 → 女 + 良　　　　　　10 strokes

("女" suggests that the character is connected with females.)

(2) 听说 tīngshuō　（聽说）

听 → 口 + 斤　　　　　　7 strokes

(3) 得 dé

得 → 彳 + 日 + 一 + 寸   11 strokes

(4) 告诉 gàosu （告訴）

告 → 𠂉 + 口   7 strokes

(The meaning side is "口".)

诉 → 讠 + 斥   7 strokes

(The meaning side is "讠". Note how it differs from "斤".)

(5) 件 jiàn

件 → 亻 + 牛   6 strokes

(6) 散步 sànbù

散 → 艹 + 月 + 攵   12 strokes

(7) 电影 diànyǐng （電影）

影 → 日 + 京 + 彡   15 strokes

(8) 咖啡 kāfēi

咖 → 口 + 力 + 口   8 strokes

啡 → 口 + 非   11 strokes

(The meaning side is "口", and the phonetic side is "非".)

(9) 宿舍 sùshè

宿 → 宀 + 亻 + 百   11 strokes

("宀" denotes a house, "百" shows a mat, and "亻" suggests a person.)

舍 → 人 + 舌   8 strokes

("人" denotes a shelter and "舌" indicates the pronunciation.)

(10) 房子 fángzi

房 → 户 + 方   8 strokes

(The meaning is suggested by "户", and the pronunciation is shown by "方".)

(11) 租 zū

租 → 禾 + 且　　　　　　　10 strokes

(12) 厨房 chúfáng（廚房）

厨 → 厂 + 豆 + 寸　　　　12 strokes

(13) 厕所 cèsuǒ（廁所）

厕 → 厂 + 贝 + 刂　　　　8 strokes

所 → 户 + 斤　　　　　　8 strokes

(14) 公司 gōngsī

公 → 八 + 厶　　　　　　4 strokes

(15) 打 dǎ

打 → 扌 + 丁　　　　　　5 strokes

(16) 电话 diànhuà（電話）

话 → 讠 + 舌　　　　　　8 strokes

(Speaking is related to the tongue.)

(17) 让 ràng（讓）

让 → 讠 + 上　　　　　　5 strokes

(18) 帮助 bāngzhù（幫助）

帮 → 邦 + 巾　　　　　　9 strokes

("邦" denotes the pronunciation.)

助 → 且 + 力　　　　　　7 strokes

民　　一 丆 民 民　　　　4 strokes

(19) 喂 wèi

喂 → 口 + 田 + 民　　　　12 strokes

(20) 位 wèi

位 → 亻 + 立　　　　　　　　7 strokes

至　フ ス 3 至 至　　　　　　　　5 strokes

(21) 经理 jīnglǐ（經理）

经 → 纟 + 至　　　　　　　　8 strokes

理 → 王 + 里　　　　　　　　11 strokes

（"里" indicates the pronunciation.）

竹

（zhúzìtóu）(The vertical stroke and the vertical stroke with a hook in "竹" are both written as a dot, when this character is the top of a multi-component character.)

丿 ⺈ 𥫗 𥫗 𥫗 竹　　　　　　　　6 strokes

(22) 等 děng

等 → 竹 + 土 + 寸　　　　　　　　12 strokes

飠　（shízìpáng）丿 ⺈ 飠　　　　　　　　3 strokes

(23) 吃饭 chīfàn（吃飯）

饭 → 饣 + 反　　　　　　　　7 strokes

文化知识　　　Cultural Notes

The Student Dormitory

One of the special features of Chinese universities is that student dormitories are usually integrated into the university campus.　Unlike most Western universities,　where dormitories usually do not meet the housing needs of all students,　in China there is usually a residential area on campus where many staff and faculty live,　and several large dormitories where it is mandatory for students to live.

Many students find living in dormitories convenient.　Since the buildings are on campus and close to classrooms and research facilities,　students may go to class and libraries on foot and save the time required to commute from off campus.　Moreover,　living in dormitories is convenient for socializing, exchanging ideas, and interactive learning.

However,　some students find sharing a room with others inconvenient at times.　For instance,　a dormitory room cannot possibly provide the privacy needed for a date.　In this lesson, Ma Dawei is eager to move out of the dormitory in order to gain some private space.

You have reached the last lesson in this volume! By the end of the lesson, you will know how to 1) make complaints and apologies; 2) send regards on someone else's behalf; 3) ask how a friend is getting along and 4) express greetings at festival times. This lesson also includes a summary and review of the major grammatical points covered in the previous lessons. With this review you will be able to see how many Chinese sentence patterns you have mastered, and evaluate your own progress. Congratulations on your achievements so far!

第十四课 Lesson 14 (复习 Review)

祝 你 圣诞 快乐
Zhù nǐ Shèngdàn kuàilè

一．课文　Text

马　大为： 力波， 上午 十 点 半，你 妈妈 给 你 打 了 一 个
Mǎ Dàwéi： Lìbō, shàngwǔ shí diǎn bàn, nǐ māma gěi nǐ dǎ le yí ge

电话。 我 告诉 她 你 不 在。我 让 她 中午 再
diànhuà. Wǒ gàosu tā nǐ bú zài. Wǒ ràng tā zhōngwǔ zài

给 你 打。
gěi nǐ dǎ.

丁　力波： 谢谢。我 刚才 去 邮局 给 我 妈妈 寄 了 点儿 东西。
Dīng Lìbō： Xièxie. Wǒ gāngcái qù yóujú gěi wǒ māma jì le diǎnr dōngxi.

大为， 我 今天 打扫 了 宿舍，你 的 脏 衣服 太 多 了。
Dàwéi, wǒ jīntiān dǎsǎo le sùshè, nǐ de zāng yīfu tài duō le.

马　大为： 不 好意思。① 这 两 天 我 太 忙 了，我 想
Mǎ Dàwéi： Bù hǎoyìsi.　 Zhè liǎng tiān wǒ tài máng le, wǒ xiǎng

星期六 一起 洗。②
xīngqīliù yìqǐ xǐ.

【抱怨与致歉】
Making a complaint or an apology

（力波的妈妈给他打电话）

马 大为：喂，你好，你找 谁？啊，丁 力波在，请 等
Mǎ Dàwéi： Wèi, nǐ hǎo, nǐ zhǎo shéi? À, Dīng Lìbō zài, qǐng děng

一下。力波，你 妈妈 的 电话。
yíxià. Lìbō, nǐ māma de diànhuà.

丁 力波：谢谢。妈妈，你 好！
Dīng Lìbō： Xièxie. Māma, nǐ hǎo!

丁 云：力波，你 好 吗？
Dīng Yún： Lìbō, nǐ hǎo ma?

丁 力波：我 很 好。你 和爸爸 身体 怎么样？
Dīng Lìbō： Wǒ hěn hǎo. Nǐ hé bàba shēntǐ zěnmeyàng?

丁 云：我 身体 很 好，你爸爸 也 很 好。我们 工作
Dīng Yún： Wǒ shēntǐ hěn hǎo, nǐ bàba yě hěn hǎo. Wǒmen gōngzuò

都 很 忙。你 外婆 身体 好 吗？
dōu hěn máng. Nǐ wàipó shēntǐ hǎo ma?

【转达问候】Passing on someone's regards

丁 力波：她 身体 很 好。她 让 我 问 你们 好。③
Dīng Lìbō： Tā shēntǐ hěn hǎo. Tā ràng wǒ wèn nǐmen hǎo.

丁 云：我们 也 问 她 好。你 哥哥、弟弟 怎么样？
Dīng Yún： Wǒmen yě wèn tā hǎo. Nǐ gēge、dìdi zěnmeyàng?

丁 力波：他们 也 都 很 好。哥哥 现在 在一个 中学
Dīng Lìbō： Tāmen yě dōu hěn hǎo. Gēge xiànzài zài yí ge zhōngxué

打工，弟弟 在 南方 旅行。我们 都 很 想
dǎgōng, dìdi zài nánfāng lǚxíng. Wǒmen dōu hěn xiǎng

你们。
nǐmen.

丁 云：我们 也 想 你们。你 现在 怎么样？你 住 的
Dīng Yún： Wǒmen yě xiǎng nǐmen. Nǐ xiànzài zěnmeyàng? Nǐ zhù de

宿舍 大 不 大？④住 几个 人？
sùshè dà bu dà? Zhù jǐ ge rén?

丁 力波：我们 留学生 楼 两个 人 住 一间。⑤我 跟 一
Dīng Lìbō： Wǒmen liúxuéshēng lóu liǎng ge rén zhù yì jiān. Wǒ gēn yí

个　美国　人　住，他的　　中文　　名字　叫　马　大为。
ge Měiguó rén zhù, tā de Zhōngwén míngzi jiào Mǎ Dàwéi.

丁　　云：他也学习　汉语　吗？
Dīng Yún：Tā yě xuéxí Hànyǔ ma?

丁　力波：对，他也学习　汉语。我还有很多　　中国
Dīng Lìbō：Duì, tā yě xuéxí Hànyǔ. Wǒ hái yǒu hěn duō Zhōngguó

朋友，　他们　　常常　　帮助　我念　生词、复习
péngyou, tāmen chángcháng bāngzhù wǒ niàn shēngcí、fùxí

课文、　练习口语。我还　　常常　　问他们语法
kèwén、liànxí kǒuyǔ. Wǒ hái chángcháng wèn tāmen yǔfǎ

问题，他们都是我的好　朋友。
wèntí, tāmen dōu shì wǒ de hǎo péngyou.

丁　云：这很好。力波，今年你要在　中国　过
Dīng Yún：Zhè hěn hǎo. Lìbō, jīnnián nǐ yào zài Zhōngguó guò

圣诞　　节，不能　回家，我和你爸爸要　送　你
Shèngdàn Jié, bù néng huí jiā, wǒ hé nǐ bàba yào sòng nǐ

一件　圣诞　礼物。
yí jiàn Shèngdàn lǐwù.

丁　力波：谢谢　你们。我也给你们寄了　圣诞　礼物。
Dīng Lìbō：Xièxie nǐmen. Wǒ yě gěi nǐmen jì le Shèngdàn lǐwù.

丁　云：是吗？　圣诞　节我和你爸爸　想　去　欧洲
Dīng Yún：Shì ma? Shèngdàn Jié wǒ hé nǐ bàba xiǎng qù Ōuzhōu

旅行。你呢？你去不去旅行？
lǚxíng. Nǐ ne? Nǐ qù bu qù lǚxíng?

丁　力波：我要去　上海　旅行。
Dīng Lìbō：Wǒ yào qù Shànghǎi lǚxíng.

丁　云：上海　很　漂亮。　祝你旅行　快乐！
Dīng Yún：Shànghǎi hěn piàoliang. Zhù nǐ lǚxíng kuàilè.

【节日祝愿】
Extending holiday greetings

丁　力波：谢谢。我也祝你和爸爸　圣诞　快乐！
Dīng Lìbō：Xièxie. Wǒ yě zhù nǐ hé bàba Shèngdàn kuàilè!

生词 New Words

1.	中午	N	zhōngwǔ	noon	今天中午，明天中午，星期一中午
2.	刚才	Adv	gāngcái	just now	
3.	邮局	N	yóujú	post office	
	邮	V	yóu	to post；to mail	
	局	N	jú	office；bureau	
4.	寄	V	jì	to post, to mail	寄书，寄光盘，寄东西
5.	打扫	V	dǎsǎo	to clean	打扫房子 打扫宿舍
	扫	V	sǎo	to sweep	
6.	脏	A	zāng	dirty	脏衣服
7.	不好意思	IE	bù hǎoyìsi	to feel embarrassed	不好意思说，不好意思去
8.	洗	V	xǐ	to wash	洗衣服，洗手，洗苹果
*9.	外婆	N	wàipó	grandmother on the mother's side	
10.	中学	N	zhōngxué	middle school	中学老师，中学生
11.	打工	V	dǎgōng	to have a part-time job	在中学打工，在哪儿打工
12.	南方	N	nánfāng	south	中国南方，去南方
13.	旅行	V	lǚxíng	to travel	去旅行，去北京旅行，去加拿大旅行
*14.	想	V	xiǎng	to miss；to remember with longing	想妈妈，想家
15.	留学生	N	liúxuéshēng	student studying abroad；international student	
				中国留学生，外国留学生，留学生宿舍	
16.	住	V	zhù	to live；to stay	
17.	楼	N	lóu	building	八号楼，四楼，留学生楼
18.	对	A	duì	right, correct	不对
19.	念	V	niàn	to read	
20.	生词	N	shēngcí	new word	念生词，写生词，学习生词，教生词
	生	A	shēng	new	
	词	N	cí	word	
21.	复习	V	fùxí	to review	复习生词，复习外语，复习汉字
22.	课文	N	kèwén	text	念课文，学习课文，复习课文，教课文
23.	练习	V/N	liànxí	to practice/exercise	练习生词，做练习
	练	V	liàn	to practice	

24. 口语	N	kǒuyǔ	spoken language　练习口语，教口语
25. 语法	N	yǔfǎ	grammar　学习语法，教语法
26. 过	V	guò	to spend (time); to celebrate (a birthday, a holiday) 过圣诞节，过生日
27. 节	N	jié	festival
*28. 礼物	N	lǐwù	present；gift　一件礼物，圣诞礼物，送他礼物
29. 圣诞	PN	Shèngdàn	Christmas　圣诞快乐
30. 欧洲	PN	Ōuzhōu	Europe
*31. 上海	PN	Shànghǎi	Shanghai

补充生词　Supplementary Words

1. 整理	V	zhěnglǐ	to put in order; to arrange; to sort out
2. 电视	N	diànshì	TV
3. 乱	A	luàn	in disorder; in a mess
4. 日记	N	rìjì	diary
5. 晴	A	qíng	sunny
6. 包裹	N	bāoguǒ	parcel
7. 惊喜	N	jīngxǐ	pleasant surprise
8. 圣诞老人	N	Shèngdàn lǎorén	Santa Claus
9. 元旦	N	Yuándàn	New Year's Day
10. 春节	N	Chūn Jié	the Spring Festival
11. 感恩节	N	Gǎn'ēn Jié	Thanksgiving Day
12. 复活节	N	Fùhuó Jié	Easter

二. 注释　Notes

① 不好意思。

"不好意思" originally meant "to feel shy", or "to find it embarrassing to do something". For example：

　　　不好意思说　不好意思问　不好意思吃

At present, this phrase is often used to express apology. For example：
> 不好意思，我的宿舍很脏。
> 让你们等我，真不好意思。

② 这两天我太忙了，我想星期六一起洗。

"I've been very busy during the last few days. I want to wash them all on Saturday."

"这两天" means "during the last few days".

③ 她让我问你们好。

"She asks me to give her greetings to you."

"问 ... + Pr/NP + 好" is a construction used to convey greetings. For example：
> 他问你好。 (He asked me to send you his greetings.)
> (我请你)问他好。 (I would like to ask you to send him my greetings.)

④ 你住的宿舍大不大？

"Is the dormitory you live in big?"

When the subject-verb phrase is used as an attributive, "的" must be placed between the attributive and the head word it modifies. For example：
> 他租的房子怎么样？
> 这是谁给你的书？
> 他常去买东西的商场很大。

⑤ 我们留学生楼两个人住一间。

"Two students live in a dormitory in our international student building."

三. 练习与运用　Drills and practice

KEY SENTENCES
1. 你不在，我让她中午再给你打。
2. 我刚才去邮局给妈妈寄了点儿东西。
3. 她让我问你们好。
4. 我们也问她好。
5. 你住的宿舍大不大？
6. 祝你们圣诞快乐！

1. 熟读下列词组 Master the following phrases

(1) 给你　　给爸爸　　给田医生　　给司机钱　　给他香蕉　　给大为中药

　　给他打了一个电话　　　　给妈妈寄了一件礼物　　给他做了一件事儿

　　给宋华买了一个生日蛋糕　　给陆雨平打了一个电话　　给马大为租了一间房子

(2) 再打一个电话　　再吃一个苹果　　　再洗一件衣服　　　再说一遍(biàn)

(3) 刚才在餐厅　　　刚才在汉语系　　　刚才在留学生楼　　刚才在陆雨平家

　　刚才去了邮局　　刚才打扫了宿舍　　刚才看了外婆　　　刚才看了电影

(4) 他问你好　　杨老师问白小姐好　　外婆问丁云和古波好　　(我)请你问林娜好

(5) 常常去锻炼　　常常回家　　常常去旅行　　常常在家喝咖啡　　常常在一起说汉语

(6) 祝你生日快乐　　祝你旅行快乐　　祝你圣诞快乐　　祝你工作快乐

2. 句型替换 Pattern drills

(1) 刚才丁力波给你来了一个电话。

　　他说什么？

　　他下午再给你打。

你哥哥	让你去邮局
陆雨平	给你租了一间大房子
张教授	请你星期四去一下学院

(2) 你的宿舍太脏了。

　　不好意思。这两天太忙了，我想明天打扫。

衣服	脏	洗
书和本子	多	整理(zhěnglǐ)
厨房	脏	打扫

(3) 爸爸，您身体好吗？

　　我身体很好。你妈妈问你好。

　　我也问她好。

田医生	陈老师
外婆	我姐姐
张教授	林娜

(4) 你每天下午做什么？

　　我每天下午锻炼。

　　晚上呢？

　　晚上复习课文。

上课	做练习
复习语法	写汉字
练习口语	看电视(diànshì)

(5) 他住的宿舍怎么样?

他住的宿舍很大。

租	房子	舒服
买	礼物	漂亮
寄	东西	贵
打工	公司	有名
穿	衣服	漂亮

(6) 今年你在哪儿过圣诞节?

我在北京过圣诞节。

我要送你一件圣诞礼物。祝你圣诞快乐。

元旦	元旦	元旦快乐
春节	春节	春节快乐
感恩节	感恩节	感恩节快乐
复活节	复活节	复活节快乐
生日	生日	生日快乐

3. 完成对话 Complete the following conversation

A：刚才你男朋友来了。你不在,我让他_____。

B：谢谢。我刚才去学院_____。

A：你男朋友今年多大?

B：_____。

A：他在哪儿工作?

B：_____。

A：他家有几口人?

B：_____。

4. 会话练习 Conversation practice

【抱怨与致歉 Making a complaint or an apology】

(1) A：你看一下你的表(biǎo, watch),现在几点?

B：_____,我刚才有点儿事儿,来晚了。

(2) A：今天星期天,我要休息一下。

B：你能不能整理(zhěnglǐ)一下你的书? 你的东西太多。

A：不好意思。我现在_____,我不想今天整理。

B：你想什么时候整理?

A：_____。

【转达问候 Passing on someone's regards】

(1) A：张先生，你好吗？

B：我＿＿＿＿＿＿＿＿＿＿＿，你爸爸妈妈身体怎么样？

A：他们＿＿＿＿＿＿＿＿＿＿。

B：你爸爸妈妈今年多大岁数？

A：我爸爸今年＿＿＿＿＿＿＿＿＿，妈妈＿＿＿＿＿＿＿＿。

B：请你问他们好。

A：谢谢。

(2) A：雨平，你怎么样？工作忙不忙？

B：我＿＿＿＿＿＿＿＿＿＿，你呢？

A：我现在在＿＿＿＿＿＿＿＿学习法语，也很忙。

B：你女朋友好吗？

A：她很好。她让我问你好。

B：谢谢。请你也＿＿＿＿＿＿＿＿。

【节日祝愿 Extending holiday greetings】

(1) A：今天是元旦(Yuándàn)，祝你＿＿＿＿＿＿＿＿＿＿＿。

B：我也＿＿＿＿＿＿＿＿＿＿。

A：我有一件礼物给你。

B：啊，是＿＿＿＿＿＿＿＿。谢谢你。

(2) A：喂，哪一位啊？

B：我是＿＿＿＿＿＿＿＿。

A：是＿＿＿＿＿＿＿啊！你好吗？

B：＿＿＿＿＿＿。今天是你的＿＿＿＿＿生日，我要祝你＿＿＿＿＿＿＿。

A：谢谢。你的生日是哪天？

B：明天是我的生日。

A：我也祝你生日快乐。

【建议与邀请 Suggestions and invitations】

(1) A：明天你有时间吗？

　　B：明天我有时间。什么事儿？

　　A：我们去游泳(yóuyǒng)，好吗？

　　B：太好了！几点去？

　　A：_____。

(2) A：星期五你忙不忙？

　　B：不太忙。什么事儿？

　　A：我们有个聚会，你能不能参加？

　　B：很抱歉(bàoqiàn)，_____。

5. 交际练习 Communication exercises

(1) Your new roommate moved in yesterday. Today you returned to the dormitory to find everything in a mess, including the kitchen and the bathroom. While you are complaining, your roommate apologizes over and over.

(2) You come across an old classmate whom you haven't seen for a long time. You ask how he/she is doing, and then ask him/her to give your regards to his/her family.

(3) On Christmas Eve, you and your friends are extending holiday greetings and wishes to one another. One of them mentions that it is his/her eighteenth birthday, so everyone wishes him/her a happy birthday.

丁力波的日记

12月18日　　　星期五　　　天气　晴(qíng)

下星期五是圣诞节。这是我第一次(dì yī cì, the first time)在中国过圣诞节。我要跟小云一起去上海旅行。现在中国年轻(niánqīng, young)人也很喜欢过圣诞节。很多商场都有圣诞老人(lǎorén, old man)。商场东西很多,买东西的人也很多。

上午十点,我去邮局给爸爸妈妈寄了一个包裹(bāoguǒ),是十张京剧光盘。爸爸很喜欢京剧,妈妈也喜欢,我想给他们一个惊喜(jīngxǐ)。我很想家,也想加拿大。

上午十点半,妈妈给我打了一个电话。我不在,大为让妈妈中午再给我打。

中午我接到(jiēdào, to receive)了妈妈的电话。我真高兴。爸爸妈妈身体都很好,他们工作都很忙。妈妈让我问外婆好。我告诉她哥哥弟弟也都很好,哥哥在中学打工,教英语;弟弟在南方旅行。我还给她介绍了我的好朋友马大为。爸爸妈妈圣诞节要去欧洲旅行,我祝他们旅行快乐。

爸爸妈妈也给我寄了一件圣诞礼物,我不知道那是什么礼物。

五. 语法　　　　　Grammar

1. 四种汉语句子 Four kinds of simple sentences

Simple Chinese sentences can be divided into four kinds according to the elements, which comprise the main part of their predicates.

(1)动词谓语句 Sentences with a verbal predicate

The majority of Chinese sentences have a verbal predicate and are relatively complex. Several types have already been studied and more examples will be introduced in later lessons. For example：

林娜的男朋友是医生。

他有一个姐姐。

我们学习汉语。

她回学院上课。

我们请他吃饭。

(2) 形容词谓语句 Sentences with an adjectival predicate

In a sentence with an adjectival predicate "是" is not needed. For example：

我很好。

他这两天太忙。

(3) 名词谓语句 Sentences with a nominal predicate

In a sentence with a nominal predicate, nouns, noun phrases, or numeral–measure words function directly as the main elements of the predicate, which especially describe age or price. In spoken language, it is also used to express time, birthplace, and so on. For example：

马大为二十二岁。

一斤苹果两块五。

现在八点半。

今天星期天。

宋华北京人。

(4) 主谓谓语句 Sentences with a subject-predicate phrase as predicate

In a sentence with a subject-predicate phrase as predicate, the thing denoted by the subject of the subject-predicate phrase is usually a part of the thing denoted by the subject of the whole sentence. The subject-predicate phrase describes or explains the subject of the whole sentence. For example：

你身体怎么样？

我头疼。

他学习很好。

2. 六种提问方法 Six question types

(1) 用"吗"提问 Questions with "吗"

This is the most commonly used type of question. The person who asks this kind of question has some idea concerning the answer. For example：

您是张教授吗？

你现在很忙吗？

明天你不来学院吗？

(2) 正反疑问句 V/A-not-V/A question

This type of question is also frequently used. The person who asks this kind of question has no idea concerning the answer. For example：

你朋友认识不认识他？

你们学院大不大？

你有没有弟弟？

他去没去那个公司？

(3) 用疑问代词的问句 Questions with an interrogative pronoun

By using "谁"，"什么"，"哪"，"哪儿"，"怎么"，"怎么样"，"多少" and "几"，this type of question specifically asks who, what, which, where, how, how about, or how many. For example：

今天几号？

他是哪国人？

他的房子怎么样？

(4) 用"还是"的选择问句 Alternative questions with "还是"

There are two （or more） possibilities in this type of question for the person addressed to choose from. For example：

他是英国人还是美国人？

我们上午去还是下午去？

你喜欢香蕉还是喜欢苹果？

(5) 用"好吗？"(或"是不是？"、"是吗？"、"可以吗？")的问句 Tag questions with "好吗？"，"是不是？"，"是吗？" or "可以吗？"

Questions with "好吗？" or "可以吗？" are usually used to ask someone's opinion concerning the suggestion put forward in the first part of the sentence. Questions with "是不是？" or "是吗？" are usually used to confirm the judgement made in the first part of the sentence. For example：

我们去锻炼，好吗？

您学习汉语，是不是？

(6) 用"呢"的省略式问句 Elliptical questions with the question particle "呢"

The meaning of this type of question is usually illustrated clearly by the previous sentence. For example:

我很好，你呢？

他上午没有课，你呢？

六. 汉字　　Chinese Characters

1. 音序查字法 Consulting a Chinese dictionary arranged by *pinyin* alphabetic order

In many Chinese dictionaries the entries are arranged alphabetically according to Chinese Phonetics (*Hanyu pinyin*). Characters with the same *pinyin* spelling are put under the same entry and then sub-divided according to their tones. Characters in the same tone group are arranged in order, according to their number of strokes. When the pronunciation of a character is known, characters are easy to find in this type of dictionary.

2. 认写基本汉字 Learn and write basic Chinese characters

(1) 才　　一十才

　　cái　　just　　　　　　　　　　　3 strokes

(2) 由　　丨冂曰由由

　　yóu　　by　　　　　　　　　　　5 strokes

(3) 州　　丶丿⺊州州州

　　zhōu　　state　　　　　　　　　　6 strokes

("川" is a drawing of a river and the three dots "、" show its islets.)

3. 认写课文中的汉字 Learn and write the Chinese characters appearing in the texts

又 (jiànzhīpáng) (the "construction" side)　乛又　　2 strokes

(1) 圣诞 Shèngdàn (聖誕)

圣 → 又 + 土　　　　　　　　　　5 strokes

诞 → 讠 + 止 + 又　　　　　　　8 strokes

(2) 刚才 gāngcái (剛纔)

刚 → 冈 + 刂　　　　　　　　　　6 strokes

(The pronunciation is indicated by "冈".)

(3) 邮局 yóujú (郵局)

邮 → 由 + 阝　　　　　　　　　　7 strokes

(The pronunciation is shown by "由".)

局 → 尸 ＋ 司　　　　　7 strokes

(4) 寄 jì

寄 → 宀 ＋ 大 ＋ 可　　　11 strokes

(5) 打扫 dǎsǎo （打掃）

扫 → 扌 ＋ 彐　　　　6 strokes

(The meaning is indicated by "扌".)

(6) 脏 zāng （髒）

脏 → 月 ＋ 广 ＋ 土　　　10 strokes

(7) 洗 xǐ

洗 → 氵 ＋ 先　　　　9 strokes

(8) 外婆 wàipó

婆 → 波 ＋ 女　　　　11 strokes

(The meaning is suggested by "女".)

羊　　　丶 丷 丷 兰 羊　　　5 strokes

(9) 南方 nánfāng

南 → 十 ＋ 冂 ＋ 羊　　　9 strokes

𠂉 (lǚzìbiān) (the "travel" side)　　丿 𠂉 𠂉 𠂉　　4 strokes

丁 chù　　丶 二 丁　　　3 strokes

(10) 旅行 lǚxíng

旅 → 方 ＋ 𠂉 ＋ 𠂉　　　10 strokes

行 → 彳 ＋ 丁　　　　6 strokes

𠃊 (liúzìjiǎo) (the "keeping" corner)　　丿 𠃊 𠃊　　3 strokes

(11) 留学生 liúxuéshēng （留學生）

留 → 𠃊 ＋ 刀 ＋ 田　　　10 strokes

(12) 念 niàn （唸）

念 → 今 ＋ 心　　　　　　　　8 strokes

(13) 生词 shēngcí （生詞）

词 → 讠 ＋ 司　　　　　　　　7 strokes

（The meaning side is "讠".)

(14) 复习 fùxí （複習）

复 → 𠂉 ＋ 日 ＋ 夂　　　　　9 strokes

(15) 练习 liànxí （練習）

练 → 纟 ＋ 东　　　　　　　　8 strokes

(16) 语法 yǔfǎ （語法）

法 → 氵 ＋ 去　　　　　　　　8 strokes

(17) 节 jié （節）

节 → 艹 ＋ 卩　　　　　　　　5 strokes

牛 (niúzìpáng)(the "ox" side) (On the left side of a multi-component character, "牛" is written as "牜".) 丿 一 牜 牛　　　4 strokes

(18) 礼物 lǐwù （禮物）

礼 → 礻 ＋ し　　　　　　　　5 strokes

物 → 牜 ＋ 勿　　　　　　　　8 strokes

（The pronunciation is indicated by "勿".)

(19) 欧洲 Ōuzhōu （歐洲）

欧 → 区 ＋ 欠　　　　　　　　8 strokes

洲 → 氵 ＋ 州　　　　　　　　9 strokes

（The meaning side is "氵", and the phonetic side is "州". The character "洲" means an islet in a river or a continent in the ocean.)

(20) 上海 Shànghǎi

海 → 氵 ＋ 每　　　　　　　　10 strokes

Beijing, Shanghai, the Changjiang River, the Huanghe River, and the Great Wall

Beijing is the capital of the People's Republic of China as well as its chief cultural and politctial centre. As the capital city for much of the last eight hundred years, Beijing is rich in historic sites, including the Forbidden City (Palace Museum), the Summer Palace, and the Temple of Heaven. Modern Beijing is fast becoming a cosmopolitan city as its economy continues to develop.

Shanghai is one of the biggest city in terms of population and the largest economic centre in China.

The Changjiang, literally, the "Long River", is commonly known as the Yangtze River in English. It is the longest river in China and one of the longest in the world. From its origin in western China, it stretches 6,300 kilometres to where it enters the East China Sea near Shanghai on the east coast.

The Huanghe, or literally "Yellow River", is the second longest river in China, flowing a total of 5,464 kilometres. The Huanghe River valley is considered by many to be the cradle of ancient Chinese civilization.

Construction of the Great Wall began more than 2,200 years ago. It ranks among the seven architectural wonders of the ancient world and is the only cultural artifact on the earth visible from outer space with the naked eye. The present Great Wall extends more than 2,500 kilometres, but there are actually over six thousand kilometres of walls, since there are numerous stretches where several walls run parallel to each other. Six thousand kilometres are more than twelve thousand *li*, so the Great Wall is often referred to as the *wanli changcheng* or the "Long Wall of Ten Thousand *Li*".

Map of China

乌鲁木齐

北京
黄河
天津

上海

拉萨
长江
重庆

福州
台北

广州
香港
澳门

生 词 索 引（简繁对照）
Vocabulary Index
（Simplified Script with Traditional Version）

词条	繁体	词性	拼音	英译	课号

A

| 啊 | | (Int) | à | ah, oh | 7 |
| 爱 | 愛 | (V) | ài | to love | 8 |

B

吧		(MdPt)	ba	(modal particle)	12
爸爸		(N)	bàba	dad	2,7
拜拜		(IE)	báibái	bye-bye(transliteration)	11
百		(Nu)	bǎi	hundred	8
办	辦	(V)	bàn	to do	13
半		(Nu)	bàn	half	11
帮助	幫助	(V)	bāngzhù	to help	13
报		(N)	bào	newspaper	10
抱歉		(A)	bàoqiàn	to feel sorry/sorry	6
北京		(PN)	Běijīng	Beijing	9
贝贝	貝貝	(PN)	Bèibei	(name of a dog)	8
本子		(N)	běnzi	notebook	10
遍		(M)	biàn	number of times (of action)	6
病		(N/V)	bìng	illness/to get sick	12
不		(Adv)	bù	not; no	2
不好意思		(IE)	bù hǎoyìsi	to feel embarrassed	14
不用		(Adv)	búyòng	need not	5
步		(N)	bù	step	13

C

参加	參加	(V)	cānjiā	to participate; to attend	9
餐厅	餐廳	(N)	cāntīng	dining room	5
厕所	廁所	(N)	cèsuǒ	toilet	13
层	層	(M)	céng	story; floor	5

差		(V)	chà	to be short of, lack	11
常常		(Adv)	chángcháng	often	10
常		(Adv)	cháng	often	10
陈	陳	(PN)	Chén	(a surname)	3,11
吃	吃	(V)	chī	to eat	9
吃饭	吃飯	(VO)	chīfàn	to eat (a meal)	13
出		(V)	chū	to go out; to come out	9
出生		(V)	chūshēng	to be born	9
厨房	廚房	(N)	chúfáng	kitchen	13
穿		(V)	chuān	to wear	12
床	牀	(N)	chuáng	bed	11
词	詞	(V)	cí	word	14

D

打		(V)	dǎ	to play	6
打电话	打電話	(V O)	dǎ diànhuà	to make a phone call	13
打工		(V)	dǎgōng	to have a part-time job	14
打球		(V O)	dǎ qiú	to play ball	6,11
打扫	打掃	(V)	dǎsǎo	to clean	14
大		(A)	dà	big, large	8,9
蛋		(N)	dàn	egg	9
蛋糕		(N)	dàngāo	cake	9
当然	當然	(Adv)	dāngrán	as it should be; only natural that	8
到		(V)	dào	to arrive	11
得		(V)	dé	to have, to get	13
的		(Pt)	de	(a possessive or modifying particle)	4
等		(V)	děng	to wait	13
弟弟		(N)	dìdi	younger brother	2,8
点(钟)	點(鐘)	(M)	diǎn(zhōng)	o'clock	11
电	電	(N)	diàn	electricity	13
电话	電話	(N)	diànhuà	telephone; phone call	13
电影	電影	(N)	diànyǐng	movie	13
丁		(PN)	Dīng	(a surname)	2
丁力波		(PN)	Dīng Lìbō	(name of a Canadian student)	7
东西	東西	(N)	dōngxi	things; objects	11

都		(Adv)	dōu	both; all	2,3
锻炼	鍛煉	(V)	duànliàn	to do physical exercise	12
对	對	(A)	duì	right, correct	14
对不起	對不起	(IE)	duìbuqǐ	I'm sorry	5,10
多		(A)	duō	many, much	8
多		(Adv)	duō	how	9
多大		(IE)	duō dà	how old	9
多少		(QPr)	duōshao	how many, how much	8

E

二		(Nu)	èr	two	5

F

发烧	發燒	(VO)	fāshāo	to have a fever	12
发炎	發炎	(VO)	fāyán	to become inflamed	12
饭	飯	(N)	fàn	meal	13
房子		(N)	fángzi	house	13
房租		(N)	fángzū	rent (for a house, flat, etc)	13
分		(M)	fēn	minute	11
分(钱)	分(錢)	(M)	fēn(qián)	(measure word of Chinese monetary unit, equal to 1/100 块);cent	10
复习	復習	(V)	fùxí	to review	14

G

该	該	(Opv)	gāi	should; ought to	11
感冒		(V/N)	gǎnmào	to have a cold/cold	12
刚才	剛纔	(Adv)	gāngcái	just now	14
高		(A)	gāo	high; tall	7
高兴	高興	(A)	gāoxìng	happy; pleased	4,7
糕		(N)	gāo	cake	9
告诉	告訴	(V)	gàosu	to tell	13
哥哥		(N)	gēge	elder brother	2
个	個	(M)	gè	(a measure word for general use)	8
给	給	(V)	gěi	to give	10
给	給	(Prep)	gěi	to; for	12
跟		(Prep/V)	gēn	with/to follow	10

工作		(V/N)	gōngzuò	to work/work	8
公司		(N)	gōngsī	company	13
狗		(N)	gǒu	dog	8
姑娘		(N)	gūniang	girl	13
挂号	掛號	(V)	guàhào	to register (at a hospital, etc.)	12
光盘	光盤	(N)	guāngpán	CD	10
贵	貴	(A)	guì	expensive, precious	10
贵姓	貴姓	(IE)	guì xìng	what's your honorable sur- name?	4
国	國	(N)	guó	country, nation	3
过	過	(V)	guò	to spend (time) ; to cele- brate (a birthday, a holi- day)	14

H

还	還	(Adv)	hái	in addition	8,11
还是	還是	(Conj)	háishi	or	12
汉语	漢語	(N)	Hànyǔ	Chinese (language)	4
汉字	漢字	(N)	Hànzì	Chinese character	11
好		(A)	hǎo	good; well; fine; O. K.	1,5
号	號	(N)	hào	number	5,9
喝		(V)	hē	to drink	2,9
和		(Conj)	hé	and	8
很		(Adv)	hěn	very	1,7
红	紅	(A)	hóng	very	9
红葡萄酒	紅葡萄酒	(N)	hóng pútaojiǔ	red wine	9
回		(V)	huí	to return	11
会	會	(N)	huì	meeting	9
会	會	(OpV)	huì	to know how to, can	11

J

几	幾	(QPr)	jǐ	how many, how much	8
记者	記者	(N)	jìzhě	reporter	4
寄		(V)	jì	to post, to mail	14
加拿大		(PN)	Jiānádà	Canada	4,7
家		(N)	jiā	family, home	8
家美		(PN)	Jiāměi	(name of a house rental a- gency)	13

间	間	(M)	jiān	(a measure word for room, house, etc)	13
件		(M)	jiàn	(a measure word) piece	13
叫		(V)	jiào	to be called	4
教		(V)	jiāo	to teach	7
教授		(N)	jiàoshòu	professor	7
节	節	(N)	jié	festival	14
姐姐		(N)	jiějie	elder sister	8
介绍	介紹	(V)	jièshào	to introduce	7
斤		(M)	jīn	(measure word of weight, equal to 500g)	10
今年		(N)	jīnnián	this year	9
今天		(N)	jīntiān	today	6,9
进	進	(V)	jìn	to enter	4,5
进来	進來	(VC)	jìnlai	to come in	4
京剧	京劇	(N)	jīngjù	Beijing opera	6
经理	經理	(N)	jīnglǐ	manager	13
酒		(N)	jiǔ	wine or liquor	9
局		(N)	jú	office; bureau	14
聚会	聚會	(N)	jùhuì	get-together; party	9

K

咖啡		(N)	kāfēi	coffee	2,13
开	開	(V)	kāi	to open, to start	7
开学	開學	(VO)	kāixué	to start school	7
看		(V)	kàn	to watch, to look at	7
看病		(VO)	kànbìng	to see a doctor	12
烤鸭	烤鴨	(N)	kǎoyā	roast duck	9
可爱	可愛	(A)	kě'ài	lovely, cute	8
可能		(OpV)	kěnéng	maybe	13
可是		(Conj)	kěshì	but	13
可以		(OpV)	kěyǐ	may	4,11
刻		(M)	kè	quarter (of an hour)	11
课	課	(N)	kè	class; lesson	9
课文	課文	(N)	kèwén	text	14
恐怕		(Adv)	kǒngpà	to be afraid that; perhaps	6
口		(M)	kǒu	(a measure word mainly for the number of people in a family)	8

口语	口語	(N)	kǒuyǔ	spoken language	14
块(钱)	塊(錢)	(M)	kuài(qián)	(measure word of basic Chinese monetary unit, equal to 10 毛); dollar	10
快乐	快樂	(A)	kuàilè	happy	9

L

来	來	(V)	lái	to come	4,7
老师	老師	(N)	lǎoshī	teacher	3
了		(Pt)	le	(modal partical/aspect partical)	5,9
冷		(A)	lěng	cold	12
礼物	禮物	(N)	lǐwù	gift; present	11,14
力波		(PN)	Lìbō	(name of a Canadian student)	1
练	練	(V)	liàn	to practice	14
练习	練習	(V/N)	liànxí	to practice/exercise	14
梁祝		(PN)	Liáng Zhù	(name of a Chinese violin concerto)	10
两		(Nu)	liǎng	two	8
林娜		(PN)	Lín Nà	(name of a British student)	1
〇		(Nu)	líng	zero	5
留学生	留學生	(N)	liúxuéshēng	student studying abroad; international student	14
楼	樓	(N)	lóu	building	14
陆雨平	陸雨平	(PN)	Lù Yǔpíng	(name of a Chinese reporter)	1
旅行		(V)	lǚxíng	to travel	14

M

妈妈	媽媽	(N)	māma	mom	2
马大为	馬大爲	(PN)	Mǎ Dàwéi	(name of an American student)	4,7
吗	嗎	(QPt)	ma	(Interrogative particle for question expecting yes-no answer)	1,2
买	買	(V)	mǎi	to buy	9
忙		(A)	máng	busy	2,6
毛(钱)	毛(錢)	(M)	máo(qián)	(measure word of Chinese monetary unit, equal to 1/10 块); dime	10

没		(Adv)	méi	not	8
没关系	没關係	(IE)	méi guānxi	never mind; it doesn't matter	5
每		(Pr)	měi	every; each	12
美		(A)	měi	beautiful	7
美国	美國	(PN)	Měiguó	the United States; America	4,7
美术	美術	(N)	měishù	fine arts	7
妹妹		(N)	mèimei	younger sister	8
们	們	(Suf)	men	(used after pronouns 我，们，他 or certain nouns to denote plural)	2,3
面	麵	(N)	miàn	noodles	9
名片		(N)	míngpiàn	calling card	7
名字		(N)	míngzi	name	7
明天		(N)	míngtiān	tomorrow	6

N

哪		(QPr)	nǎ	which	3
哪儿	哪兒	(QPr)	nǎr	where	5
哪里	哪裏	(IE)	nǎli	no (an expression of modest denial)	11
那		(Pr)	nà	that	3
那儿	那兒	(Pr)	nàr	there	10
奶奶		(N)	nǎinai	grandmother on the father's side	3
男		(A)	nán	male	2,8
南方		(N)	nánfāng	south	14
呢		(MdPt)	ne	(a modal particle used for elliptical questions)	1,2
能		(OpV)	néng	can; be able to	11
你		(Pr)	nǐ	you	1,3
你们	你們	(Pr)	nǐmen	you(pl.)	6
年		(N)	nián	year	9
念	唸	(V)	niàn	to read	14
您		(Pr)	nín	you (polite form)	3,4
女		(A)	nǚ	female	5
女儿		(N)	nǚ'ér	daughter	11

O

| 欧洲 | 歐洲 | (PN) | Ōuzhōu | Europe | 14 |

P

朋友		(N)	péngyou	friend	2,4
漂亮		(A)	piàoliang	pretty, beautiful; nice	9
瓶		(M)	píng	bottle	9
苹果	蘋果	(N)	píngguǒ	apple	10
葡萄		(N)	pútao	grape	10

Q

起	起	(V)	qǐ	to get up, to rise	11
起床	起牀	(VO)	qǐchuáng	to get up	11
钱	錢	(N)	qián	money	10
请	請	(V)	qǐng	please	4
请问	請問	(V)	qǐngwèn	May I ask...?	4,5
球		(N)	qiú	ball	6
去		(V)	qù	to go	6
全		(A)	quán	whole	12
全身		(N)	quánshēn	all over (the body)	12

R

让	讓	(V)	ràng	to let; to allow; to make	13
人		(N)	rén	people, person	3
认识	認識	(V)	rènshi	to know (somebody)	4
容易		(A)	róngyì	easy	10

S

散步		(VO)	sànbù	to take a walk; to walk	13
嗓子		(N)	sǎngzi	throat	12
扫		(V)	sǎo	to sweep	14
商		(N)	shāng	trade; commerce	10
商场	商場	(N)	shāngchǎng	market; bazaar; shopping mall	10
上		(N)	shàng	above; last	9
上		(V)	shàng	to ascend; to go to	11
上海		(PN)	Shànghǎi	Shanghai	14
上课	上課	(VO)	shàngkè	to go to class (both students and teachers)	11
上午		(N)	shàngwǔ	morning	9
烧	燒	(V)	shāo	to burn	12

谁	誰	(QPr)	shéi	who; whom	3,7
身		(N)	shēn	body	12
身体	身體	(N)	shēntǐ	body, health	12
什么	甚麼	(QPr)	shénme	what	4,6
生		(A)	shēng	new	14
生词	生詞	(N)	shēngcí	new word	14
生日		(N)	shēngri	birthday	9
圣诞	聖誕	(PN)	Shèngdàn	Christmas	14
师傅	師傅	(N)	shīfu	master worker	10
时候	時候	(N)	shíhou	time; moment	6
时间	時間	(N)	shíjiān	time	6
事儿	事兒	(N)	shìr	matter; affair; thing	13
是		(V)	shì	to be	3
寿面	壽麵	(N)	shòumiàn	(birthday) longevity noodles	9
书	書	(N)	shū	book	10
舒服		(A)	shūfu	comfortable	12
属	屬	(V)	shǔ	to be born in the year of	9
数	數	(N)	shù	number	11
水		(N)	shuǐ	water	12
睡		(V)	shuì	to sleep	11
睡觉	睡覺	(VO)	shuìjiào	to sleep	11
说	說	(V)	shuō	to say; to speak	6
司机	司機	(N)	sījī	driver	11
四		(Nu)	sì	four	5
宋华	宋華	(PN)	Sòng Huá	(name of a Chinese student)	5,9
送		(N)	sòng	to give (as a present)	10
宿舍		(N)	sùshè	dormitory	5,13
岁	歲	(M)	suì	year (of age)	9
岁数	歲數	(N)	suìshu	years (of age)	11
孙女儿	孫女兒	(N)	sūnnǔr	granddaughter on son's side	11

T

他		(Pr)	tā	he; him	2,3
他们	他們	(Pr)	tāmen	they; them	2,3
她		(Pr)	tā	she; her	3
太		(Adv)	tài	too; extremely	6
疼		(A)	téng	painful	12

天		(N)	tiān	day	6
天气	天氣	(N)	tiānqì	weather	6
听	聽	(V)	tīng	to listen	13
听说	聽説	(V)	tīngshuō	to be told	13
头	頭	(N)	tóu	head	12

W

外		(N)	wài	outside	8
外国	外國	(N)	wàiguó	foreign country	8
外婆		(N)	wàipó	grandmother on the mother's side	3,14
外语	外語	(N)	wàiyǔ	foreign language	3,8
玩儿	玩兒	(V)	wánr	to have fun, to play	11
晚		(A)	wǎn	late	5,11
晚上		(N)	wǎnshang	evening, night	11
王小云	王小雲	(PN)	Wáng Xiǎoyún	(name of a Chinese student)	5,8
为	爲	(Prep)	wèi	for	11
为什么	爲甚麽	(Qpr)	wèishénme	why	11
位		(M)	wèi	(a polite measure word for person)	13
喂		(Int)	wèi	hello; hey	13
文学	文學	(N)	wénxué	literature	7
问	問	(V)	wèn	to ask	4,7
问题	問題	(N)	wèntí	question	11
我		(Pr)	wǒ	I; me	1,5
我们	我們	(Pr)	wǒmen	we; us	2

X

西		(N)	xī	west	12
西药	西藥	(N)	xīyào	Western medicine	12
洗		(V)	xǐ	to wash	14
喜欢	喜歡	(V)	xǐhuan	to like, to prefer	8
系		(N)	xì	faculty; department	7
下		(N)	xià	below; next	9
下午		(N)	xiàwǔ	afternoon	9
先生		(N)	xiānsheng	Mr.	4,10
现在	現在	(N)	xiànzài	now	6
香蕉苹果	香蕉蘋果	(N)	xiāngjiāopíngguǒ	apple with a banana taste	10

香蕉		(N)	xiāngjiāo	banana	10
想		(V/OpV)	xiǎng	to think; to miss/to want to do sth.	12,14
小		(A)	xiǎo	little, small	8
小姐		(N)	xiǎojiě	Miss; young lady	5
写	寫	(V)	xiě	to write	11
谢谢	謝謝	(V)	xièxie	to thank	5,6
星期		(N)	xīngqī	week	9
星期日		(N)	xīngqīrì	Sunday	9
行		(V)	xíng	to be O. K.	6
姓		(V/N)	xìng	one's surname is.../surname	4
休息		(V)	xiūxi	to take a rest	12
学	學	(V)	xué	to learn, to study	7
学生	學生	(N)	xuésheng	student	4,5
学习	學習	(V)	xuéxí	to learn; to study	4,7
学院	學院	(N)	xuéyuàn	institute; college	4,7

Y

鸭	鴨	(N)	Yā	duck	9
杨	楊	(PN)	Yáng	(a surname)	4
药	藥	(N)	yào	medicine	12
要		(V)	yào	to want/must; to want to do sth.	2,10
要		(OpV)	yào	must, to want to do something	12
也		(Adv)	yě	too; also	1
(一)点儿	(一)點兒	(Nu-M)	(yì)diǎnr	a little bit	11
一共		(Adv)	yígòng	altogether	8
一起		(Adv)	yìqǐ	together	12
一下			yíxià	(used after a verb to indicate a short, quick, random, informal action)	7
衣服		(N)	yīfu	clothes	12
医生	醫生	(N)	yīshēng	doctor; physician	3
医院	醫院	(N)	yīyuàn	hospital	12
音乐	音樂	(N)	yīnyuè	music	7,10
应该	應該	(OpV)	yīnggāi	should; ought to	11
英国	英國	(PN)	Yīngguó	Great Britain; England	4
英语	英語	(N)	Yīngyǔ	English	11

影		(N)	yǐng	shadow	13
邮	郵	(V)	yóu	to post; to mail	14
邮局	郵局	(N)	yóujú	post office	14
游泳		(VO)	yóuyǒng	to swim	6
有		(V)	yǒu	to have	6
有点儿	有點兒	(Adv)	yǒudiǎnr	somewhat; rather; a bit	12
有名		(A)	yǒumíng	famous	10
有意思		(IE)	yǒu yìsi	interesting	6
语法	語法	(N)	yǔfǎ	grammar	14
语言	語言	(N)	yǔyán	language	4
愿意	願意	(OpV)	yuànyì	to be willing to do sth.	12

Z

再		(Adv)	zài	again	5,9
再见	再見	(IE)	zàijiàn	good-bye	5
在		(V)	zài	to be (here, there); to be (in, on, at)	5
在		(Prep)	zài	at; in; on	10
脏	髒	(A)	zāng	dirty	14
怎么	怎麼	(QPr)	zěnme	how	10
怎么样	怎麼樣	(QPr)	zěnmeyàng	how is it?	6,9
张	張	(PN)	Zhāng	(a surname)	7
张	張	(M)	zhāng	(a measure word for flat objects)	8
找		(V)	zhǎo	to look for	13
找(钱)	找(錢)	(V)	zhǎo(qián)	to give change	10
照片		(N)	zhàopiàn	picture, photo	8
这	這	(Pr)	zhè	this	3,5
这儿	這兒	(Pr)	zhèr	here	5
真	真	(A/Adv)	zhēn	real/really	8
知道		(V)	zhīdao	to know	5
中国	中國	(PN)	Zhōngguó	China	3
中文		(N)	Zhōngwén	Chinese	7
中午		(N)	zhōngwǔ	noon	14
中学	中學	(N)	zhōngxué	middle school	14
中药	中藥	(N)	zhōngyào	traditional Chinese medicine	12
住		(V)	zhù	to live; to stay	14
住院		(VO)	zhùyuàn	to be in hospital; to be hospitalized	12

祝		(V)	zhù	to wish	9
祝贺	祝賀	(V)	zhùhè	to congratulate	9
专业	專業	(N)	zhuānyè	major; specialty	7
字		(N)	zì	character	11
租		(V)	zū	to rent	13
昨天		(N)	zuótiān	yesterday	6,11
坐		(V)	zuò	to sit	5
做		(V)	zuò	to do; to make	8,10

补充词汇
Supplementary Words

词条	繁体	词性	拼音	英译	课号

B

词条	繁体	词性	拼音	英译	课号
包裹		(N)	bāoguǒ	parcel	14
包括		(V)	bāokuò	to include	13
杯	盃	(M)	bēi	cup of	10
本		(M)	běn	(measure word for books and notebooks)	10
笔	筆	(N)	bǐ	pen	10
表	錶	(N)	biǎo	watch	11

C

词条	繁体	词性	拼音	英译	课号
茶		(N)	chá	tea	9
唱歌		(VO)	chànggē	to sing (a song)	11
车	車	(N)	chē	car; vehicle	8
吃饭	吃飯	(VO)	chīfàn	to eat (a meal)	11
春节	春節	(PN)	Chūn Jié	the Spring Festival	14
词典	詞典	(N)	cídiǎn	dictionary	8

D

词条	繁体	词性	拼音	英译	课号
打的		(VO)	dǎdī	to take a taxi	11
打针	打針	(VO)	dǎzhēn	to have an injection	12
大便		(N)	dàbiàn	stool	12
电脑	電腦	(N)	diànnǎo	computer	8
电视	電視	(N)	diànshì	TV	14
肚子		(N)	dùzi	abdomen; stomach	12

F

词条	繁体	词性	拼音	英译	课号
方便		(A)	fāngbiàn	convenient	13
份	——	(M)	fèn	(measure word for publications such as newspapers)	10
复活节	復活節	(PN)	Fùhuó Jié	Easter	14

G

| 感恩节 | 感恩節 | (PN) | Gǎn'ēn Jié | Thanksgiving Day | 14 |
| 工程师 | 工程師 | (N) | gōngchéngshī | engineer | 8 |

H

孩子		(N)	háizi	child	8
汉堡	漢堡	(N)	hànbǎo	hamburger	9
合适	合適	(A)	héshì	suitable	13
化学	化學	(N)	huàxué	chemistry	7
化验	化驗	(V)	huàyàn	to have a medical test	12
回答		(V)	huídá	to answer	11
回信		(N/VO)	huíxìn	reply/to reply	13

J

教育		(N)	jiàoyù	education	7
经济	經濟	(N)	jīngjì	economy	7
惊喜	驚喜	(N)	jīngxǐ	pleasant surprise	14

K

开车	開車	(VO)	kāichē	to drive a car	11
开刀	開刀	(VO)	kāidāo	to have an operation	12
可乐	可樂	(N)	kělè	coke	9
客厅	客廳	(N)	kètīng	living room	13

L

礼物	禮物	(N)	lǐwù	gift; present	11
历史	歷史	(N)	lìshǐ	history	7
凉快	涼快	(A)	liángkuai	cool	12
律师	律師	(N)	lǜshī	lawyer	8
乱	亂	(A)	luàn	in disorder; in a mess	14

M

卖	賣	(V)	mài	to sell	10
米饭	米飯	(N)	mǐfàn	(cooked) rice	9
面包	麵包	(N)	miànbāo	bread	9

N

| 难 | 難 | (A) | nán | difficult | 11 |
| 牛奶 | | (N) | niúnǎi | milk | 9 |

P

啤酒		(N)	píjiǔ	beer	9
便宜		(A)	piányyi	cheap; inexpensive	10

Q

巧		(A)	qiǎo	coincidental	13
晴		(A)	qíng	sunny	14

R

热	熱	(A)	rè	hot	12
热狗	熱狗	(N)	règǒu	hotdog	9
热心	熱心	(A)	rèxīn	enthusiastic	13
日记	日記	(N)	rìjì	diary	14

S

生活		(N)	shēnghuó	life	12
圣诞老人	聖誕老人	(PN)	Shèngdàn lǎorén	Santa Claus	14
售货员	售貨員	(N)	shòuhuòyuán	shop assistant; salesperson	10
书店	書店	(N)	shūdiàn	book store	10
书房	書房	(N)	shūfáng	a study	13
数学	數學	(N)	shùxué	mathematics	7
水电费	水電費	(N)	shuǐdiànfèi	utility	13

T

套		(M)	tào	suite	13
体育馆	體育館	(N)	tǐyùguǎn	gym	10
跳舞		(VO)	tiàowǔ	to dance	11

W

外公		(N)	wàigōng	grandfather on the mother's side	8
晚上		(N)	wǎnshang	evening	9
文化		(N)	wénhuà	culture	7
卧室	臥室	(N)	wòshì	bedroom	13
物理		(N)	wùlǐ	physics	7

X

西餐		(N)	xīcān	Western food	9

吸烟	吸煙	(VO)	xīyān	to smoke	11
系主任		(N)	xìzhǔrèn	chairman of the department	8
下课	下課	(VO)	xiàkè	to get out of class; to finish class	11
小便		(N)	xiǎobiàn	urine	12
血		(N)	xiě	blood	12
新		(A)	xīn	new	13
选修	選修	(V)	xuǎnxiū	to take an elective course	7
雪碧		(PN)	Xuěbì	Sprite	9

Y

牙		(N)	yá	tooth	12
爷爷	爺爺	(N)	yéye	grandfather on the father's side	8
音乐	音樂	(N)	yīnyuè	music	7
英文		(N)	Yīngwén	English	12
元		(M)	yuán	(the same as "块", but used in written language)	10
元旦		(PN)	Yuándàn	New Year's Day	14

Z

哲学	哲學	(N)	zhéxué	philosophy	7
整理		(V)	zhěnglǐ	to put in order; to arrange; to sort out	14
支		(M)	zhī	(a measure word for stick-like things such as pens)	10
中餐		(N)	zhōngcān	Chinese food	9
助教		(N)	zhùjiào	teaching assistant	8
作家		(N)	zuòjiā	writer	10

汉字索引

Character Index

作者简介

刘珣 Liu Xun,北京语言文化大学教授,中国人民大学、北京外国语大学、哈尔滨工业大学兼职教授。1997 年任"国家对外汉语教学学术研究专家咨询小组"成员、"国家汉语水平考试委员会顾问委员会"成员,1989 年至 1991 年任美国纽约州教育厅中文教学顾问。曾在南斯拉夫、美国、新加坡、泰国及香港、澳门任教或讲学。从事汉语作为第二语言的教学、理论研究、教材编写、研究生培养及教师培训工作近四十年。主持或独力编写过《实用汉语课本》(第 1—4 册)、《儿童汉语》、《汉语初阶》、《交际汉语一百课》等对外汉语教材,出版论著《对外汉语教育学引论》、《对外汉语教学概论》并发表论文多篇。

张凯 Zhang Kai,北京语言文化大学汉语水平考试中心副教授。自 1989 年从事语言测试研究至今。主要论文有"关于结构效度"、"对外汉语教学学科的基本问题和基本方法"。

刘社会 Liu Shehui,北京语言文化大学副教授。曾在法国巴黎第七大学和突尼斯布尔吉巴语言学院任教。参加编写对外汉语教材《基础汉语课本》和《实用汉语课本》。参与策划和编写《中国古代文学作品选》、《中国现代文学作品选》和《中国当代文学作品选》,并主持编写《世界汉语教学概况》和《世界汉语教学书目概览》,发表过多篇有关现代汉语句型研究和对外汉语汉字教学的论文。

陈曦 Chen Xi,北京语言文化大学副教授。曾在比利时国立根特大学任教。主要研究方向为汉语及对外汉语教学,主编中级口语教材《步入中国》,出版专著《汉字演化说略》并发表"汉语形符内部系统初探"等学术论文多篇。

左珊丹 Zuo Shandan,北京语言文化大学讲师。曾在日本东京大学、东洋大学和荷兰莱顿大学任教。参与编写对外汉语教材《桥梁——实用汉语中级教程》和大型工具书《中日辞典》。发表论文"论对外汉语中级阶段的教学原则与方法"、"汉语的活性与文学语言实验"、"文学语言的日常化"等,出版过小说集《水下有座城》。

施家炜 Shi Jiawei,北京语言文化大学讲师,主要研究领域为第二语言习得与语言教学。发表论文"外国留学生 22 类现代汉语句式的习得顺序研究"、"跨文化交际意识与第二语言习得研究"、"第二语言习得内在过程研究综述与展望"、"来华欧美留学生汉字习得研究教学实验报告"、"韩国留学生汉语句式习得发展的个案量化研究"等多篇,出版译著《跨文化交际:话语分析法》。